You Always Think of Home

You Always Think of Home

A PORTRAIT OF CLAY COUNTY, ALABAMA

Pamela Grundy

Foreword by Wayne Flynt

Photographs by Ken Elkins

The University of Georgia Press

Athens and London

© 1991 by the University of Georgia Press
Athens, Georgia 30602
All rights reserved

Designed by Sandra Strother Hudson
The paper in this book meets the guidelines
for permanence and durability of the Committee
on Production Guidelines for Book Longevity
of the Council on Library Resources.

Printed in the United States of America
95 94 93 92 91   5 4 3 2 1

Library of Congress Cataloging in Publication Data

Grundy, Pamela.
    You always think of home : a portrait of Clay County,
Alabama /
    Pamela Grundy ; foreword by Wayne Flynt ;
photographs by Ken Elkins.
            p.   cm.
    Includes bibliographical references and index.
    ISBN 0-8203-1304-1 (alk. paper)
    1. Clay County (Ala.)—Social life and customs.
2. Interviews—Alabama—Clay County.   3. Clay County
(Ala.)—Description and travel—Views.   I. Elkins, Ken.
II. Title.
F332.C62G78   1991
976.1′58063—dc20   90-43615
                                              CIP

British Library Cataloging in Publication Data available

Frontispiece: Jody Watts

CONTENTS

FOREWORD

I forget how the courtship began. Perhaps it was my first mile of wading Hatchett Creek, seining its rapids for bait with which I would challenge its catfish, bream, and bass. The fish were a lot like the people: a bit small compared to another variety; lean from fighting the rapids and floods; tough and smart; survivors.

Or perhaps it was my first trip to Brownville–Hatchett Creek Presbyterian Church, where my wife's family holds its annual reunion on the Sunday before Labor Day. The church is a bit like the people, too: simple; unadorned; sturdy; sitting on a hillside; a bit forlorn and deserted by neighbors now, but manifesting great dignity and a hint of better days once upon a time. The small cemetery is immaculate, a sign that these people know their past, treasure it, and take care of their own in life and in death.

The first lesson I learned about Clay County came in that cemetery. We had finished one of those gargantuan dinners so renowned among Southerners. The children had moved out of the tabernacle, built onto the church near the turn of the century, and up the hill behind the church, where once cabins sheltered some of the thousands who attended camp-meeting revivals. The children began to catch lizards that darted among the tombstones ("finger sitters" the kids called them, because when rubbed on their stomachs they would lie quiet and still).

I wandered into the older section of the cemetery, where tombstones informed me that some of the inhabitants were born in Ireland or Scotland and fought in the Revolutionary War to free America from British rule or in the first Creek War to free this land from its original inhabitants so new ones could settle in their place.

One marvelous obelisk, made of marble and towering above the rest, told me these people took pride even in perverse wrongmindedness. The memorial contained inscriptions on all four of its faces.

Sergeant Malcolm Patterson was born July 17, 1839 and was slain in the Battle of Sharpsburg, MD. in defense of his own sunny South. Sept. 17, 1862. Aged 23 years and 2 months. We know not his resting place as we did not recover his body from the battlefield. But have every reason to feel and know that he died as true soldiers die.

Captain Archibald A. Patterson was born July 12, 1832, and was slain in the Battle of Murfreesboro, Tennessee. December 31st, 1862, and was buried near that place not far from the bank of Stone River. Aged 30 years 5 months and 19 days.

Col. Thomas H. Patterson, was born Jan. 13, 1831. He also was slain in defense of his beloved country near Atlanta, Georgia, July 30th, 1864 where his remains are now interred. Aged 33 years 6 months and 17 days. The Sweet Remembrance of the just will flourish while they sleep in dust.

Only the mother of these men rested beneath Clay County soil, memorialized on the fourth face when she died not long after her three sons fell in combat.

The lesson about roots was not the only secret that the cemetery yielded that hot September afternoon. It also told me a great deal about their religion. Often simplistically dismissed as Calvinistic, escapist, otherworldly, and emotional, their understanding of ultimate reality cannot be so easily captured in caricatures of camp meetings that once met here. True, the hills once rang with denunciations of sin and calls for repentance while nearby horse traders and gamblers plied their trades and young folks courted. True, they did talk of Beulahland and a land where "no storm clouds roll." But such talk was the way powerless people coped with mortality. Their hope was in the world to come, a hope that allowed a semblance of sanity in a world of poverty, capricious nature, and early death. The three Patterson men died because humans could not sort out their differences short of cannon and rifle. The four children of I. W. and M. E. Jones rested here because there were too few doctors of too limited learning. Their three daughters died at ages seventeen and twenty, their son at age twenty-two. M. Y. and J. P. Swindall buried two infant sons beside the little church: John Manly, who was born on 1 September 1884 and died on 21 October 1886; and an unnamed son who was born and died on 9 April 1887. Such a world provided more questions than answers and drove people either to Calvinistic resignation or self-destructive anger.

Hatchett Creek taught me a third lesson about the county and its people. During one of my frequent fishing trips on a blistering summer day, I had emerged from the creek, dragged my tired body and long stringer of fish through the solitude of a tall forest, climbed an embankment, and begun the mile-long walk back to my ancient Volkswagen. Hair disheveled, legs wet and covered with mud, I was a forbidding sight and hoped to meet no cars. Only one did pass, a long American type, Pontiac or Buick as I recall. A handsome black man, casually but neatly dressed, drove. The car must have traveled a hundred feet before I saw him apply the brakes, and a good deal farther before he came to a full stop. He put the car in reverse and slowly backed toward me. As he approached I noticed an attractive black woman in the passenger seat and two teenage girls behind. The predominant expression on all faces except the driver's was boredom. The man engaged his power window and inquired pleasantly, "Did you catch those in Hatchett Creek?"

"Yep, it's a grand place to fish," I replied cheerily, determined not to confirm my appearance as a "redneck cracker." He responded to the friendly tone and asked if I knew where a certain family lived in Clay County.

"No I don't," I replied. I was not a resident and had driven from Auburn only to fish. But I gave him the name of Mira Carmichael, an elderly white woman who kept the county's genealogy and topography in her amazing mind. I was confident that she would be able to answer his question.

He was not anxious to move along and volunteered that the family he searched for was his own. They had moved away when he was only a boy, bound for the auto factories of Detroit. He remembered only snatches of an impoverished childhood in Clay County, but among his memories were recollections of happy hunting trips with his father, fish fries, dogs with wagging tails and barks of greeting, and a close family bound together in love. He had been to Florida's Disney World on vacation and wanted his daughters and wife to see the land from whence he came. They obviously were not impressed. His explanation complete, and with one last envious glance at my day's catch, he put the car in drive and sped off in the direction of Miss Carmichael's house.

Mira Carmichael lived with her two sisters near Hatchett Creek, in a simple frame house built by her grandfather before the Civil War. All three were in their eighties. The Carmichaels were one of the best-known families in the southern end of Clay County, having sent forth generations of physicians, university presidents, and Presbyterian laypeople. It is largely through the prodigious efforts of the three sisters that Brownville–Hatchett Creek Presbyterian Church remains alive now that nearly all the population of Brownville has moved away. I knew Miss Mira's enlightenment on race, religion, politics, and economics, and was certain that she would greet this black migrant with the same respect and dignity that she extended to everyone. Once she discovered he was from "down home," talk of common acquaintances and old times, good and bad, would erase barriers of accent and color.

After all, Clay County not only provided America Hiram Wesley Evans, who in 1922 became imperial wizard of the Ku Klux Klan; it also furnished Hugo L. Black, associate justice of the Supreme Court and the twentieth century's most distinguished defender of Bill of Rights freedoms. One of these treasured notions, the separation of church and state, he undoubtedly learned as part of his Baptist upbringing in Clay County.

So much for images. Important as they are, life in Clay County is about reality, tough reality as hard as its rocky soil. Barren land is the most elemental reality. Land in Clay County conforms generally to one of two types. Nearly half the 603 square miles are creased with mountains and valleys—steep hills susceptible to erosion, which make row crops and pasture impractical. Slightly more than half the land consists of plateaus dissected by valleys that are suited to pasture, hay, and other crops. Soils in both areas are acidic and lack organic matter and fertility, making commercial farming impossible on most of the land and difficult on the rest. Agricultural production now occurs on only 45,000 of the county's 386,000 acres; three-fourths of the total acreage is devoted to commercial timber. Although pioneers to the southwest in Alabama's Black Belt built plantations on rich prairies that yielded abundant crops, those who settled in what is now Clay County clawed a living from steep, rocky land. The early settlers shunned the area—virtually the last occupied by Creek Indians before their expulsion from the state—in favor of the more hospitable and easily cultivated lands farther west. For late arrivals it was the poor hill country of Clay County or nothing at all.

Unlike the Black Belt counties with their fabled Greek Revival mansions, opulent styles of life, and preponderance of black inhabitants, Clay County became a bastion of small-farmer democracy. Created in 1866 of lands taken from adjacent counties, Clay contained only 9,560 people on 1,274 farms in the 1870 census. Nearly 90 percent of the farms consisted of less than 50 acres. Crops differed as much as residents. In a state which proclaimed cotton king, corn reigned on the pinnacle of Clay County agriculture. Local folk consumed most of the crop, either eating it themselves or feeding it to their livestock. Ground into meal, corn furnished grits and bread; roasted, it supplied important vitamins; fermented and drunk as liquid, it quickened the spirit and made a person forget his troubles. Cotton was a wonderful revenue producer, but local soils did not favor it. In 1880 Clay County produced less than half as many bales as the average county in Alabama. No railroad crossed the county, and without navigable rivers or railroads, transporting a five-hundred-pound cotton bale to market was no easy task.

Taxes complicated problems of poor soil and transportation. Reconstruction legislators transferred taxation primarily from slaves and luxury items to property and tripled the rates. As a consequence, farmers needed ever more cash income to hold onto their lands. Cotton presented virtually the only feasible money crop, although Clay County was not well suited to it, so Clay County farmers found themselves caught in a steady downward cycle of indebtedness, foreclosure, and farm tenancy. In 1880, 73 percent of county farms were owner-operated; by 1890 that figure had fallen to 63 percent. Compared to the state average, twice as many Clay County farms were in debt, and citizens paid the third highest interest rates on their debts, an average of 11.44 percent annually.

Mitchell Garrett, who later obtained graduate degrees and became a respected writer and college professor, grew up the son of a land-owning Clay County farmer and Primitive Baptist preacher. But he remembered landlords who took "all [a tenant's] movable property except his poor clothing and his scant furniture" for debts, then "set [him] adrift to repeat the performances somewhere else." He recalled one sharecropper family that exhausted its supply of bacon, sorghum, and cornmeal and had to subsist on sweet potatoes for two or three weeks. The children became potbellied and sometimes ate the "dry, red clay daubing that chinked the crevices in the rock chimney which stood outside the end of the house. They crumbled off small chunks of the dry clay with their fingers and allowed it to melt in their mouths like fudge."

Cascading rates of tenancy fueled agricultural revolt that swept across Alabama during the last two decades of the nineteenth century. In fact, Clay County was often referred to as the "cradle of Alabama populism." As five-cent cotton sent small farmers crashing through the bottom rung of landholding into sharecropper status, they enlisted beneath the banner of rustic revolution. Summoned to war by the *People's Party Advocate*, published in Ashland in the early 1890s, they formed a solid phalanx of reform for the Populist gubernatorial candidate Reuben Kolb and the reformers who sought to overturn conservative planter-industrialist rule of the state. Many of them considered agricultural conditions too drastic for even the moderate nostrums advanced by Kolb and preferred the more radical strategies of one of their own, Joseph C. Manning. Called variously "the Clay County evangelist," "the evangel," or simply "the apostle," Manning was perhaps the finest orator the agrarian movement produced in Alabama. Under the effect of his tutelage and plummeting cotton prices, Clay County became one of the most persistent Populist counties in the state.

Perhaps the failure of Populistic reform was a harbinger of what was to follow in the twentieth century. Modern technology began slowly to transform the county and further erode the economic base. The advent of tractors and cotton pickers required ever larger amounts of land to make the new technology cost-effective. In 1910 the number of mules and horses peaked and shortly thereafter began to decline. By 1925 twelve tractors broke land in the county. Two decades later more than a hundred chugged across the rural landscape. The radio began to reduce rural isolation; between 1925 and 1945 the number of sets increased from 28 to 1,341. Electricity and telephones also made their appearances, further accelerating the pace of change. Tenancy rates rose to 48 percent in 1910, then declined during the war before increasing again in the 1920s and early 1930s. Both county population and the number of farms peaked in 1920. Nearly a third of those farms disappeared in the next quarter century as farmers left for industrial jobs in the South and elsewhere, and those who remained behind consolidated land. By 1959 fewer people farmed in Clay County than had done so in the first 1870 census.

The county's first modern paved highway allowed ambitious residents to leave their rural homes for Talladega and high-paying war industry during the 1940s. Foremost in the emigration were the young. The farm population below the age of thirty-five dropped by almost 50 percent between 1940 and 1945. By 1970 the average age of the county's farmers was fifty. Other residents remained in the county but commuted each day to factory jobs in adjacent counties. Women, in particular, found expanded opportunities in sewing plants.

By 1945 more than a third of the county's farmers earned some income from nonfarm work. Swift Packing Company opened a poultry processing plant in the 1960s, and the value of poultry production topped eleven million dollars, placing the county in the top third of Alabama's counties. Those who did not find their economic salvation in poultry turned to forestry. Most tree-producing acres are small wood lots still owned by county residents, although some land has come under the ownership of large outside timber companies. Nearly half the county's farm land is officially designated now as woodland. Blueberry production has recently helped to diversify agriculture, but despite efforts to stabilize the agricultural base, farming accounts for only 20 percent of the county's land area.

If economic change characterizes the agriculture of Clay County, cultural persistence marks its social order. A county that contains only two communities deserving the designation "towns" can hardly claim to be urban. Nor does it even try. Lineville and Ashland remain tiny merchandising centers, and residents eager for a movie or nice restaurant usually head for Anniston, Talladega, or Sylacauga.

Locked within their rural domain, folkways flourished well into the post–Second World War era. Camp-meeting revivals, protracted meetings, quilting bees, house raisings, and neighborly concern tending sometimes toward meddlesomeness remained a sacrosanct tradition. Churches tended to be small and rural. People got to know their neighbors quite well and learned to rely on them in times of trouble. Homecomings, decoration days, family reunions, and Sacred Harp singings not only supplied avenues of entertainment before radio, movies, and television, they also contributed to a sense of belonging, of shared community and common purpose. Folks might disagree on politics or on the rightful method of baptism (immersion or sprinkling), or whether church services should allow musical instruments or even shouts and speaking in tongues. But that people should help their neighbors in times of trouble and live upright, orderly, and respectable lives was pretty much a principle subscribed to by all.

Because they had fewer of this world's resources than their neighbors in more affluent regions, Clay Countians learned to make do with what they had. They became, to use the local term, "jacks-of-all-trades," capable of building a house, digging a well, mending a saddle, repairing a motor, plumbing a house, or preaching a sermon without the benefit of very much formal education or training. And as an increasingly standardized world emerged from the new technology of the twentieth century, folkways formerly considered quaint or even eccentric suddenly came into a certain kind of fashion. In 1926 some women in the county formed the Clay County Basket Association and began to sell pine-needle baskets. So distinguished was the craftsmanship and so beautiful the design that articles about the basket makers and their creations appeared in newspapers as far away as Montana and New York. Two Chicago women became brokers for the basket makers, obtaining space in department stores along Fifth Avenue, Broadway, and Savoy Plaza in New York City. In 1927 the women's association earned thirteen thousand dollars divided among five hundred Clay County women. The 1960s revival of interest in folkways again focused attention on such locales as Clay County, Alabama.

The fickle grasp of progress, which transformed sylvan landscapes into aesthetically numbing malls, passed by places like Clay County. These places continue to beckon us to times past and communities forgotten. They also remind us of human relationships endowed with special kinds of meaning. They speak of a spiritual sense of community fast being lost. They recall us to a time when families tolerated more tensions before they split, and where the rhythm of life made time for good conversation, hunting, and fishing. They convey a politics where constituents, unimpressed by sophisticated television campaigns, expect to make up their minds about whom to vote for only after they have heard all the candidates in person.

Not all goes well in this land, and Clay County is no rural Eden. Spouses betray marriage vows, neighbors once shot and lynched each other, religious bigots ostracize the unorthodox, and political demagogues plant seeds that bloom more profusely than local crops of corn and cotton. But in these ways Clay County residents are neither better nor worse than most people in other places and times, and Clay County's excesses have specific causes and explanations.

It is such a world as this that Pam Grundy discovered, loved, and tries to describe to others. At times it seems a grimy, unkind world, mean-spirited and not inclined to provoke nostalgia. Elsewhere it is an amazingly sensitive and perceptive world, proving once more that plain people sometimes have insights too deep for philosophers, historians, and theologians. But above all, the emotion that bursts forth from these pages is the one about which William Faulkner wrote, a sense of endurance. It is that remarkable capacity of dogged persistence that Pam Grundy best captures, and it is that characteristic that makes these people so memorable.

WAYNE FLYNT

ACKNOWLEDGMENTS

It would be close to impossible to list all the Clay County residents who, wittingly or not, helped in the preparation of this book. But more than any others, Mildred Farrow, Morland Flegel, Ruby King, and Lewel Sellers took hour upon hour to talk, to explain and to remember, and their contribution far outstrips the words that are included here.

Outside support also came from several sources, but particularly from my parents, Scott and Lois Grundy, and from Elise Sanguinetti, whose faith in the county and the project never wavered.

Finally, although the voice of Howard Hamil does not make an appearance, my perspective on the county would have been far narrower without the help, the advice, and the encouragement of one of the best friends I have ever known. Although Ken and I hope that this book belongs in some small way to the entire county, Howard has more than earned its dedication.

INTRODUCTION

Whenever I told anyone that I was working on a book about Clay County, I was immediately asked if it would be a history. Not that much of note had ever taken place within the county lines. But there, as everywhere, history was made by men and women, in this case by the ancestors of present residents, and, an account of the diligence and often bravery with which they carved homes from what had been a wilderness, persisted and even sometimes prospered through the vagaries of weather, the swings of economic cycles, and the fluctuating winds of social change would say something about who they were, and perhaps who their descendants are. That such a small and isolated place might draw the interest of a wider world had not crossed many minds.

So when a refugee from small-town Alabama journalism, a Texas native with an aversion to stereotype, an Ivy League education, and little in the way of conscious system started showing up on doorsteps, I doubt most people knew quite what to think. But perhaps the county's greatest charm lies in the endurance of its old-fashioned manner, reflected in the unspoiled countryside, in the comings and goings around the classic courthouse square, and most of all in the gentle hospitality of its inhabitants, accustomed to country ways of helping out. This book owes much of its existence to the generous, if somewhat bemused, politeness of people who told a listener about their lives mainly because she asked them to.

Neither of the two most widely dispersed Deep South images—of Greek-columned plantation homes and of blacks and whites in battle on firehose-washed downtown streets—could represent Clay County. Most antebellum residents were white subsistence farmers living in log houses, and although the county managed to produce both Ku Klux Klan Imperial Wizard Hiram Evans and integration-minded Supreme Court Justice Hugo Black, the small black population within its borders posed few threats to the balance of county power.

Indians held the hilly terrain first and longest, and it belonged to the last swath of land left by the Creek Confederacy in 1832, when its final members turned toward exile on Oklahoma reservations. On those departing heels

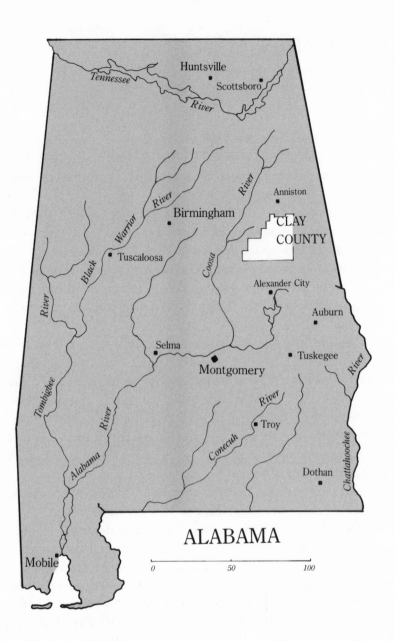

Tennessee River

Huntsville

Scottsboro

Warrior River

Black

River

Birmingham

Tuscaloosa

River

Anniston

CLAY
COUNTY

Coosa

River

Alexander City

Auburn

Tombigbee

Selma

Montgomery

Tuskegee

River

Alabama

River

River

River

Conecuh

Troy

Chattahoochee

Dothan

ALABAMA

0   50   100

Mobile

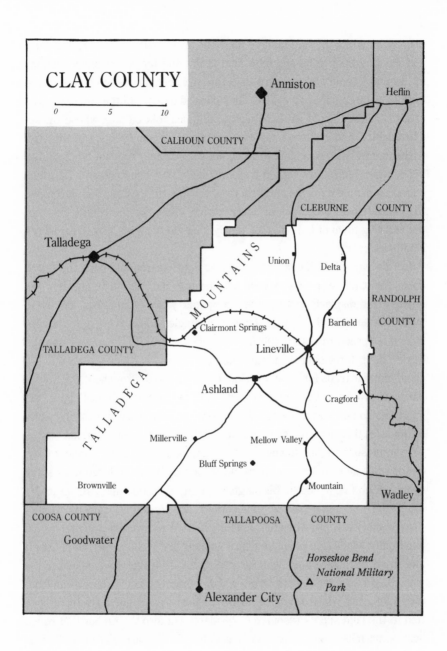

CLAY COUNTY

0   5   10

Anniston

Heflin

CALHOUN COUNTY

CLEBURNE COUNTY

Talladega

M O U N T A I N S

Union

Delta

RANDOLPH COUNTY

TALLADEGA COUNTY

Clairmont Springs

Barfield

Lineville

T A L L A D E G A

Ashland

Cragford

Millerville

Mellow Valley

Bluff Springs

Brownville

Mountain

Wadley

COOSA COUNTY

TALLAPOOSA COUNTY

Goodwater

*Horseshoe Bend
National Military
Park*

Alexander City

poured hundreds of land-hungry migrants from farther east. Those early and wealthy enough to purchase land in flat and fertile southern sections of the state could look forward to prosperity, but those who halted in the hills were often happy to get by. They cleared patches of the trees, planted crops that they could eat, and nurtured a rich folk culture whose music, Christianity, and crafts remain essential parts of county living to this day. Alabama had become a state in 1819, but Clay County was not created until 1866, when legislators carved it from neighboring Randolph and Talladega counties, named it for the antebellum statesman Henry Clay, and, in a move that would spark a century of bitter rivalry, chose for the county seat not the existing town of Lineville but newly founded Ashland, named for Clay's Kentucky estate.

In this part of Alabama, where slaves were scarce and corn the major crop, the Civil War was largely felt through its long-term effects—the poverty and displacement brought on by four years of hardship, and by so many soldiers' deaths. And as families struggled to recover from the conflict, the spread of cotton culture trapped many in its downward spirals. Taxes, debt, foreclosure, and the indignities of sharecropping contracts became familiar trials for county residents, as they did throughout the South. Farmers protested where they could—during the state's brief Populist revolt Clay County was a stronghold, and one resident became a leading party orator. But the moment came and went, while old problems carried on.

In some surrounding towns, in Talladega, Sylacauga, and Alexander City, cotton mills and iron foundries had after the war begun to forge what some spoke of as a new South. Birmingham in one direction and Atlanta in the other were booming past all expectation, and in nearby Calhoun County the company town of Anniston, founded in 1881 to process iron ore, would eventually swell to a population that topped thirty thousand, its factories and shops coming to dominate the area. But Clay County, which before the war could boast no trading river, which would not get a railroad line before 1906, and which would never be crossed by a major highway, stayed tied to the land and its resources. Residents cut into the timber that rolled across the hills, mined in erratic spurts for the rich array of minerals that lay beneath the soil, and continued—often with little or no real return—to cultivate their crops and gardens.

Alternative employment would not reach the county until the years that followed World War II, after the ravages of the Great Depression and the sudden attractions of high-paying war-production jobs had reduced the county's population from the twenty-two thousand it held at its peak to less than seventeen. The handful of factories that became established—producing cabinets, clothes and small rubber tires; processing eggs and chickens—could only slow migration trends, and population slipped under thirteen thousand by 1960, although returning retirees and some people moving out from town have brought a small increase in recent years. (More whites seem to have left than blacks, and the black share of the population has more than doubled since the Civil War, reaching just beyond 16 percent.) Departing farmers abandoned rocky land not to tractors but to trees, and by the 1980s barely a fifth of the county's soil remained in cultivation, growing mainly cows and chickens. With the earlier isolation broken by better roads, more travel, and the reach of television, inhabitants have mixed aspects of their heritage with elements of the changing outside world, and today their lives reflect the varying patterns such amalgamations have produced.

The history many residents envisioned would probably have traced classic American lines of progress and development, describing how hard work and community cooperation brought the county from a collection of homesteads and rough farms into a more prosperous and comfortable modern world. I do not try to draw conclusions of such sweep. Neither can I reproduce the remarkable vitality of the voices on the tapes I made, or the unfathomable individual complexity behind every statement and life story. But if these fragments of conversation, chosen as much for their beauty of expression as their content, and more to reflect the strength and flexibility of culture than the drawbacks of economic or political arrangements, give even some small hint of the struggles and the passions this small place has nurtured through the years, they will have done the job I hoped they would.

You Always Think of Home

1

2

3

4

5

6

7

9

10

12

13

17

18

19

21

22

24

30

31

33

34

38

39

41

42

44

45

A sense of great age lies over the Clay County hills. In places, when you leave the state roads and pass by weed-choked glades and the hulks and skeletons of bare-board houses, only the paving beneath the wheels suggests that what might be called progress has touched the place at all, that it has not lain forgotten since the days when farms were measured not in acres but in mules, and the world beyond the South seemed almost too far away to be imagined. The undergrowth has given trees the look of great primeval monsters, even some still-lived-in houses seem barely able to beat back an advancing wilderness, and the passing sway of fashions, wars, convictions, economic change, and modern troubles seems to have no place at all.

But if you listen, that is not what you hear.

I Think I Had
a Good Life

Preceding page: Monroe Wood

MRS. J. T. M. (ANNIE MAUDE) KENNEDY
Eighty, retired farmer, Mountain, white

I was born in Clay County, about eight miles east of here, in 1906. It'll be eighty-one years the thirtieth of June. I was born and raised on a farm; I've always lived on a farm. My dad passed away when I was two and a half years old, with typhoid fever, in 1908, in December. And he had insurance, and my mother bought an eighty-acre farm in Tallapoosa County and fixed his grave with that—it's got a huge monument, a marble slab—and I lived there until I married, and we still lived in Tallapoosa County one year, moved back to Clay County one year after I married. My husband was born and raised in Clay County about two miles from where we lived. I had met him about two year before we were married. I met him at church, at an all-day Sacred Harp singing, about a mile down here at Bethany Primitive Baptist Church. We moved up here on the hill where that huge oak tree was, and we moved here will be sixty years ago in November, two days before Thanksgiving, 1927, and we lived here ever since, and I've lived alone will be twenty year the eleventh of July. My husband passed away in the hospital in Birmingham after a nine-year-and-one-day illness.

I stay busy, I really do. If I couldn't stay busy I don't think I could stay here by myself. My son lives up on the hill and he comes by every morning at five-ten to check on me on his way to work, to see that I'm OK. The other son is waiting for him when he gets to work to see if I'm OK and if I need anything. Got four children, mighty, mighty thankful for them, and they are really good to me.

I've been in club work. Back years and years ago 4-H Club was started as a Corn Club for boys, Tomato Club for girls, and I was a Tomato Club girl. From 1915 till 1920. We had to have so many tomato plants and we had to put up at least thirty jars of tomatoes in some form or other, and I won several prizes on my Tomato Club work. In 1924 we organized our Home Demonstration Club. Now it's Homemaker's Club, and we meet the second Friday in every month. I haven't missed very many meetings, and I know that I'm a better homemaker, a better mother, and a better person by being a club member. I've done a lot of arts and crafts that we learned there, and canning, sewing, just a lot of different things.

We always meet and have pledge of allegiance to the flag, and then we have devotional and prayer, a song and then devotional and prayer, and people, one of my sister-in-laws told me one time, says, "Y'all just go to club to gossip and tell jokes," but we've never gossiped and we've never told jokes. Our club is more like going to church. Of course we have a social hour and enjoy that, just like meeting in one's home, but as for the other part, we don't.

Of course used to everybody farmed, but now the majority of them work away from home, at public works. There's still some farming goes on. Glenn, my son, has sixteen acres of corn planted, and he raises cattle. Lot of people have cattle, and most everyone has a garden and that helps out. And they share—if they have more of something that a neighbor doesn't have, they share that with them.

We have got a good, caring community. Cooperative community. When someone's sick, there's always someone there, when there's death we all gather in and carry food to the home, even if it's two days and nights there's always food carried in to the home, and that's worth lots. Lot of communities don't do things like that. And the majority of the people in the community was born and raised, either the husband or the wife or maybe both of them here, in old family-settled places.

*   *   *

I read a lot. I enjoy reading. I read a chapter in the Bible every night before I go to bed. I don't usually go to bed till nine or ten o'clock at night. I'm very fond of Paul's writings. And Proverbs, I enjoy Proverbs a lot. Well, just the Bible, I like it all. A lot of people say they don't like the Old Testament, but I do. That's the beginning and if you'll study it, you'll find that if you'll take and read all through a book, like say Genesis, or Proverbs or something like that, you get a lot out of it by studying it. You've got to study to learn, and I've heard a lot of people say, "Well, I just can't understand the Bible," but it's like everything else, we've got to study it too, I understand. I'm a-reading First Timothy now. I've been a-learning a lot; he went through a lot, lot, lot. You can read any book and a lot of people thinks we have trials and temptations now, which we do, especially the young people, there's so much more temptation than there used to be. But we don't have the hardships that they had, the pioneers of our country and the writers in the Bible.

I get a lot of papers. Usually, when the papers come I always turn to the obituaries first. I have friends a lot of places and I always turn to that and see, especially if I have a friend that's sick. It's always sad when you see somebody's passed away, it always makes you feel sad. Now I had a brother that passed away the thirteenth day of April, and it was hard. He was five years younger than I was. It was hard to give him up, but he suffered so much till I felt that God was good to him and to his family. He stayed in the hospital six weeks. His wife went home one day. He had cancer. He was in a coma twenty-eight days, and just slept away, the thirteenth of April.

I've always gone to funerals. A lot of people don't let their children, when they're small, go to funerals, but personally I think that's wrong. I think a child should be taught about death, same as it is about life. I've always gone to funerals as long as I can remember. My mother was a person that would explain things to us, and I always tried to explain them to my children and to my grandchildren—that we're born to die, and that's just life, that's as natural as being born.

Of course I regret my husband being taken but I know it was God's will for him to go or he wouldn't have gone. Until I married John Kennedy I always thought I wanted to be a nurse, but I decided I loved him more than I wanted to be a nurse. So we got married, had four children, we had a very, very happy life.

Let's study about something else for a while.

*   *   *

I don't believe, like all these big crusades and all of these, when all these maybe five or six hundred go up to profess that they've been saved, I don't believe God saves that many people at one time. I don't think so. I think maybe it's more emotional than it is really feeling that God has forgiven them of their sins. And if I'm wrong I hope God will forgive me, but that's the way I feel about it.

I was eleven years old when I was saved. We lived over near Motley, and it was in April was when it was, and it was just a feeling I never had had—

of course I had known for a long time that something was working with me, but I didn't know what it was. And then it was just like stepping out of a dark house into the bright sunshine, and I knew God had saved my soul. I was at home. I was helping my mother wash clothes. And then you didn't have a washing machine, and we drew water out of the well, and I was drawing water for my mother to wash her clothes with, and it's just like I said, it was just like I was in a dark room, just walked out in the sunshine. But I didn't join the church till mid-August. I wanted to be sure that what I had was what I was supposed to have. I was eleven years old.

*   *   *

I've had a happy life. I don't find one thing to regret. I'm proud that I'm a Clay County girl.

MONROE WOOD
Sixty-six, retired army-depot worker, Delta, black

I grew up—well, partly born and raised up here around Delta, in the Delta community. And I was a real small kid, I can barely remember when we first moved in there, but I grew up to be a pretty big-sized boy. We moved from one place to another, stayed here five years, over there three years, over there two years, here and yonder, different things. My daddy was what we call a sharecropper. So in 1934 we wound up down in this area.

Then I wound up there in the army, and stayed in the army three years, two months, and some days, and then I moved over into Clay County. Me and my wife farmed for a few years after I come out of the service, and then I went into public work. Worked for Hodges Construction Company, worked for them about three years, then I got a job at Bynum, the army depot, stayed there thirty-one years, and then I retired, but we've been living right here for something like twenty-eight, twenty-nine years.

Plowing mules, picking cotton, pulling fodder. Wasn't much sharing then, you just made crops. My daddy raised us all during that depression, and it was rough. No money, fifty cents a day. You just couldn't hardly make it. We grew peas and we grew sweet potatoes and we grew sorghum syrup. My dad put out enough sorghum to make a hundred gallons of syrup. We had plenty sorghum syrup, corn bread, and sweet potatoes. Milk—we had a couple of milk cows. Never did starve, but you got tired of what you had, but you couldn't do no better. You'd miss about two meals and it got good to you again, you'd go back to eating again.

Back at that time, every house in this country there was somebody living in it. At that time this country was thick settled, all the way back to the river. The church would just fill up. But we ain't got the people any more. All the older people died, and the younger people left here. I had in mind of leaving, but the army got me and me and my wife hadn't been married but about a year, and after I stayed three years in the army I come back, and you could draw ninety-seven and a half dollars a month to farm, so I said, "Well, I'll try that." So I went back to farming, and I was able to take care of myself, and we done better. I had in mind of leaving, going back up in Ohio, had some brothers up there, that were doing pretty good, and they offered me a chance, but my mama and all my brothers and sisters, younger ones, was here, and so I got that job at Hodges Construction Company. I worked there a couple of years, then I went to Bynum. Then after three years I was at career condition, you know, so I said, "Well, I can stay here until I retire." And the longer you stayed the more money you made. And that money was getting in circulation good then. So we bought this place, and we moved here. And I bought the Luker place right yonder adjoining this— we go plumb to the highway, to the blacktop there. So we got a few cattles here and a few hogs, and, well, I don't want to go nowhere else now. I'm settled at home.

I always had a dream and a view that I wanted this thing, but I couldn't see it noways possible I could ever accumulate it with the wages we was making at that time. I couldn't see this far ahead, you know. I always, after I growed up and got grown, I said, "Lord," I said, "maybe someday I'll have a farm of my own and if I make anything it's mine." And I kind of looked forward to that and, well it was as I was telling you, you couldn't see far enough ahead to tell whether you was ever going to own it or not, you was living in hopes.

It's been a long drawn-out thing, a long struggle. But at this old age now, we've got it pretty well beat. And I was telling my wife yesterday, another year, I'm going to sell most of my cattle, just keep a few. And if I want to do any work I'll do it, and if I don't I won't. I'm going to go down to that fish pond there and sit there and fish, and go down to the river and fish, and get me one of these lazy things to hang out here in the tree and get up there and lay flat on my back and swing. Getting too old to work.

*   *   *

Way back, my daddy was fortunate enough that—I don't know anything about it, but his daddy was a white man. He was born way back yonder in slavery time. But his daddy being a white man, he really never was a slave, he got to go to school some. The most of the black people my daddy's age couldn't read, couldn't write, so the man said, "You owe me this, and you owe me that," they didn't know no difference. They worked happy, made a crop this year: "Well, you come out of debt but you didn't clear nothing." "OK, try it again another time, yes sir!" And they said the same thing. "You come out of debt, but you didn't clear nothing. OK, try it again another year, you'll do better next year." They didn't know whether they was paid fair or not, but people were happy.

People visited one another then, too. I remember my daddy would get all us kids in the road and walk on to the neighbor's on Saturday—when you'd laid by a crop you didn't have nothing to do nohow—walk over there and sit till nine o'clock Saturday night, walk back home. People come visit us. Now nobody visits nobody. They ain't got time to fool with you. I ain't got time to go over yonder, sit with him. I don't want him here to sit with me, I got something to do. And people work twelve months a year now. You're in a public job, you're going to work twelve months a year. Back then, by the Fourth of July we was done laying by, we didn't do nothing but fish and run up and down the road all summer, gather a crop. We'd hunt in the wintertime. There were no jobs. There wasn't nothing to do.

These jobs didn't come along until World War II come along, and then they set up these defense plants, and everybody went to working day and night, and it was a continuous thing. Used to be, you didn't never hear tell of nobody working at night, but now there's as many jobs run at night as there is in the daytime. Some places run twenty-four hours a day.

*   *   *

If I need anything these white people got around here, I can get it. We've been here since 1934. Of course, back in them days didn't nobody have nothing, you couldn't help one another if you wanted to. People with money at that time were scarce. But the relationships was good, all the way up through now.

I got neighbors around here, they'll do anything in the world for me, the white people, do anything in the world for me, and I do the same thing for them. Gay Taylor over here, Guy Fuller over there, Willard Fuller over there, and Brinton East over there, and all of them around here. I can go over there today—if I get stuck somewhere, tractor in a hole or a minor breakdown, I can go over to Gay's and he ain't at home and the tractor's out there, I can get it and go on back and use it, carry it back, tell him about it. He'd do me the same way. I wouldn't want to live in a better community than we live in.

Back yonder, when Martin Luther King was marching here and yonder, I pulled in Lineville one day, went to the doctor's office, was sick. Come back out, had a flat tire. Asked the guy about fixing a flat tire, he said, "Go to Martin Luther King's shop, let him fix it for you." You know, like that.

But I couldn't tell no difference among these people out in here that I grew up with. They never did show no partiality or that they were prejudiced towards me because Martin Luther King done all this. They didn't have nothing to do with it.

But there was people that did, and you drive different places, and, well, in Anniston there was two or three places around there, they didn't even serve the black man. If you had a black face they wouldn't even serve you— and public places too. But things is changed considerably. Always at that time, you know, the black had to take the back end of everything, he went to the back of the bus, he went to the back end of the cafeteria, and it was always like that. But things has changed. Even at Bynum.

When I first went to Bynum, we had drinking fountains: black only, white only. Bathrooms: black women, white women, black men, white men—all of it was segregated. The cafeteria: a brick wall down the middle. White people went in on that side, black went in on this side, you couldn't even see one another. When Kennedy got to be president, they blotted out all of that colored on the drinking fountain, and white only, painted all that out, locked two of them bathrooms, had men only, women only, knocked the partition out of the cafeteria, the cafeteria only for everybody, so, in other words, I saw a lot of changes through the years.

Well, it bothered me. I'd get stubborn, you know, and I'd have to walk clear from here to my barn to where it said "colored drinking fountain," and me working here and one sitting right there said "white only." It bothered me enough so I'd go over there and get me a drink of water. Won't walk way down yonder to get no water, all of it the same water. And some of the guys: "Why don't you get you a cup?" "Why don't you get you a bottle?" Says, "I don't want to drink after you no more than you want to drink after me." I said, "When I mash that button, that water comes up, I drink it. When I cut it off, the rest of the water's still way down there. You ain't drinking behind me. You're just getting you a drink of water."

But I just took a lot of things that went on. Even the supervisors at that time, something come down over yonder, real hot, got red tags on it, got to be shipped—"Hey! Three or four of you niggers come over here and pack this hot order out for me." I didn't like it, but I had to take it because I needed the job. I was trying to buy a home, I was trying to educate kids, and I needed the job. But I was looking and hoping for a brighter day, and I lived through all that stuff, and I saw a time come under John F. Kennedy.

They had a team to come in there from Washington. I didn't know nothing about them, they was just a bunch of people. And they come in there, and they stayed on the depot about a week. They come in there, and they drank water at this fountain, and they drank water at the next fountain, and they said, "Can't see no difference, this is colored water, this is white water, can't see no difference in it, what's wrong?" I didn't know what they was after.

Anyway, they hung around there for a few days, and this guy got up one day and made the speech. He quoted the ten commandments that's in the Bible. And he said, "We's supposed to keep these ten commandments." He said, "We done added on three, and that makes thirteen." He said, "Number one"—I can't remember but two of them—he said, "Number one, thou shalt not call a black man a nigger. Number two, thou shalt not call a man a boy. Because everybody is wearing a badge, and his name is on it. If you don't know his name, walk up to him, look at his badge and get his name and then call him by his name." That number three, I don't remember what it was now, but anyway they went all over the depot making that speech. And when they left there, they painted out all them signs there, just painted out all that "colored" on this and "white" on that, and done away with all of this.

And Mr. Mintz, he was the big brass chief, he got up on Friday—called everybody together, about three hundred people in that building—called us all together and said, "Fellows, I don't like this no better than y'all do," but said, "that's the law," said, "I've got to help enforce it." Said, "All these drinking fountains in here belong to the government, everybody in here working for the government, all them bathrooms around here belong to the government. We going to close up two of them, one for men and one for women. And if you've got to have a private bathroom, or a private drinking fountain, I can get your separation papers fixed up before quitting time. Then you'll have to go home, because that's the only place you're going to have it private." Said, "Now I don't want to hear no squabbling about it, and if you can't stand it I'll get your separation papers fixed up for you so you can go home." And after a week or ten days—they'd cut that cafeteria partition—for about a week or ten days, there wasn't nothing but a few of us blacks in there. But after that they began to come back, filled the thing back up, the white did. And there wasn't no squabbling, everything went on smoothly.

*   *   *

Well it's still some squabbles about it. There's places they don't want a black man to live yet in some of the cities. Well in Lineville too, they don't want you to live in a certain area, you got to move over yonder. But I always felt thisaway about it. Now there's two or three houses down there in Lineville for sale. And if I wanted to buy one of them houses, and wanted to move in there, I would buy it and move in. And then me and that carbine would protect it. I just feel like that, whatever's mine is mine. In other words, a man got a right to own whatever he is able to buy, wherever he want to, in my book.

But I wouldn't want to get in no trouble, especially now at this age. When I was younger, I might have took a chance on it, but now I'm happy right like I am.

BRUNA LAMBERT
Seventy, retired, Lineville, white

I was born not too far from Cragford, and I lived there about five years, and then my daddy moved us to south Alabama, in Coffee County, and saw-milled for seven years. And then the Depression come on, and we come back home to the old farm, and lived there and survived for several years. That's all we had, was just what we made at home, just about it. My daddy was a carpenter and a sawmiller too, and he made eighty cents a day as a carpenter during the Depression. I didn't hardly have shoes to wear. And we didn't have too much to eat, like we had been used to. We just didn't have it back then, and, man, it let me down a country mile. The old place was growed up, and I had to cut all the bushes down and everything to farm. It was a bad time there. I done most of the farming. My daddy would work out, he'd work at the sawmill, or carpentry work, anything he could.

My grandfather married a Morris the first time, and he had five children by the Morris woman, and she died, and he married a Miller the last time, and she was my daddy's mother. And Grandpa went to the Civil War—he had five slaves—and he went up in Tennessee. He got shot at Jonesboro, in a battle there, with a minié ball. It's a round ball, like a marble. Went in the left shoulder and stayed in there. And it didn't kill him—he come on home, and the brother-in-law did too, George Morris, they come home and they lived down there close together. But Grandma Miller, that he married the second time, her daddy was in the Civil War in Mississippi, him and another man, and they come back, and they stopped over there, near the old place I lived at, called Teague Mill. And they worked for wages—their shoes were wore out and their clothes was, and they stopped there. And they lived in Georgia. And they never did go home. They married there and stayed there. But that was strange, that anybody wouldn't go home after a war. I'd of swam the Pacific Ocean to get home.

People was ill toward the North when I was a kid, because the North come down here and overrun us, and Sherman come through, and you know what Sherman done. He was rough. Burnt everything that was left behind, even where the women and children was, and the slaves was, to depend on, they'd burn all the barns down and the big mansions down and everything else. See they never have forgot that. In fact they ain't forgot it today. Just like I don't forget the Japanese. I wouldn't buy their Toyotas or none of their cars at all. No, I won't. I don't like them that good. They took a chunk of my life away from me. And I ain't going to forgive them for it. And the Civil War, you see, people that remembered anything about that, knew what that was. My daddy was born after it, but his people talked it, all the old people still living. They knew about it.

I've thought more about my grandpa in the last year than I ever did. You get older, and you think about how they lived. And then, see, I went through the war, and then I think about the war he went through and what they had to fight with and what they endured and what we did.

In 1942 I went to World War II. I stayed almost four years. Got drafted. I stayed in combat two and a half years. I got four ribbons, Presidential Citation ribbon, and I got nine battle stars, a silver and four bronze. And I made three landings.

That was a trying time. I had a terrible time over there. I had appendicitis about three months after I was over there. We had beef dinner, breakfast and supper. Didn't have no leafy vegetables or nothing, and the diet I think caused a lot of us to have appendicitis. And when I done that I got weak. I weighed a hundred and seventy-two pound when I went overseas, and when I come back I weighed about a hundred and thirty. And I was weak and my nerves were shot to pieces—I had a nervous breakdown after then.

See, the war in Europe was different from the Pacific. That was just an altogether different thing. The terrain was different. It was cold over there. When they come home, their cheeks was red and rosy, and pretty color, and we was just swarthy as we could be, yellow—we took stuff to keep from having malaria—and we was yellow as gold. And I weighed about a hundred and thirty pound. And they said, "Where y'all been?" We looked bad. We was bad, too. When I was getting my discharge and come out there was an officer stopped me right there, said, "Why don't you go down there and sign up for disability?" I said, "I don't want no disability. I want to go home." And I needed one then. I sat there at home a year and a half before I could quit shaking.

I don't regret it. I'm glad I put my part in the war. Fill that space, because I think I was supposed to go. I was in that bracket to go, and we had to go. But it sure did slow me down. It took out four years of my life; it just slowed it down the worst you ever seen.

*　　*　　*

I enjoy life now as good as I ever did, I reckon. I go dance on Friday night, and I go dance on Saturday night. Me and Betty. She's the woman I go with. We think a lot of each other. If I say go or anything, she's ready to go, we go. We're going on the Fourth of July to my cousin's to a barbecue, and then my sister will meet me there, and she lives in Mobile, and we'll go to Gulf

Shores and stay a week. And we go down to Wayne and Shirley's and dance in the nights. He's got about a three-piece band. Got a good dance floor, it's not too big. Last time we were down there, Wayne picked up the fiddle and said, "I'm going to play some high-stepping music." And everybody fell off the floor except three couples. And when they started one of them got off right then, and the other stayed about halfway down, and me and Betty stayed there and danced till he quit. Buck danced. We have a good time.

I think I had a good life. When I was young, when the times was good, we had a good life in south Alabama. I thought we lived better than most people did, because we had a new car and Daddy had a payday every week or two weeks, and I'd get to go to the show for a dime and buy a Coke or something for a nickel. I didn't buy no Cokes, because my mama wouldn't let us drink Cokes. They was dopes. That's what they called them back then, dopes. And I bought a Nehi orange. And Daddy'd give me a quarter when we'd go to town, and, boy, that was big money. I had a good time. I'd play there, and my cousins—my mama's sister and her husband, they come to town too, and we'd meet there, the kids would, and we'd have a big time. Usually go home with them, or they'd come home with us, or go to Daddy's nephew's, or somewhere down there. We just had a good time.

Then I come on back and I thought I had a good time during the war. I'd come home some then, and I went with a girl in Millerville, and me and her was madly in love with each other. But we just, something, I don't know what, just drifted apart and she finally married this air force man in Orlando. She went down there and went to school, business school, just before we went off to the war. I always grieved about that, and the war come on too, and I thought about her a lot.

We had a big love affair going, and a good thing. And I always dreamed about that—that was a fantasy, you know. I married my wife. I loved my wife with a different love to that—it was strange. It was substantial. And since my wife died, this woman's daddy died, and they brought him here to Benefield Funeral Home in Lineville, so I went up there one day and I looked back and seen them. I said, "That has to be her." I couldn't even pick her out. Come back to get some water at the water fountain and I got up and met her there—I was back there with the undertakers. I go up there and hang out with them some. And I said, "Are you Nadine?" She said yes. She didn't know who I was, and stood there a good little bit, and I waited. And I told her, I said, "I'm Bruna." And she walked up and put her arms around me and held me a long time. She was married and had three children grown. She was about sixty-something years old, I guess.

I had a big picture of her, and I told her little girl—she had one that was eighteen years old—and I told her, I said, "You ought to have seen your mother whenever I went with her." I said, "I've got a big picture of her." She said, "Oh, I'd like to see that picture." I said, "I'll be back in a few minutes," and I just turned and walked out and come to the house and got it. Carried it back, frame and all. And Nadine looked at me and said "Bruna, you don't love me any more, you're giving my picture away." I said, "Well, I think we ought to pass it on."

But you know, I always wondered about everything, but after I seen her, that left. I needed to see her.

And I go with Betty now, and I love Betty. But that's a different love. You wouldn't think so, you'd of thought if you love anybody it'd be the same. But it's different. I love Betty. Betty leaves and goes to Birmingham to her daughter's up there, or anything up there, she goes up there and eats first Wednesday in the month. Each time I know she's gone I miss her.

No matter where you are, you see the hills before you, not the harsh and pointed slopes of mountains in their strength, but the final breaths of the Appalachian chain before it gives way to the flat land that runs three hundred miles below it to the Gulf. The soil is red, and rocky, and hard to plow, and even when farming was the major occupation, the farms were small, returns were low, and as alternatives arose, in the saw and cotton mills of the 1920s, the war plants of the 1940s, or the sewing factories that spurred Southern growth after the boys came home, residents rose to seize them, and to leave the county behind. When migrants returned to visit, often in cars bought with their new-found wages, the sight, said one man, made you get hungry for something. The concrete rewards of farming—generally a house, and food, and precious little more—no longer seemed enough.

Clay County's population now is close to half its former size, and large swaths of open land lie between the small, home-built farm houses, the graceful, white straight-boarded structures, the new brick dwellings that boast neat fences and horses in the field, and the corrugated sides of the cheaper make of mobile home. Around these buildings floats the flotsam of a farming past: old plows turned into mailboxes, rows of hanging birdhouse gourds, rusted coils

*of wire, mammoth tin-roofed barns shaky and just short of collapse, like the
faint shadows that haunt old photographs before the last trace of silver fades
from view.*

*Old enemies still in places linger strong, in homes where poverty keeps tight
its tenacious grip; in the drinking, fights, and shooting that recall earlier,
rougher times; and in the spirits of those—often black but also white—who
hunger after change but so often find despair, the fight has proved so long and
hard. The marks of slow decline mingle with the scattered signs of progress,
and the streamlined modern churches, the videotape and indoor tanning businesses, the satellite dishes reaching toward the airwaves in the sky, cannot
block out the empty shop fronts on the courthouse square, the worry in the
voices of those unable to find work, the overgrown old grand hotel, that looks
as if it had been closed a hundred years ago, instead of just fifteen.*

*But still those left keep holding on, some almost more through chance than
conscious wish; some with the passion that they harbor deep for woods and hills
and open spaces; some because they can't imagine living anywhere but home.
And although a niche in such a changed and changing world is hard to find
for a small place not on the way to anywhere, a place where people often have
more generosity than education, the distance the county has traversed since the
days of sharecroppers and mules has been a long one. Unsuccessful students
from poor and troubled homes have special spots in school, and all the care
their teachers have to give, to help them learn, and perhaps escape some of the
problems to which their birth once seemed to doom them. When old men get
together, they talk not of a fickle crop that they will have to live on, but of the
details of caring for their lawns. And on the first day of school, waiting for the
bus, kids compare the labels on their shoes and in their clothes, gesturing with
fingers that the sharpness of a cotton boll has never touched.*

BRUNA LAMBERT

There's one man over by Cragford, William Mayo, had a pistol that killed
two black men, killed two black people in Georgia, *it* had. I don't know who
killed them, and he got it and it killed his brother and it killed him and then
it killed Skint Walker at Cragford. Dee Walker owns it at Cragford. I'd like
to have the pistol, but I know I can't get it. I've got the one—over there
where Daddy lived, Buck Mitchell run a big store, and that was Goldburg

and had a post office in it. I got the one he had. It's a lemon squeezer, genuine pearl-handled, nickel-plated. He killed hisself with it. So I got it, it's in a safe deposit box. I don't keep it at the house.

I'd like to have the one that Dee Walker's got at Cragford. I'd like to have that one, and I know where there's another one at that killed a man, I would like to have it, and this one here, I'd like to have them three guns. You got a history on them. You've got something to talk about, you can tell about it, you see.

I Remember When
There Was More Folks
Come to Cragford

There was a time when the community of Cragford stretched for nearly twenty miles. When, in 1906, the Atlanta-Birmingham-Atlanta railroad marked a path through the county's eastern edge, naming its depot for the craggy peaks the rails ran by, the stores and businesses that lay scattered through the nearby country came to cluster near the tracks. Behind them came the farmers and the salesmen and, with Prohibition, the whisky drinkers, settling comfortably beyond the sheriff's reach. On Saturdays, activities in Cragford could rival any in the county, and when, each summer, the Christian church held its all-day singing, the hills around were thick with wagons and waiting mules.

But now, in the summer of 1987, when you make the turn at the empty schoolhouse, passing between the Baptist church and the well-kept Baptist graveyard to descend the short road into town, you will have seen almost all that remains. Perhaps a dozen houses line the hill, some with neat rows of front-yard flowers and clean side-garden patches, but others shuttered, less well kept, with weeds growing in the yard or belongings spilled in disarray on the front porch. As the paving levels out, downtown comes into view—a handful of brick, wood, and cement-block buildings that line the two sides of the street before the land drops down to rows of near-deserted railroad tracks. Only three doors stand open, at a garage, a struggling country store, and a small white post office that only concentrated effort has kept from being closed. Most of the business has moved to larger towns that cars now place in easy reach, and the death or departure of old residents, and the scarcity of new ones, have left the street empty enough for each passer-by to be remarked upon.

On the bench outside the general store, most mornings and some afternoons, a group made mostly of old men sits in the shade, exchanging thoughts and talking of a past painted in brighter colors than the present day—a time when there were often fights, and once a shootout, on the unpaved downtown street, when federal agents prowled the woods, and when, a hundred years ago, a group of men hunted down a murderer and hanged him a few feet from where they found his victim. Sitting with them, looking at the row of aging shop *fronts and tin awnings altered mainly by the wear of time, it is not hard to picture how it was. Rather than changing with the years, Cragford seems to have simply aged. The people who ride downtown are all the same ones, only older, and the community is bound together most of all by memory.*

WAY I GOT IT, HE KILLED THIS WOMAN

IN MEMORY OF

THE TRAGIC DEATH OF
MRS LOBINA KNIGHT
MITCHELL
JUNE 30, 1881
BY THE CRUEL HANDS OF
CHARLES J. WALDROP
AGE 24 WHO WAS
HANGED ON THIS SPOT
BY THE PUBLIC
JULY 3, 1881
ERECTED BY
M. D. AMASON
COMMISSIONER DISTRICT
NO. 3
CLAY COUNTY ALABAMA
1949

The spot sits quiet now, and the three-foot slab of granite, scarred at its center by a pistol shot, forms the only clue to mark it off from any other swath of clear-cut ground, growing back in ragged clumps of sumac and scrub pine. Few people drive along the red-dirt road—the handful who live back farther in the woods, and now and then someone who has heard the century-old legend and come to see the place where Charles Waldrop swung till he was dead. The silence, which the constant hum of nearby bugs serves only to intensify, seems to extend back toward that span of long-dead summer days, as though memory had managed to transcend time's passage. But the hand-carved letters on the stone tell only the beginning.

Waldrep, the murderer, ravisher, bigamist and tramp, was captured near Hogansville, Ga., on Friday night after having murdered Mrs. Al W. Mitchell, near Wesobulga, Clay County, Alabama, on Tuesday before. . . .

There Was More Folks Come to Cragford / 25

He denied having outraged Mrs. Mitchell, and let us hope he did not, yet circumstances pointed so strongly against him that no one believed him innocent. Those who heard his confession believe from his manner of delivery, that he lied liberally, and that many other crimes could be traced to his hands. His own confession was enough, and with his Maker and self let all accounts be settled!

He was carried to where he committed the murder, where he was hanged in the presence of about 2,000 people. Thus ended the earthly life of one whose life had been a continuous crime against the laws of God and his country. Let his fate be a warning. A Bigamist, a Tramp, a Ravisher, and Murderer and hung, all before his 24th year! Waldrep made other statements while on the scaffold, but we do not feel authorized to repeat them.

Roanoke Leader
Randolph County, 1881

People around here remember.

No one who saw the 1881 lynching near here is still alive, but most everyone in Cragford and other parts of Clay County knows something about the incident.

"It's all just hearsay now," says L. D. (Dee) Walker, 87.

Michael Anderson
Talladega Daily Home
Talladega County, May 20, 1987

WALTER ROLAND (SHINE) MORRIS
Seventy-five, retired, Cragford, white

Way I got it, he killed this woman; he thought she was another woman. Was mistaken in who he killed. And after he done that he run away—went back to Georgia. And they went over there and got him and chained him— locked him, they said, with trace chains, and put him behind the wagon and drug him till they got him back over here where they hung him. Yes, sir. There've been some mean things happened as far back as we ever had any history.

You'd hear different ones talk about it now and then. My daddy said he was over there when they hung him. Said the first time the rope broke, and he said somebody else there told them that he had a rope that'd hold him. And they got this grass rope, or whatever it was, put it on him. Said his nose was bleeding then. That other one bloodied his nose and all. Then put him back up there and knocked the prop out from under him, hung him. Said them boys all around there got pieces of that grass rope, wanted to keep it—a man was hung on it and all of that crap. But that's boys for you, they want to do something. He said, he told me, "A boy that bad, I don't want none of that rope."

He said there was a lot of people there. That was a new thing, you know. I guess there was a lot of people wanted to see it done. Right on the side of the road. Right where he killed that woman. Yes, sir. They just went and brought him back to the spot he done that on, see. To do the hanging.

Mildred Farrow told me, said some old fellow was in that store down there one day and said he had his skull. I wouldn't of wanted it, would you? I reckon some of that woman's people, that he killed, had his skull. I don't know how he got it. I wouldn't of wanted it.

We liked to hear it. That was something new, you know, to everybody back in that day. I don't know a lot about it. That was before my time. All I know about it is just hearsay.

RUBYE DENNEY
Seventy-three, senior citizens' companion, Shiloh, white

It was all what I was told by my grandfather, Barcellus Knight, and he came to live with me in '31. He lived with me for twenty-five years. Everybody that come along wanted him to repeat it. They come along as long as he lived here. And when something would come up, something bad, a killing, why he'd repeat these things to me and say that if they would do what they did back then, and let people see it, maybe we wouldn't have so much.

There was one thing that come along that really disturbed him, and he talked about it right sharply, was rumors that the Ku Klux had did something to somebody in Talladega or Sylacauga, something bad somewhere. He said that was no way to do things. That if a person had did a crime worthy of that, there should be enough reliable men to go and not cover their face, like they did at the hanging. That was his remarks on that.

*   *   *

She was his sister. He was just a child. He was thirteen years old when this took place. And I was a-told that she was a-going to her sister's, and she had some sewing in her apron, some apples, and she met this man and he asked her name and she told him. And he told her that she had caused him to stay in jail. And he attackted her. She was expecting her first child. And she was going to her sister's, and my grandfather said that it was in the summer and they was working in the bottoms, a bottom land where they were working, and a black man told them to listen. He heard somebody scream. But summer school was in progress, and they thought it might be children. But when she didn't come for lunch, they went to search for her, and some man's mule that couldn't stand blood found her. They found her by a stump with her clothes over her head. And she'd been stabbed several times.

Then they began to hunt, they went everywhere, and wherever they went people just quit and went hunting him. And they went to this place where they found him.

Granddaddy said that some of them said he ought to be burned. But said that some old man, Granddaddy told me his name, but these names, after thirty years, you don't remember names. He said that he talked to Granddaddy David Knight, and said, "Uncle David, death is in the law. Just hang him." Somebody said that it was a lynching. Granddaddy said it was not a lynching, that they had a judge and jury, they just didn't have it in the law court. People were appointed and he pleaded guilty to the crime. Said he told them that his first wrongdoing was smoking cigarettes, and stealing a horse. Then he said that he told that this man had hired him to kill and he had killed the wrong one. And they were about to get the other man. And he changed his story and said that he thought she was a Mrs. Mitchell that caused him to lay in Dadeville Jail seven months. They traced that later, and that was fact.

He told them that he knew he didn't have enough friends to bury him, so he would give his body to Dr. Gay—I think it was Dr. Stonewall Gay, I'm not sure, but anyhow he lived at Wadley—for five dollars for his widowed mother. And all he could eat before he died.

The first rope broke. When they hanged him the first rope broke. And somebody else supplied another rope. And I've been told that they cut that rope up and scattered it amongst the people. And he said that the man that was going to put this rope around his neck, his wife told him that if he put that rope around his neck, that she would leave him. And he told her to go on, that he was doing it for her and the good women of the country.

They say—well, they tell so many thousand, I don't know, but he said there were just people everywhere just come and camped, to see that. I never did see the chain. Dee Walker, my cousin, had the chain and lock. They taken a crib door from a Walker home down there and made the scaffolding. Them trees died. Those two trees died, that they hanged him on.

They gave him to Dr. Gay, and my grandfather said that he could remember seeing him as they carried him. They stuck his feet in a two-horse buggy, and he could see them as they went down the road. They say that his skeleton is at Wadley, at the Masonic Hall. I don't know. But Granddaddy had told me when he lived with me that if I ever wanted to see it, that it was upstairs at Lineville, in Dr. Gay's office, but I never had the nerve to go and see it. It was intact then, it was all together. They give it to him for medical purposes. Granddaddy said that her friends went to help boil him. To get the skeleton. I was told it was done in a washpot. That's what I've been told all these years. I worked at Wadley, and they told me that was his skeleton in the Woodland Lodge down there. Skull. But whether that be so, I don't know.

It was hideous. To think about it. Because I don't like the word *cremate*. I wouldn't want to be cremated. And to think, something like that. But she had five brothers, and the older ones were ready to do anything. Because he had killed their sister. And stabbed her several times and all. Granddaddy said he went there to tote lighter knots to help burn him. They thought that would be what they'd do. And this old man, he said that would just be a heathen way of doing things.

*   *   *

There're still generations in the family that are concerned. I don't suppose that nobody outside of the family is. I have seen people that their people remembered it. From years back that are old people now. And somebody'll mention it and they say, "Well, I remember my granddaddy, he went."

I don't know if it'll keep going or not. But it's history now. It's history. Things happen on. It's sad. It's sad to think about taking a life. You think about—you hope that the Lord forgive him before he died. You hope that He did. And that we don't know. If we go by the Bible, we know that we've got to forgive. And that there's a chance that he was forgiven. I think my grandfather said that he said he was sorry.

JAMIE BURDETTE
Twelve, student, Cragford, white

All I know is that it's a lynching and they said that a woman was taking some apples, I think it was, and the colored man was walking down the dirt road and then I think a fighting took place and she was throwing apples at him, and I think she might of got strangled. Or he might of stoned her to death, I don't know. A lot of people came from around Clay County and Randolph County to where it took place.

I read the *Talladega Daily Home*. I didn't know about it till then. I think it was wrong what that man did. I don't know if the other people were right. I wasn't living in them days.

RUBYE DENNEY

I was upset when they said he was a black man, because he was not a black man. This Mr. Anderson that wrote the article in the *Talladega Daily Home*. I wanted people to know that it was not. We have good black people. And I had talked to my father, and he said, "Well, you ought to call them and tell them that he was not a black man." I called Mr. Anderson, and he said he understood. He just took it for granted or something. He didn't know why, but he thought that they told him it was a black man. Then next day he retracted it, and said according to Rubye M. Denney he was not a black man. But it did disturb me that they said that, because he was not black. It was wrong. It was not true. It was not a black man. And we didn't want it told it was a black man. Because there's lots of crime, things that goes on that's not black people. So I didn't want it.

I DON'T KNOW THAT I EVER SAW
A BETTER PLACE

Shine Morris, standing in his worn and somewhat cluttered house, holds a flashlight in his hand. The lines carved deep in his old, red-brown face, the seams of his new overalls, and the startling strong blueness of his eyes lie shadowed as he plays the beam along the walls. Outside, bright day strikes on the corrugated roof, but in the house the brown of never-painted boards seems to suck up all the light, and when Shine can't remember where he's put things, he needs the flashlight to help find them.

Of all the layers of time that lie within Clay County's lines, Shine, despite the riding lawn mower he so loves to use, inhabits one of the most remote. While his friends have gladly slipped on trappings of modernity, while some people bristle at the thought that Clay County might be considered poor or backward, and many well-dressed children betray their rural background only in a few distinctive turns of speech, Shine has no phone, drives no car, and has left his house much as it was when his mother died there years ago. When he can't get a ride to town, where he goes most mornings to sit outside the open store and listen more than talk, he sets off on his own, in the slow gait that age has left him with, and the mile or so of distance can take him half an hour to traverse.

He has a wife and daughter in far-off Tuscaloosa, and lived with them a while, he says. But one day he came back to his boyhood home; his garden, goats, and geese; his dog and his old friends. He likes it here, he says in his short bursts of sentences, broken with halting laughter and syllables that have the hollow, hanging sound of echoes from somewhere far away, because even after all these years, it's still like he remembers it used to be.

SHINE MORRIS

I was raised here. My daddy built this house in '25—we moved here in '25. I was born in 1912. Twentieth day of April. I've been here going on seventy-six years. I was forty-four years old before I ever got married. Forty-four years. I've always been a home boy.

I lived over yonder where my wife lives ten years. In Tuscaloosa. She's got her place and I've got this one. I've been here about ten, twelve years. She lived over here four years. Worked in the hospital up there. She didn't like it. She's a registered nurse. She was always used to big places.

It's quiet around here, see. Makes a big difference. Over there, it's just one house on top of the other, like doorsteps going down. I don't like a place like that. She comes over once in a while.

I don't do nothing. I'm retired. I've got a little junk. Have my garden. That's what occupies me. I've got a little of everything. I've got beans up there. If it'd rain, it'd make some beans. I don't think it's ever going to rain no more. Been here for about nearly a month it ain't rained.

I was born in Randolph County. My daddy owned a whole section of land down there at the bend of that river. Owned over a hundred acres of bottom land. My great-granddaddy entered all that. We farmed it. Horses and mules. All this land in cultivation. Not growing up. I expect I got over a hundred cords of trees on it now.

I used to work for these boys cutting logs. Used a cross-cut saw. We was cutting logs out of that big old long-leaf timber. Little old six-and-a-half-foot saw wouldn't even reach—wouldn't even start through them. They went to Georgia somewhere and bought a nine-foot cross-cut saw to cut them trees down with. They was whoppers. But you don't see no more timber like that. Ain't none nowhere hardly now. Just pine trees. And they ain't worth a flip. Might make paper, that's about all. Everything has changed lots, from the time I come along till now.

I ain't got all that many years in front of me. That's a lot to study about, ain't it? Not got so many more years in front of you. After you had all this that you lived. My daddy lived to be a hundred and one years old. And three days over. That's a ripe old age, ain't it? Ain't many people ever done that. That's longer than I'm going to live. There was six of us boys, and I'm the only one living. All the rest of them are dead. Six boys and four girls.

You can think of a lot of things that happened. First one thing and then another. You take a lifetime, you know. When you grow up and work and do all these things. You can recollect all that. And chances are, you can recollect what happened way back there quicker than you can now. My daddy was a hundred and one years old, and he could sit down and talk and tell you things that happened—you'd never dream he was slipping. But anything that recently happened, he'd forget that the next day. That shows you the difference.

I was up here in Ashland one time, and they had an old nigger up there, a big old nigger. Called him Shorty. They had a bear trained to wrassle with you. The sheriff up there at that time told old Shorty, "You wrassle that bear, throw that bear"—a big old round platform, they had him on—said, "you'll have the bluff on these niggers." Said, "They'd be scared of you." Old Shorty put that muzzle on—they put a muzzle on him to wrassle with that bear. Old fellow went to putting it on Shorty. Shorty said, "Man," said, "put the muzzle on the b'ar! I ain't going to bite the b'ar!" That bear throwed him two or three times off of that platform. He was stouter than Shorty was [laughing]. "Man, put the muzzle on the b'ar! I ain't going to bite the b'ar!"

They had a leash on it. It was a big old thing. It'd stand up higher than you could reach. A big old bear. There's some of them fooled with him. He'd throw all of them—that bear was trained to throw.

This woman that stays over here at the dam said that here a while back she was down there—I don't know whether she was picking huckleberries, blackberries or what—said there was a black bear down there. She seen it. Run off toward the lake, she said.

I used to be bad at fox hunting. Run the foxes off. We had some mighty good races around on these hills. There was a bunch of us boys that got in that business one time. There was an old woman one time up here at Clairmont Springs, at a fox hunters' convention. She was from Tulsa, Oklahoma. She had five of the prettiest July dogs you ever seen. Had a big Cadillac automobile and had a big trailer on that thing. She picked me to help her manage her dogs. So I stayed with her two days and nights up there. She stayed the two days and nights, decided she'd go back home. Her husband was dead. I was just a kid of a boy—eighteen, nineteen year old, something. She tried to get me to go back to Oklahoma with her. I've studied about that a lot. That might of been my best bet that I'd ever had. That old woman might of willed me every durn thing when she died. You couldn't of told about that. When she got ready to leave, she come around and give me twenty dollars. Helping her with her dogs. You know she was worth all kinds of money, or she wouldn't of been that far off. Yes sir.

It's quiet. Nothing to bother you. Unless that bear comes along. Get a bear up here, he might get up some disturbance. I've been expecting one since that woman seen that one down yonder. Might graze out up thisaway. But he ain't showed up yet.

I don't know whether I could shoot one or not. I might not have sufficient shot to kill him. Might have to just run. I don't know. Too old to run [laughs]. If he's done rambling around, he could ramble around here. Might show up anywhere, you know.

What's that dog into now? I hear him scratching. He's all the time busy. He's all the time a-hunting rats. I can hear them at night. He favors a police sort of, but he ain't no size. He's little.

You know, I used to sawmill. Get in that old mill and whup the mules. I soon learned that that's foolish. I'd of done a heap better petting them. And felt a heap better over it. They do just as much with one a-petting them as they would otherwise. You take stock, they've got feelings just like human beings. If you'll work one long enough, you'll learn that. A fellow I used to work with'd go to Montgomery and get them old outlaw mules, bring them back up there. We'd wrap them up with harness, carry them in the woods. Some of them'd work pretty good, some of them didn't want to do nothing. We'd whup them, we'd do every way to get them to go. I can recollect there used to be two or three different sawmills in this country. Big timber back then. You could hear them old boys with them old drays, hauling logs. Whups a-crying everywhere. Whupping them old mules. But that was all foolish, and we'd of done just as well a-petting them.

I've been noticing some big old yellow butterflies, up here flying around. I just wonder what kind they are. In Mexico, don't they have all the butterflies lodge up down there in the wintertime, somewhere down there? I believe I read about that. They come from way up North, stay on all the winter. I didn't think a butterfly'd live that long.

Skinner! Come out of there! Come on!
He found a rat down there somewhere, he's working her. Get out of there! He's good to mind.

It don't worry me to be by myself. I mess around. I stay out here on the back more than I do around yonder. Think of one thing and then another.

I've told my daughter I want to do so and so, paint so and so. "No,

Daddy," says, "I like it like that." Says, "That's the antique about it." These teenagers, they see things different to what we would. I told her one day, "I'm going to clean that old range stove up, get everything off of it and everything, and repolish it." "No, Daddy, that's the antique about it."

One fellow living by hisself, there's too durn much to do. You find a job any which way you turn. I get out working in my garden and see lots of things I need to do.

I don't know that I ever saw a better place. Of course, where there's sweet there's bitter, you know, always. You ain't going to get everything just like you want it.

He's coming out now. Going to run that rat out.

VIEW FROM MAIN STREET

To the right of Cragford's central street, just before a cement bridge arches over the sunken railroad tracks, cars of all makes and descriptions cluster round a long, low building with three bays open to the summer air. Beneath a bright red Coca-Cola sign, large letters spell out "Buster Robertson Garage." Robertsons have been fixing vehicles at Cragford through four generations, and people for fifty miles around will bring their cars to Buster, even when they have to wait two weeks for an appointment.

Inside, a huge, loud, rusting fan shudders as it struggles to cool the air between the cars covering the floor and the scattered stacks of parts and tools that hint at too much work to pay attention to appearance. Larry Robertson, Buster's son, has his arms plunged past the elbow in the mass of tubes and wires beneath one open hood, and from another corner comes the sharp sound of machine on metal.

It's pretty hot, Buster remarks, but neither temperature nor words slow his brisk walk as he disappears behind a wall whose calendars, orders, and mementos proclaim allegiance to Cragford, to the Auburn Tigers, and to the Winston Cup car-racing series. The local men that have gathered near the door sit quiet in the sticky heat, concentrating movement on occasional remarks or trips to purchase sodas, but even when Buster pulls up to a stop, either briefly, to pass on a bit of news, or for longer, to listen to some tale of automotive woe, he cannot be still. His eyes dart back and forth beneath the bill of the cap he always wears, the weight of his small, neat, compact form shifts from one foot to another, and when he speaks words tumble out in bunches, run together almost as a single breath, as though he doesn't have the time to say them even slightly slower.

BUSTER ROBERTSON
Fifty-nine, garage owner, Cragford, white

One day I sat down and figured my customers at the garage. I cover a seven-county area. I get as much out of Clay County as I do in Clay County.

Maybe more. It's just the reputation, built up. You see my father was in this business all his life, and I worked with him, and then I took over, and I've had it twenty years now myself. My son's planning on taking over when I retire. Which won't be that long. Even my grandfather was in the blacksmith and wagon business—repairing wagons. When my father came along, in his age, that's when automobiles came in strong. He picked it up then. We started out under a hickory-nut tree. No garage. Worked there one year, and then he built a garage. The old garage is still standing there on the farm where my mother lives.

We was mechanically minded. It just come on down. I had six sisters—there wasn't but eight of us total—and even the girls were mechanically minded. Two of them could really of made mechanics.

Things have spread out more, just like everything else. Anniston is closer now than Ashland used to be, really. The Clay County people have really spread over the years. And those people have told other folks, and they still come back themselves, and that's where a lot of the business came from.

The other thing that built my business up so was when automatic transmissions first came out. I was the first one in the whole county that started doing that work. It's still a big part of our business. Tune-ups are the same way. I was the first one that had a diagnostic machine in the county. And I'm the only one that's got one now like this one. We've kept up all through the years by going to school, correspondence and that kind of thing. Just like the beaucoups of magazines I take all the time. You have to to keep up with it now. It's really hectic right now on account of electronics.

My son Larry finished school at Auburn and taught and coached for three years. It was just in his blood. That's all it could of been. He wanted to see if something else, I guess would satisfy a desire, but it didn't, because he came back.

LARRY ROBERTSON
Thirty, mechanic, Cragford, white

I guess coming back wasn't really something that I made a decision on. It was something that was just an understood thing. There's a lot of people say it's in your blood. My grandfather, I was real close to him. I was raised pretty much at the garage. And then as I got older I sort of got the feeling that if tradition was going to hold on, or if we were going to continue with the family thing, that I was going to have to get into it sooner or later. But I realized that there really didn't have to be any rush, because when I got out of college Daddy was still real active and there was no big rush that I had to jump into it right now, unless something had happened to him. I really wasn't pushed either way. It was just sort of—I guess it was just a feeling more than a thought process.

I don't know exactly why I came back that quick. I just got sort of discouraged at what I was doing. I wasn't really happy. I taught math at Talladega High School. I taught there for three years and I coached football and basketball both. But after the second year I didn't really enjoy it that much. At Christmas and summers I came back here and worked, and I halfway kept up with the changes in the vehicles and all, so it wasn't that hard to move back as far as the work went.

I knew moving back would be a big change because there's a lot of things left to be desired in living here. You know, fast food and stuff like that that you just don't have. Movie theater. Any time that you want to do anything, you've got to go somewhere, as far as those types of things. You've got to go somewhere. Here a while back, I was talking about somebody that was living in Birmingham and how few miles they had on their car. And I said well what the difference is, for them to go out and eat, for them to go to a movie, it's two miles. For us to go out to eat and go to a movie it's forty. And it makes a difference.

I like it here, because I pretty much always liked space. I was raised here, and we always had plenty of room. If you walk out the back door, wasn't nobody going to be there. And you had a lot of privacy, and I always enjoyed that. That's one thing I like living here more than anything we've had is the privacy you have. I can go in the back yard, and nobody's going to bother me.

I always have enjoyed doing mechanic work. It's the feeling of accomplishment. There's a lot of problems sometimes, and when you solve them, or if you fix a car, you can envision what you've done. And the satisfied customers always makes you feel good. Of course anybody knows when you work with the public you can't satisfy everybody. But you can satisfy a lot of people.

I don't know whether it's so much a knack for fixing vehicles as it's a knack for not failing. A person, when he's around a lot of people, and they try to do their best to fix whatever it is, or to take a problem head on and work for it, he's going to do his best for it. I think that's more a part of it than really having just the ability to do mechanical-type things. It's just a drive to fix whatever it is. If we were in any other kind of business, I think it would still be the same. I don't really get the feeling that we have a knack for mechanical ability. My son has a knack for taking things apart and putting them together. But that's because he sees me do things like that. We fix the lawn mower, we fix this. He sees that. It's just because of his environment. Not necessarily a natural thing for him. I have two sisters, and they're not extremely mechanically inclined. So I don't know.

I try not to get too fast-paced. I feel like I'm a little slower than Daddy because I don't want to become like that. I try to look at his life and see some things that I wished he had done when I was a child that maybe I could do. I wish when he was younger that he had spent more time with us, me and my two sisters. But he couldn't to a certain extent. As far as being a must for him to succeed in the business, it was probably more of a must than for me. Because I do have something I can fall back on. To him, he didn't have the opportunity to go to college. He pretty much had to make a go of what he was doing. And that put him in a fast pace right there, he was in a pressure-type situation. He had to provide. So he worked daylight to dark and beyond every day, and we didn't get to see him very often.

I don't think in terms of failure. Every once in a while it crosses my mind, but the only time I've ever thought about—this is sort of bad thoughts, I guess—but the only time I've ever thought about having to go back and teach would be that I was injured in some way that I wouldn't be able to do manual labor. That's the only thing that's really crossed my mind.

I realize that in the years to come it's going to be harder and harder to run a business like we run because of the advancements in cars, but I guess I'm hardheaded enough to believe that I can fix them. I don't see that I will fail.

Across from the garage, in the cavernous darkness of the general store, what work there is breaks only now and then into the great space of waiting—for deliveries, for customers, and for the phone. Outside, the building still holds to some of its old grandeur, displaying the solid, straight-lined red-brick form that marks so many American main streets. Inside, a sparse assortment of merchandise congregates on largely empty shelves, and the intervals between customers can seem to last forever.

Although Dee Walker, whose name survives in fading letters on the building's northeast side, opened the business in the inauspicious years of the Depression, his trade in crops, in farm supplies, and in the water pumps that new-strung electric lines had just brought into vogue made him one of Cragford's richest citizens, the kind of man whose presence, though he is in his eighties and rarely ventures from the house he built up on the hill, still hangs over many conversations.

But now, although residents have much more cash to spend, the store cannot compete with the savings and selection found easily elsewhere. Mildred (Mimi) Farrow, who waits on the customers, has the short white curls and the bright, hearty manner of a storybook grandmother. She spends much of her day listening to her neighbors, encouraging them in their stories and their projects, sharing when she can, and helping out in times of trouble. The store still helps to focus the community—the bench by the now-empty gas pumps in summer and the squat, wood-burning stove in winter set the scene for conversations, stories, and recollections. But the Cokes and snacks the talkers buy don't add up to a living.

So the warm circle of Mildred's smiles and support does constant battle with the sense of dim foreboding that seems to hover on the building's ceiling and in its darkened corners. Uneasy waiting can seem all the longer when other members of the Farrow clan drop by—some working now, some not, but all with tales of drifting from job to job with the county's usual uncertain prospects. Mildred bears hardship with patience, only rarely letting worry break onto her face. But as summer fades to fall, her business hours grow ever more irregular, pointing toward the inevitable day when the store will have to close, and the post office and garage will be the only spots in Cragford left to come to.

MILDRED FARROW
Fifty-eight, store clerk, Cragford, white

We got married in 1946. My husband came home on leave. Rough, it was. He wasn't wounded, luckily. He had been a farmer. He had saved a little money when he was in service, and we invested it in some property. We farmed for a while, and then it got where you couldn't make a living at it, so we went to mill work.

He went to the mill and went to work, and I went to Higgins. The sewing plant. He worked in Lanett. Down in the valley. Fifty miles. For a long time, there were ten of them, and they rode in a station wagon. He hauled them back and forth to work for about eight or ten years. Everybody would meet at the house that was catching a ride, and they'd ride from there. They worked the night shift. So they'd leave about nine-fifteen, and they had to be at work at ten-thirty. They'd get back in the next morning about seven.

I worked days. With three kids I couldn't work nights. I stayed at home and worked up there in Lineville, and I'd have time to get the kids on the bus before I'd go to work. I didn't have to go to work till seven o'clock and the bus'd come by about twenty till. Everybody around us was working back then. Just everybody around me went to work. We went to work for fifty-five cents an hour. That was some extra income for the family. The husband just stayed on the farm and kept working and the wives worked at public works to gather up extra money.

You hate to go away and leave your kids. But still, you wanted to educate them, and they had to have clothes, they had to have other things that you could not buy when you was just depending on farming. Because by the time you bought your seed, fertilizer, poison, and all the equipment and everything that always tore up, went with the farming, you didn't have any money left. So that was the main thing. And I always carried my kids places and did things to make up for the time I was away from them, working. Bought them a lot of stuff too. Spoiled them.

Where my husband worked, they made mail bags. And he'd been there twenty-three years, and they decided they could have the mail bags made overseas cheaper than they could make them here, so they closed the mill down. And he was right in the last bunch to be laid off, but the mill is standing idle today. There was fifteen hundred of them laid off. And right at a time that it was hard to pick up a job anywhere else. And gas was already getting high. It had jumped up to a dollar a gallon then. A hundred miles round trip, you don't make much money.

He stayed idle a pretty good while, about two years, and just did odd-and-end jobs. And he went to work for the government. He put on storm windows and doors and stuff like that. Winterization for homes. He worked there until last year when he got hurt.

He had gone down in the woods where my son was cutting some pulp-wood and firewood. And it came a little whirlwind and blew the top out of the tree down on him. Broke his arm up and knocked a kidney loose. Broke some ribs and knocked it all loose and he never has got able to go back to work. He was going to work until he was sixty-five. And after that happened, his doctor just told him his working days was over. He would never be able to do anything else. So he went ahead and retired. He was sixty-three. And Social Security has been so low on him. They'd taken a profile back—they can go back any amount of years that they want to. But they just go back three years now. And they take your lowest years. And of course they took that year that he was laid off in April and that give him that whole year, just nothing. And boy, it just knocked his Social Security to nothing. It has really been hard on us and I have just had to work. We just get odd jobs, first one thing and then another to make ends meet.

We had a big layoff at Higgins—got on short time. It was in '69, '70, along there. And I went from there to the mill and worked with him five years. And I quit and came to Amerace, at the rubber plant. And I worked there five years, we had another layoff, and I went from there to Ben Franklin supermarket, and Ben Franklin sold out to Valu-Mart and I stayed there a year, and they staggered our hours so bad. Some days I'd just get two hours. And I couldn't drive ten miles for two hours of pay. So I asked them to lay me off. So I was laid off two years. And then they didn't have a supply girl here—this store belongs to somebody in Atlanta—and so he got me to work till he could know what he's going to do with the store. It's been two years, and it's still here. But I think he'll close it up. Not enough business for anybody to make a living.

When Corbin got laid off in the mill, they were guaranteed that their insurance wouldn't be canceled. And he had our cancer policies, he had life policies, and everything with them, and they were not supposed to cancel. OK, they carried it one year, and then they dropped it on every employee. We couldn't even pay it, and the company certainly wasn't going to pay it. They said it was due to government regulations. And they dropped it on everybody. And we couldn't even pick it up or anything. He had a retirement plan down there and they lost that. All these years they had been paying in on the retirement and they didn't get that. They said it wasn't due to the companies, it was government regulations. I think they should have gave them their retirement. I think that's awful, they done paid all that in for all those years. There were two or three investigated on it, to see if there's anything that could really be done. I don't guess they did anything; we never did hear anything of it. We didn't because you'd have to of gone and hired a lawyer and went through all that and everything, so we just didn't do it. We figured if somebody found a loophole—if one got it everybody'd get it. They never did because we never heard anything about it.

In the fifties and the sixties were the easiest years. It was real good till '75. And from '75 to '85 it's been a hassle. Such a price hike came in, and it was just hard to pay for things or make ends meet on low income. You just had to really watch your dollar. Of course, I think that right now, everybody else is having to watch their dollar. It still hasn't changed any. There're a lot of people out of work; there're a lot of people that doesn't have anything. I guess we're fortunate that we're living on a farm and can raise our garden and have vegetables and stuff to eat, where people in the crowded city don't have a thing.

We're stable. We're living. And right now I don't think that anybody that is just working—an ordinary working person—is getting rich. I think if you're paying your bills and living, you're doing good. You're doing as good as your next-door neighbor.

I guess in a way we're fortunate. There've been a lot of people in worse shape than we have been. We've always managed to keep swimming.

MARK SPRAYBERRY
Mildred Farrow's grandson, twenty-one,
sewing-plant worker, Cragford, white

I lived here when I was born, and then we stayed gone until I was about five and then we moved back. And then we moved when I was about six to North Carolina, then we moved to Carrollton, Georgia, and then we moved to Nebraska, and then when I was ten, or about ten, we moved back here.

After high school I went to work in Alexander City, at Russell Manufacturing, where I work now. Tallapoosa County. I worked for about three or four months, and my job was terminated because it was just temporary. I came back here, pulpwooded until about November, and then that November I went to Texas with my uncle and stayed out there eleven and a half months, moved back here and got a job at Russell again. And I stayed about seven months, came back up here and went back to pulpwooding. And then I went to work for a construction company, went to Texas, Virginia, and Florida, all around like that. They laid me off, and I went back to work at Russell, and I've been working there ever since.

I load trucks—I work in the shipping department. I'm a checker now. I don't have to load so much; I just check the boxes off as they come through. I want to get a job driving a truck, but right now I've got a secure job, and I don't want to leave it. I love big trucks. I've been fascinated with them— ever since I was fourteen years old I've wanted to, and my stepfather taught me how to drive when I was about sixteen, and every chance I get I jump in one and drive it.

Second shift, it's like sleep, work, sleep, work, sleep, work. You don't have time to do anything. I have to work from three-thirty until eleven-thirty. Takes an hour to get down there and an hour to get back. It really messes up the whole day and night and everything. My girlfriend works during the daytime. I go by where she works and see her for a while, and then she comes and sees me at break. Sometimes I stop by on my way home.

I pulled a tendon in my knee, on the outside here, last month. And I had a little tear in the cartilage, and they had to go in there and they bound the cartilage back where it'd grow back smooth, and they wrapped that ligament with something, they overlapped it and then wrapped it up, so it's supposed to grow back. I was out for about three weeks. A big setback. They said I didn't get it on the job. I didn't fall or anything, or hurt it. It just started hurting.

Getting a job at Russell nowdays, you have to know somebody. It's getting just like the power company or something like that. You don't know somebody that can pull some strings or get you in the door, you're just wasting your time filling out the application. They pay more than most of the other sewing plants around there; they work regular, where the rest of the plants are on and off. As far as around here, Russell's about the best thing you can do, other than drive a truck or something like that. A thousand people a day, that's about how many come through their doors.

I'd like to go to college, but ever since I've graduated from high school I've immediately had bills to pay and then it'd be so hard to work full-time to pay bills and pay my tuition and all. I'd probably fail. Two weeks after I graduated I moved into an apartment. I had a truck, rent, utilities, stuff like that.

I'd like drafting, architecture, something like that. When I get my bills paid off that I have now, I plan to go back to school. Probably I'll go to trade school, take either electronics or drafting. They've got a new thing down at the mill where they're taking younger people and putting them in this program in electronics, or being a fixer or a mechanic. And they're sending them to school, paying their tuition and all and paying them to work while they're doing it. That's what I'm trying to get on now.

I'm probably going to get married about a year from now. And in ten years, I plan to have a nice house, a couple of kids. The American Dream, so to speak.

WE WENT RIGHT ON TOGETHER

You would not see the graves unless you looked for them—nine spaces laid out on a rise above the road, the letters on some stones broken and faded to illegibility, but the encroaching vegetation still neatly cleared away. Back farther from the road, barely visible foundation lines mark the former heart of Cragford's black community, the church that filled the isolated grove with Sunday morning song. The railroad workers were transferred away, the share-croppers left with the demise of cotton culture, and the gravestones, the van-ishing foundations, and a few rarely evoked scraps of memory are all they left behind.

The road to Lineville runs eleven long, twisting miles to where the flowers outside a sheltered home have run a little wild as well, crowding up against the screened-in porch. Inside, fragments of black Cragford can with some effort be recalled, although the frailty at the edges of Tom Johnson's voice and the ghostly air of his wife Eunice's thin body, her white hair, careful movements, and floating, unjointed conversation, suggest that not much time will pass before the images on which they keep a fragile hold will also fade away.

EUNICE JOHNSON
Seventy-eight, retired housekeeper, Lineville, black

Lord, it's been so long since we lived in Cragford. I don't know how many years it's been. We moved to Cragford from Lineville. Ain't no colored peoples down there at all now.

I worked there for Mrs. Carter, and Mrs. Romaine. I worked for every white man there was there. Housework, and wash some, iron, do every-thing else. And Mr. Nichols' oldest boy got killed in service. I got his picture in yonder somewhere now. I look at him sometime and cry. I done tended to him so long. I was just like in the family, because I stayed with them folks long as we lived down there. Dennis Nichols was his name. When they told me that boy was dead, I like to fell dead too, because I was just in the family, you see. They was just as crazy about me as I was them. I think I have his picture somewhere, but I don't know where it's at now.

When we lived down there, there wasn't no difference hardly in the white and the colored, they just went on together. You didn't ever know Jim Gates, I don't guess. That was one of our best friends. He's dead now. He didn't miss a day coming to our house. If he worked that day, he was coming by there at night and set a while before he left. Yes ma'am, I loved Mr. Jim Gates, I don't care if he was a white man. Jim'd come there sometimes and sit till eight or nine o'clock with us.

We tried to do the best we could, and they was nice to us. We visited them white folkses houses anytime we got ready. And they'd come to our house. Yes ma'am. They'd come to our house and we'd go to theirs.

You could catch the train and come back here to Lineville. And I never did have to run nowhere either. Because didn't matter where I was going, the train wasn't going to leave me. They wouldn't leave me, them white men, they'd say, "Yonder she come!" I had three little boys at Cragford and they'd wait and get them children and put them on the train. Say, "We ain't going to leave you," say, "Yonder she come." Sometime I'd be further than down here at them houses, but they never did leave me. No. They'd know I'd be coming and they'd help me get them childrens up on the train. No, they never did leave me, I have to give that to all of them white folks.

*   *   *

When they told me that they had done killed Martin Luther King, it like to killed me. I've got some pictures sitting on the couch. Got all of them sitting in there. And you see them, right there. Them's the Kennedy brothers, them white boys. They killed them too. Killed them Kennedy brothers. But you see Dr. Martin Luther King's right there with them. There's them over yonder. I've got about five or six of them sitting in there. I reckon everybody thinks, "She sure does love them pictures," but I sure do keep them.

But you know, I don't care where you go, some folks are going to think they're better than others. Don't care where you go, some's better than others. But all those folks we come up with was nice to us. And Mr. Jim, he'd come over and set with us every night till bedtime. When they told me that man was dead, I couldn't help from crying. I had to cry. I don't care what color he was. He sure did get off with me.

TOM JOHNSON
Seventy-nine, retired railroad worker, Lineville, black

We've been up here forty-two years. A long time. All them people that I knew when I was down at Cragford, mind you, is dead. Ain't no colored down there at all.

I worked on the railroad. I worked on the railroad forty-four years. I moved from Lineville. I was working on the section here, and I got laid off, and I went to Cragford and went to work. Then my job was cut off there, and I moved here to Lineville.

When they first made the church down there, they made a little log cabin. And we just kept on building until it come to be a pretty good-sized church. And we had two, three preachers down there. It's growed up down there now. The church is almost rotting down, after we all left out from there. When we first had a church, we just had a house. And it was a lot of peoples come over there then.

We just got to moving away, and the section got cut off and we moved away and didn't leave nobody. We had singings down there. We had a nice time down there then, and there'd be a lot of white folks come there and hear us sing.

*   *   *

Now back here when I started on the railroad, I couldn't get no, what I call a section-foreman job. They wouldn't let us do that. Now, they got black men running these machines and things. When I come up, they wouldn't let me do that. They just wouldn't allow us to run them. Just wouldn't give you the opportunity to try.

I started in 1926, working. I was a laborer. And they'd hire a white man to come out there and work, and first thing you know he'd be working a job where he'd get more pay. And I have learnt them how to work. But see, they wouldn't let me do that work. But I learnt them how. And five or six months, they'd jump up and get them a job making more money. I learned a lot of whites how to work, how to do the work. That wasn't fair. I felt like after I help him to learn the work, then he'd get out there and work me, and I done learnt him how to work, why couldn't they let me do that work too? I learnt him. I learnt him how. Why couldn't they let me have it? And after I learned him how, he tried—I'll just tell you how it is—he got where he wanted to tell me what to do. And I knowed more about it than he did. But still, I had to go on doing that. I could do any kind of work that he done, but because I was black they wouldn't let me have it. Wasn't nothing you could do about it. Wasn't a thing you could do.

You'd think about it. When they did give better jobs, and didn't give them to you. It'd make you think.

*　　*　　*

It was a nice place to live, Cragford. Down there, when we was at Cragford, take the blacks, they could go around and visit the whites. They was just as good to us as you'd want anybody to be. We went right on together.

PROGRESS IS WHAT IT IS

Shade falls on the bench behind the rusting gas pumps, where Mike Carter, eighty-nine, sits talking in the slow and husky voice that comes part from being white and Southern, and part from being old. Across from him, in a chair, sits L. B. (Junior) Gibson, a younger, if not quite sprightly, seventy-five. It is a lovely day in early summer, the street awash with sun not yet too hot, and the men look perfectly in place, as though they had spent the afternoons of the past fifty years in just that spot. But neither of them lives in Cragford now, Carter explains. They just like to come down to the store, to see people, to talk, and to remember. As they converse, with each other and with passers-by, their words come at an easy gait, sounding like lines in an oft-practiced play, and in the silences, through which you hear the lawn mower Delon Farrow is riding next door, it seems as though someone simply has forgotten for a moment what he is supposed to say.

Mike: I just come down here with L.B., just he wants to come. We just sit here and chat. I usually know somebody here, but nobody's here today. I know everybody that was born and went to school here. Meet your old friends here, talk to them. Things that's past and gone and then present things—oh just anything we can get up a conversation about, that's what we talk about. Politics is the biggest thing, especially on election years.

A loud rattle comes from near the Robertson garage, as Allwin White, whose hair is also gray, pushes an ancient lawn mower across the street.

Allwin: I read in the paper last night that Anniston's still a little under the normal rainfall. And so's Birmingham. But the creek's full. It's running normal.
Mike: Well, that's good. What's that one over yonder, what creek's that?
Allwin: That's Whiskybulga Creek. And this other one right over there behind the schoolhouse, that's White Oak Creek.

Mike: That's like that liquor we used to have around here in Clay County. Cragford Clay County Corn is what it was.

The water conversation continues, but Carter is laughing to himself.

Cragford Clay County Crooked Creek Corn is what you called it.

He pauses.

I started on my first corn still down at New Hope. I was running with the other boys, and they was at it, and they learned me how. We drank it then. We drank that whisky then. But I ain't taken a drop in forty year. I had a family, and they was coming up and I didn't want them to see me drinking.

I've been here on Saturday evening when you couldn't turn around here for the people with cars, and wagons. Drunk. Clay County Cragford Crooked Creek Corn. *He laughs again.* I done made a bit. You take some meal and cook it. Sour it. Put some malt in there and let it work about two days. And then go back and put sugar in there and let it work about eight more. And put it in the still then. Turn water on the worm, to cool it, to evaporate it, to cause it to make alcohol. Easy as anything.

Lord, I couldn't start to tell you how many did it at that time. Every other hollow you go to you'd find a still. We sold some, enough to pay for our materials and things to make it out of, and we'd drink the rest of it. There's not much whisky now. They drink it now, but they drink it at home. I've seen more fights right out there when that was just dirt out there, right there in them streets. Get drunk and get to fighting.

L.B.: What do you think about me? I'm seventy-five years old and if you was to take a gun right there and say, "I'm going to kill you if you don't tell me what whisky or beer or anything like that tastes like," I'd say, "Well, you just have to kill me for it." Never tasted it in my life. I just never did have no taste for it. I had plenty of chances, you understand. I had a brother that drank a whole lot, but I never did.

Mike: We had a pretty good sale for it. I know what they call Morris Bend down here, I know I've seen fifteen fifty-gallon barrels in there lots of times. Ten dollars a gallon. Me and another fellow took two fifty-gallon barrels down there in an old pickup one night, carried it to Wadley. This fellow poured syrup all over the stopper, and all over the barrel.

I've had pretty good races, two of them. They just somebody reported it. And they run in on me. They used to couldn't catch me though—there wasn't no use for them to try. A fellow that used to be the sheriff here in this county, he was close as this here. And I saw him. And he reached up and grabbed at my overalls—I had on a pair of overalls. And he grabbed hold of one strap but I give him that strap and kept going. I run and got away. They'd send you to the penitentiary for that then. I had a brother went. Then I was police chief at Lineville five years. I had to catch some mighty good friends of mine.

L.B.: This here dope business, that's what's giving trouble now.

Mike: That marijuana, and stronger stuff. They're catching two growers every week nearly. Right down there on my son-in-law's place, they caught a bunch about a month and a half ago. He's disabled and don't get about much. They had it planted over there, and he found it and called the sheriff.

I'm sure sorry that so much of this dope has got in our schools.

L.B.: They got it in all the schools from the sixth grade up.

Mike: I tried to buy a cigarette of that stuff two or three years ago. I wanted to try one joint of it. And the girl who was selling it wouldn't let me have it. I just wanted to know what it tasted like. She wouldn't let me have it. She was selling it right enough. But she wouldn't let me have any. Said, "You don't need any."

*   *   *

L.B.: I just like it down here. I don't know—I just like it. I come thirteen years, and I just got used to it. Come with the man that carried the mail. Back then we had more mail than we got now. They changed all that around. It's different from what it was.

I never did live here, but coming with him every day except Sunday for thirteen years, it just give me a—something that I like about it. I couldn't explain it. I couldn't tell you to save my soul, what it was. But I just fell in love with it, is all it was. I'd love to live here if I could, but my health's bad. I have to stay up there in the project, close to the hospital. You got nobody in them projects to talk to.

Olen Farrow, another long-time resident, appears at the end of the street, walking toward the store.

Olen: Hi, Mike. Hi there.

L.B.: Hello, old man.

Mike: You doing all right?

Olen: Well I'm doing, I don't know if it's all right or not.

Mike: Well, it's the best you can, ain't it?

Olen: I hear you.

Mike: Well, all right.

After a few minutes Farrow comes out of the store, and inquires about chewing tobacco.

L.B.: No, sir. Don't carry any of that. I can't use that.

Mike: Me, either.

L.B.: I used to could.

Mike: I used to too.

L.B.: I used to plow a mule, too, but I can't do that no more.

Olen: I hear you talking now.

L.B.: I used to plow a mule. To death.

Olen: I used to plow two of them.

L.B.: Me too.

John Stanford, who lives just up the street, is walking by, and joins in.

John: That old hotel's going down in a hurry, I'll tell you.

He points to the two-story building by the store.

L.B.: Yeah, it's going down.

Mike: That's an old building.

Olen: That house there out yonder's going down too.

L.B.: It needs a top on it, that's what it needs.

Mike: It's old. That building's been there about as long as you have.

John: It's older than I am.

Mike: That's what I'm talking about.

John: And the railroad's just about gone.

L.B.: They're not running nothing but local trains over it now, ain't no more through trains. Manchester-Birmingham. Cut that out.

Mike: That was the first building they built in Cragford. *He points to an empty space.* Right there.

Olen: That's the drugstore, there.
Mike: And the bank was over there. These buildings was all built the same time.

The bank, they note, failed during the Depression.

Mike: Two or three got in there and got their hands in the cash drawer and got it all.
Olen: That's the way a lot of them go.

There is a long pause.

Mike: That was during Hoover's days.

Another pause.

I remember when there was more folks come to Cragford than there is goes to Lineville now.
John: Yeah.
Olen: Ye-ah, boy.
Mike: Yes sirree.
Olen: I've seen mules tied all over these hills.
Mike: I have too. I've come to the gin right down there and get there about one or two o'clock in the morning and it'd be dark and before you get to the cotton gin there'd be cars parked all the way up this hill. Used to be a pretty good hill from here down there. But it's not any more. *Pause.*

I've known fellows to run corn down there until way in the night. Lots of times.

The conversation quiets again, and Farrow and Sanford drift away.

L.B.: I wish it was back like it was when I come down here several years ago.

Mike: The people was more better. They was neighbors, and if I needed something all I had to do was to call them down. You can't call nobody today.

L.B.: Now they don't pay you no attention.

Long pause.

Mike: Progress, that's it. Progress is what it is.

Having a Job
Beats Hunting One

Preceding page: Brenda McDonald

WALTER FARR, JR.
Sixty-one, retired school administrator, Barfield, white

There are people in this county who claim that their ancestors were plantation owners and slave owners, but I don't really know about that. I doubt it. Clay County and Randolph County were pro-Union, by the way. Of course it was Randolph County at the time, and the majority of Randolph County people were pro-Union. So when people in Clay County start bragging about my great-great-grandfather, and his slaves or plantation, I look at these log houses, with the dog trots, and I just kind of chuckle. Now I might be wrong, and we might have had one or two, but you've been in this area. You haven't seen any plantations. We were poor hill-country farmers. Let's face it. A lot of people in this area took land that nobody else would have.

Making a living in Clay County has never been an easy proposition. From the days when farmers came to settle the uneven land, cut down the trees and burned and dug out the resistant stumps, until now, when women labor for production pay and some inhabitants commute two hours each way to jobs, work in the county has almost always meant hard, physical, and tiring effort, with relatively low return. If recent decades have raised wages, they have done less for stability—after struggling through the slow and painful death of cotton farming, residents now face the loss of many of the factory jobs that replaced the crops and mules. With frequent plant layoffs, and many occupations depending on the weather, the county unemployment rate has only in good times been out of double figures, has topped fifteen percent in several of the past decade's years, and has swung as many as ten points from month to month. "I guess maybe I'm looking for too much," an unemployed and close to desperate woman says about her search for work. "I'm thirty-nine years old. I need something with a retirement plan and a decent salary and that works twelve months out of the year and has some hospital insurance." There are many in her situation.

An assortment of small businesses lies scattered through the countryside, ranging from a cabinet-making firm with sales throughout the country to a store stocked with dented cans of food. But few serve much beyond a local clientele, and many have given ground to larger, outside firms. Where men with their own small trucks once cut down the county's trees, sawed them into the five-foot length their vehicles could hold, and took them to the pulpwood yards, most such operations have lost out to large conglomerates, which run expensive rigs that carry massive loads of uncut trunks. Chicken growers, just about the only full-time farmers left, never own the birds they care for. The mammoth firm of Tyson Foods brings growers baby chicks to raise and picks them up several weeks later, paying according to the weight they've gained. A disaster, such as hail or killing heat, is the grower's loss, and if for some reason Tyson cuts the stream of chickens off, there is nowhere to turn, and a sixty- to seventy-thousand-dollar investment per chicken house is lost.

In such troubled circumstances, finding a niche with some stability, let alone one you can love, calls for dedication, responsibility, and sometimes courage, and the success that people have achieved reflects all of these qualities. Although the death of full-time farming took with it much of the passion that even now gets people out at the first hint of spring to break their garden plots, to set out tomato plants despite the threat of frost, work still brings forth strong emotions—pride in the quality of what you make; the satisfaction of a long day in the sun, building something that will last; and everything tied up with making steady money in a place where that can be a real accomplishment, no matter what you do.

A woman whose back had slipped two discs, who had found no work for months and hated not only being poor but being idle, rejoiced to find a sewing-plant position, even though it meant a hundred-mile round-trip commute, and leaning over her machine produced a stream of nearly constant pain. A former pulpwood cutter, who now can hardly walk because of the hard and risky tasks he undertook, still eyes rich timber stands with a deep-down kind of longing, and at night he dreams of being in the woods, and of the slow, descending crash of falling trees.

HUBERT GREEN
Seventy-four, truck farmer, Ashland, white

I used to raise these Clay County yellow-meated watermelons. They've been here ever since I could remember. My daddy died when I was young, and I taken the habit up and raised them I'd say fifty years ago. Been raising them ever since, up till two years ago. My seed run out on them. Anything'll run out. They taken the blight, and diseased up more, and we don't have the ground now like we did then. There's just more disease in it. And everybody else's around here has got that way, nearly. There's seed, but they don't make like they used to.

I heard somebody say that they got together and improved the seed up to this, but I don't know how. I think it got in the Owen settlement down here, was the first ones I ever knew a-raising it. He built his seed up. They crossed them up some way and got a yellow-meated one after so many years.

I saved my own seed. You couldn't order them. You just cut them and lay the seed out on a paper, and they'd dry up just like any other kind of seed. I used to just go to the patch and get them, and there'd be a tub and put it out in front of the air conditioner and it'll dry out. Everyone in Clay County raised and saved their own seed. There's no company never did put these seed out.

I'm a-raising a different watermelon now. It's Crimson Sweet, and I like it better than I do the yellow-meated one. They don't have this disease in them, and they don't take the wilt like the others. They're wilt-resistant. Of course I order my seed now. I didn't save none of them this time. It's lots of trouble to dry a watermelon seed out.

Lots of them still call for yellow-meated ones. I think the Owens still try to raise them, but they wasn't any good this time, I heard them say. Now one fellow, he still raises them, but he carries them down to south Alabama. Better land for it. They are a sweeter melon, now, they're a good melon. But everybody'll tell you their seed run out.

I ALWAYS WANTED TO BE A FARMER

LEWEL SELLERS
Eighty-six, retired farmer, Millerville, white

Papa was born right over here, just across the creek. My grandfather died when he was twelve. Uncle William, I believe he was fifteen. They had my grandmother and two old maid sisters. And they were on the mercies of the world. Somebody come and took up a pair of mules and a good horse that my granddaddy had, told them that they owed him for it and he'd have to take it. They've questioned that a lot since they've got grown. But they let him have it. See, Uncle William was fifteen, and my grandmother didn't know anything about it. Anyway, all they had left was an old steer. And Uncle William had about five or six acres of corn. They had a fence around it. At that time all your fields were fenced—the stock was branded, and it ran and rambled everywhere.

And he looked over there one day, and there was a bunch of cows and hogs in his corn field. And he couldn't get them out. Went down there and told Uncle Frank Monroe. He was one of the most prominent men in this community at that time. He had a grist mill and a flour mill, and had a good many sharecroppers down there. He was no kin. But he was a mighty good man. They always called him Uncle Frank. He said, "This man's cows are in the field and I can't get them out." So Uncle Frank went and told the fellow, "Get them out of there." Well, come to find out that he'd had a nigger tear the fence down for his cows and stuff to get in that corn patch.

Well, in two weeks they was back in there again. Uncle William went down and told Uncle Frank that they was in there. And he says—he called them Tommy and Willie. Says, "Willie, can you shoot your daddy's old musket?" Uncle William said, "I can but I can't load it." He said, "Go get it and bring it here." So he loaded it and he said, "You go back, Willie, and just kill whatever you can get. Bring it back and I'll load it again, and you just keep on." So he killed an old cow. Killed an old hog. And killed a pretty good-sized yearling. And by that time word had got to this fellow up here that he'd better get them out. And he got them out and they never got back in again. Now what he'd had in mind up there was to starve them to death and get the place. Well, he never bothered them any more after that.

There was lots of good people around here, and then people who took advantage of the lower class. That old man up there did. I remember Uncle William telling me he took everything. They rented a crop from him, and the fall of the year he took everything they had and all he left them was a wash pot. Even took the furniture out of the house. But he died, and everything he had went away. His children never amounted to anything.

*   *   *

I always wanted to be a farmer. When I was a little kid, I played farm. I'd have me a fence with strings in the fields, and where I'd be a-plowing. I just wanted to be a farmer so bad.

I'll go back and tell you how I got started. I had three old bachelor uncles. One of them was running a store over here in Millerville. He was well-to-do. He had a place of business in Millerville, and he bought Uncle Frank Monroe's gin and sawmill. And he owned a lot of land. I'd go up there and hang around the store. Well, a man come through back then in the spring of the year—these mule and horse dealers, they'd come through with ten and twelve behind the buggy in a string. They'd buy, swap, sell, and do whatever you had. Well, this old fellow stopped there at Uncle Sam's store. And he had a bunch of them. And kidlike, I was going out and looking at them. I was ten years old. I was looking at them and finally that fellow said, "Here, son, let me put you up on this little mule." Had a little mule there, weighed about eight hundred pounds, I guess. Perfect pet. And he untied him from the train and said, "Ride him around here. He's gentle; he won't throw you." So I rode that mule around there, and I was thrilled. Finally he says, "Sam, buy this mule for that boy." And Uncle Sam says, "That boy don't need no mule." And kept on and finally Uncle Sam said, "Would you love to have that mule?" I said, "Yeah, Uncle Sam, I *would*. Uncle Sam, buy me that mule."

Anyway, he bought the mule. And now he said, you're going to pay me for this mule. It was a hundred and fifty dollars. Well, Uncle William and them fixed me a cotton patch right up there—that was before we had the boll weevil. And I felt like I was doing big. I made me a bale of cotton. Sold that bale of cotton. Next year I made me a bale. I was farming.

When I finished high school, I went to Jacksonville Teachers' College. The first school I taught, I taught it over here in Millerville. I got sixty dollars a month. I was staying at home; didn't have any board to pay. Well, I started buying land. I bought forty acres from Aunt Margaret out here. And give her four hundred dollars. I just kept staying at home—I stayed there and taught for a good many years. Well, as fast as I could make any money, I put it in land. Thirty dollars an acre was the most I paid for any of it. I got lots of it for five dollars an acre. Then when I was teaching, I farmed too. I had sharecroppers on all this land. At one time I had eight plows a-running.

*   *   *

When my son Tommy first come back here, we were the biggest farmers in the county. We've put most of it in the soil bank now; it's all gone. We're going back into timber. For I guess about ten years we growed between two hundred fifty and three hundred acres of corn, and grain sorghum and other stuff. We had a good bit of row crops. At one time I had over twelve hundred acres.

I was just big, and then Tommy wanted to be a farmer. But that's the worst mistake I ever made. You can't make it now. We can't make it—he can't. And I've hurt. I was the cause of him coming back. Because I wanted him to come back. He wanted to. And I thought then it looked like there was plenty—well, I was making money. I made money farming. I quit teaching when the war come along. Went to Talladega, to that defense plant. I stayed home and worked over there all the years, and kept my farming going. Mary Ruth and I had a good nigger, hired him by the month. He and Mary Ruth kept everything going. I had a great wife; wonderful wife.

If anybody'd of told me twenty years ago it'd be like it is now, I wouldn't of believed him. I believe between Ashland and Goodwater, Tommy and Earl Mattox, up the road here, are the only farmers that's making their entire living off of farming. All the rest of them got jobs somewhere else. It's gone back to timber land.

I miss Mary Ruth so much. She was a good mother. And if I'd of listened to her, Tommy wouldn't of been back. She said, "It won't work. Things are not going to stay like they are. Haven't ever have, there's been ups and downs, ups and downs all through there." Yes, she was great. Worked hard and helped to save. She made all the girls' wedding gowns. No, I take that back; she bought Colleen's. And what she made looked just as good and cost much, much less.

DAVID AND DARLENE UPCHURCH
Thirty, cattle and chicken farmers, Barfield, white

David: My daddy's been in the chicken business for thirty-three year now. So I was raised on a poultry and cattle farm. And all through high school I wanted to be a farmer, and chicken farming's about all there is here in Clay County. My daddy never had done anything but farm. He and my granddaddy had a general store that they run, but they've always farmed. We're the fourth generation on this place here. Hoping to carry it on, let our boys have it sometime.

We got married in '76, after I got out of high school, and in '77 we rented two chicken houses about a half a mile from here, and we grew pullets. And got on our feet to where we could build our own chicken house. I'm wanting to build another one now, and it costs right at sixty-four thousand dollars. The first one, we've got about twenty-eight thousand in it. But we had used equipment. The second one was about thirty-four. That sixty-four, that's everything new. But we've always got out and found folks that had some equipment that we could use, and buy it from them. And we've always tried to just do it slowly, as we could, and not jump in and build lots of them and have a high interest rate to pay. The most we've ever borrowed is six thousand dollars. Built the first one in '80, and then built the second one in '85, and as soon as they'll let me build another one, I'm going to build another one. We grow for Tyson Food. And right now, they're not building. But this spring, they're hoping to build more.

Now I think they're building the houses on about a ten-year payback period. When my daddy built his last one, some twenty-three year ago, his first batch of chickens paid for the house and equipment. So that's the difference in now and then. It's a lot more expensive nowdays. There's some risk in it. They just guarantee us the next batch, that's all. No long term. But most farming is a risk. That's the way it's always been. You never know.

We get our baby chickens when they're just hours old. They bring them on a bus and put them in the chicken house. And we get rid of them about eight weeks old. They weigh six to six-and-a-half pound at eight weeks old.

All roosters. Roosters are for deboning—they take them to Ashland, to the processing plant, and debone them.

They furnish chickens, feed, and medicine. We furnish housing and lights and gas and the upkeep. That's the way it's always been. See, we grow them under contract, on feed conversion. The two chicken houses have thirty thousand capacity, together. We get about five batches a year, around a hundred and fifty thousand a year.

I've got a full time job at Higgins Slacks at Lineville. Mechanic. Of course it's close by; I can run home if I need to. Darlene's usually here except on days she carries the mail. She carries it about eighty-five days a year. I'd like to go full time. If we had one more house, it would support us. Might get by now, but it'd be tough.

A lot of folks don't count it as real farming, but it is. Growing animals— I consider that farming. And this last year we won the state Outstanding Young Farmer contest, and we were judged against nine other commodities, growing corn, cotton, peanuts, fruits, and vegetables, so the judges believed it was farming.

I enjoy it. I always have enjoyed being out, watching things grow. These chickens grow off so fast.

Darlene: You can tell a difference in them from one day to the next. You can really tell a difference. We've got one house that's a week old today, and we've got one house four days old, and in the next week you'll really be able to tell the difference in them. In this next week they'll really change their size every day.

He goes out there about six-thirty every morning, to make sure everything's OK. Then he goes on to work—he has to be at work at seven o'clock. I get Randall off to school, and then Jason sleeps a little later, and I get him up and me and him gets out there and sees about them. David comes in for lunch, and if anything needs seeing about that afternoon, I go back out there. If it don't, he comes in and he goes out there until dark. And he goes out there after dark and puts them to bed, he calls it.

David: Just go see that everything's all right. You sleep better knowing that everything's all right. That's the main thing—make sure the feeders are working properly and no water's running over.

Temperature is most important. We've got to keep the houses around eighty degrees. Eighty-five when they're babies, and then drop it on down— you can get it as low as seventy-five. Temperature and ventilation, keeping good feed and clean water. Just seeing after them is most important. Being there.

In the summertime, if it gets to ninety-five degrees, and you have big chickens, you'll lose thousands sometimes. We've never had anything like that. Hope we don't.

Darlene: The most we've ever lost was about four hundred and something. A lot of the other farmers around here was losing two-three thousand. And it was bad on the paycheck.

David: We've got brood cows. Raise the calves and sell them. We've got thirty head of brood cows. We spend all summer getting hay up for them, and winter feeding it. When the price is good like it is this year, you can make money. Some years you can't. But we don't have a lot of fertilizer. We use our chicken litter—about three times a year we clean out. And we use that on the pasture for fertilizer. That comes in handy because commercial fertilizer's so high.

Darlene: Some people have cows just for hobbies, but that's somebody that's got a good-paying job.

David: If I wasn't making money on them, I wouldn't keep them. I'd just sell mine. No use doing it if you can't make money on it. That much work. I'd rather chicken farm. Them cows, they can get out of the fence. You always know where the chickens are going to be. There's a lot more to keep up in the cattle.

Darlene: The cattle are not as time-consuming as the chickens are. So we can work it in there, along with everything else. I was thinking the other day, if we didn't have but two jobs, we wouldn't know what to do with our time.

David: It's hard to slow down, I reckon. I come in from Higgins, put my boots on, and go out the back door. I stop at dark. Go from sunup to sundown.

Darlene: And as the days get longer, he still stays. In the wintertime we eat supper around six-thirty, seven o'clock. In the summertime it's nine o'clock. We're constantly having to keep up with different things. We have to tell each other what we've done out there, changed or whatever. If the service man comes and tells us something different to do, or give them vitamins, or they're going to vaccinate them or something.

David: Daddy's feeding the cows now, during the winter. He feeds them about two o'clock every afternoon. Lots of times my brother's there to help him. The cows are having calves now, so we have to go back and check them just before dark. You just sort of fit it all in when you have to.

We don't do a whole lot else. We go to Anniston, go out to eat every now and then. Go to meetings. During the summer we go to the backwater down here and fish and play. But mostly just work.

Darlene: We go to church.

David: We just have to enjoy each other, I reckon.

ESTELLE AND JOHN HEARD
Fifty-five and sixty, retired pulpwooders, Delta, black

John: My brother was pulpwooding for a guy, and he got me a job helping him pulpwood. And we pulpwooded several years for him. I ran a power saw. I cut them down by myself and cut them up. And the other guys loaded it on the trucks and carried it away. I cut an awful lot of them. Sometimes I would haul them to the wood yards. Sometimes I'd do all of it. But most of the time I ran a power saw.

So I cut for him a long time, and then I decided to cut for myself. I believe I was thirty-four. I bought me a truck of my own, and I cut for several years for myself. Until I got sick and I had to go to the hospital and was operated on. Well I came back out and I pulpwooded a little bit, but I finally got where my health was no good, and I had to quit. I can do a little work, but not much, now. I go gather a little firewood. They retired me on Social Security about nine or ten years ago. I'm sixty-one the twenty-second of this month. So that brought me down to where I am now. Sitting down doing nothing.

There were quite a few like me. Most little guys had just two or three working. My brother-in-law, he had four or five helping him. But I never did that. Mostly myself. Cut them down, and loaded them, and then carried it. I guess that's why I can't go now.

Estelle: I helped him sometimes. Helped load it. Yes sir, when he didn't have a loader, I'd have to pick it up and load that wood. By hand. I had five kids, but they'd mostly be going to school. The baby we carried with us.

John: I worked all the year round. Unless I was sick or something and I couldn't go. Bad weather I couldn't go. Rain or something.

Oh yes, I enjoyed it. I dream about it at night. I talk about it in my sleep. That's what my wife says.

Estelle: "Watch it, watch it!" he'll say. "Oh mercy! Look at the wood over there!" And when he's awake we'll be riding down the road going to church, and he'll see a batch of pulpwood; he don't take his eyes off the wood. He don't look at the road, he looks at the wood and says, "I wish I was in that batch of pulpwood."

John: Yes, I loved it. I really did.

Estelle: He liked to work like he wanted to. He could go early if he wanted to. Quit when he wanted to. If he had two loads early, he quit early. If he didn't, he'd stay there till he did.

John: I borrowed the money from the guy at the yard that I sold it to. I borrowed the money and bought the truck. It was nice. You can't do it now. You can't find no timber now. Peoples don't want to sell none. See, most of the big guys have took over now. They go cut it tree length. They just cut the whole tree and carry it. They get more for it than we got for it. They could pay more for it than little guys could. Now every guy that pulpwoods has got big trucks—trailers you call them. There's not very many small ones.

That's about all a black man could do. Pulpwood or sawmill, one or the other.

Estelle: Or pick cotton. The women picked cotton and the men pulpwooded. I remember me and my twin sister picked three hundred pounds apiece, every day. We'd go in groups, and we'd see who could pick the fastest. And whoever picked the fastest they'd give them the prize, or the most money, or whatever. Tell them that if you pick a bale of cotton by two o'clock you can quit. And that'd be three hundred pounds apiece. So we did.

John: That was all there was to do before the pulpwooding came along.

Estelle: That was about all. Oh, Lord, it was rough.

John: First pulpwood I ever cut, I cut it with a hand saw. We didn't have a power saw. That was hard work. But I enjoyed it. It was a good, healthy job, as far as that. You got plenty of exercise. And see, I was young. We had to carry it out with our hands. And I'd show them how strong I was, you know. In a way it was fun, to us young boys. We would see which one could carry the largest one. It was fun. It wasn't hard at all after I learned the power saw, to cut it. It wasn't any trouble.

Estelle: Especially with a loader. A loader helps a lot.

John: A power loader, run by the motor on the truck. You just pile it up and put the cable around it. Load it on. You wouldn't have to carry it. A cable goes around it. Bundle up a big bundle, and just pick it up and just set it on the truck.

Estelle: You hook it together and work it from the top and wind it like drawing water out of a well.

John: Have you paid attention to these pulpwood trucks with a big long beam hanging on the top? That's what it is. That's the loader.

Estelle: I liked it, but it was rough. And then he began to get feeble, and then I'd want to go so I could watch him. To me it was fun. When he cut it down, he wasn't able to cut it fast enough to pile it in piles for the cable. I'd take it up as fast as he could cut it. I'd tell him, "Hurry up! I've got through! I'm waiting on you!"

John: My brother'd be a good one for you to talk to. He'll get two or three loads of wood a day by himself. Yes sir. That's hard work, when you get like that. It's dark when he leaves; it's dark when he comes back. I don't know why he does that. Everything he's got is paid for. A truck top blowed up with him. And he got seven hundred thousand dollars. And he still goes out there like he ain't got a dime.

Estelle: We didn't really work that hard. Just to make a living and pay bills. I mean, I can understand a person working to get ahead. But good Lord, you work and kill yourself and die and not enjoy it.

John: Pulpwood business is gone though, now. I reckon that's about all I can say about it. You have to watch out for snakes.

THEY NEEDED TO WORK

V. L. LETT
Seventy-three, retired, Highland, white

The first real thing that happened around here that the ladies could work at was the Higgins slacks plant at Lineville. There's a lot of people works at that. I have a neighbor out here, she's been working out there I guess almost since it started. She's been working for over forty years. At the same place.

I guess they liked the work, because it helped out. They said they had to work awfully hard. They had to make their own production and they had to work real hard. But they needed to work. Women's always had work. Even back when I was coming up and we farmed, everybody had to work. You had to work in the fields. I guess it's a little easier some of it now.

The swift and careful hands belonging to Clay County's women have always been a major source of family support. Out on the farm, unnumbered wives and daughters picked and churned, helped to haul timber, and sometimes held the traces of a plowing mule. When in the 1920s rural crafts came into vogue, they learned to weave pine-needle baskets, sold them via a cooperative in department stores across the country, and the money their handwork earned was often the first real cash their households ever saw. The 1940s brought war-production jobs, and afterward, when Clay County snared its share of the small apparel plants that sprang up across the South, most of the positions called for women's skills. Leaving babies with their mothers, or with ladies who organized the precursors of day care in their homes, they went to sew for the unheard-of sum of fifty-five cents an hour. Since then, they have in many homes brought in the only income that families could depend on, a welcome addition to the work men picked up here and there—the construction, farming, and pulpwooding which offered few future guarantees, and only rarely insurance or retirement.

The machines and high production quotas that prevail today mean that the jobs demand speed and precision, and leave many of the workers—particularly older ones—profoundly tired. But the hard work performed within the plants is often somewhat lightened by the advantages of friendship, and by the many ties that women form with one another. If workers are bound together in no formal way (at one plant the owner smoothly says that if his workers needed a union they would get one, although plenty of employees recall when, years ago, some people who discussed organization were immediately fired), small-town connections mean that most of them know and like each other. The rhythms of the work, along with the break at lunch, leave time to talk, to swap news and crochet patterns, to share a new recipe's results or to gather a collection for a fellow worker who is sick—the kind of socializing women often miss when they stay home.

As one worker puts it, you look forward to Friday evening, and to Monday morning.

ANNIE PEARL ROBERTS
Fifty-eight, Higgins sewing plant worker, Highland, white

The plant opened up in '46, and I went to work in June of '47. I lacked a few days of being eighteen, but they hired me. I didn't like school—I went through the tenth grade and I quit. And I went down there and put in an application. So you had to be eighteen, but I lacked just a few days and this girl got married on the job, sewing on tickets, so I got her job and I've been on it ever since. I've been there forty years in all. I done got my twenty-five-year pin.

You start off at three thirty-five and you go to four-fifty. You make production, you can make more. Now back there in the repair section, they may be set four-eighty. Some is set rate. When we catch up our job and they carry us to another one, we've got to do fifty-six percent of production. Or either we go back to three thirty-five.

You've got to learn how to handle a machine. Handle the material. And the different styles, there's a certain way you sling them. You pick them up and there's a certain way you've got to put them. Each operation has a certain way to do everything. Some jobs are a lot harder than others. That seat-seaming is hard. And that pressing's hard. And them back pockets is hard. There's a lot of it in there hard. That trimming looks simple, but it's a job—you get every string off in a certain length of time.

We've got four types of work in my job. That's what we get paid by. One of them, we put a ticket on the band and a label on the side of the ticket. There's another one we drop the ticket and put a label on this side. Then one we just put tickets on. And then there's another one that you drop the ticket. And we have to keep them separated. We get paid by that, so many an hour. The regular ones is three hundred and five pair an hour. The other one, that you put the ticket on the band, is a hundred and eighty-four an hour. That you just drop the ticket is two hundred an hour. And that you drop the ticket with a label is a hundred and fifty-four an hour. But we're all used to it. If the machine does good and the material sews good, you can do all right.

You've got to keep your mind on your business. If you don't, you get them on wrong. And each cut has a certain kind of label. Some don't have any labels and some does. And you have to keep up with that. We've got a book, just like in school. We've got I believe it's four or five different type labels. I don't like to miss a day, because somebody'll turn the knobs on the machine, tear it up. They get ahold of it and turn every knob on there, and it'll take you a while to get it straightened out. They know if I ain't there, there's something wrong.

I love it better than anything. I guess like anything else, when the machine acts up and you get bad work, it's rough. But you know what you're going to do every day. We have different cuts, different pants, different material, but still we know one machine where we'll be at. Where those spare hands don't. They go all over the building. I'd rather have tickets than anything. I just hope I can stay there until I retire. I'm fifty-eight, and I hope I go to sixty-five. I hope it'll run from now on, but I hope I can retire then.

Now some had to stay out yesterday. Or go home at dinner. Nothing to do. Sent two in our section home at dinner. It's rougher. All of it is rougher. See, there's a lot of sewing plants has shut down. And they're shipping from overseas too, and that hurts us. We've had a good company. We'd work when the rest failed. That meant a lot.

It wasn't on production when I started, but later years, when we got out here in the new building, they put it on production. You have to get it or get out, because they won't put up with you not getting production. I think after you get a certain age they don't hire you. Because this production is set up at speed, and when you get any age, you can't cut that speed. I've wore out one ticket-tacker, and I'm on another. They wear out. The speed does it.

I just can't turn off as much work as I did. That makes a difference. The older you get, the harder it is to make. A good many of the old ones is on the repairs. Before you leave there, if you don't make production, if they can use you, they'll put you there.

You come in tired and give out, you've got supper to cook, dishes to wash, and answer the telephone half a dozen times. You've got to get in wood, and take out ashes. Get splinters in. And maybe you wash and hung out this evening, got to get that in tomorrow evening. Some evenings you may go by the grocery store, go by the hospital. So it's a full-time job. When you work down there, you don't feel like doing nothing else much. I may eat a sandwich sometimes, or soup, but I don't cook every day. It's eight hours. And that cement floor.

I always look forward to Monday morning and Friday evening. Because we know if we don't work, we don't get paid. I look forward to vacations. Look forward to Christmas. Because I tell you, the same thing day in, day out, gets old. And you need a little time off to do the things you have to do.

Shoot, yes, I like it. Having a job beats hunting one. And we have good insurance.

JAN AND WENDELL WHITE
Twenty-two and twenty-three, Higgins workers, Pine Grove, white

Jan: I've been working at Higgins a little over four years. I worked about a year part time, up to right before I got married. I had started to Southern Union Junior College, and we just go till lunch there. I went up and put my application in, just to work part of the day, and that's how I got started to work up there.

My mom still works there, and Wendell's mom does too. And I just decided it would be easy for us to ride together on days I didn't have to go to school. My mom side-seams. She's been doing that for over twenty years. She went to work I think when I was about seven months old. I stayed with my grandmother.

Wendell: I stayed with my grandmother, too. Up until I got pretty good-sized, and then I stayed by myself. I had a sister, and we just stayed at home. Sort of took care of ourself. I had some grandparents who lived right straight across the road. So there was really somebody close by all the time.

Jan: That's the way it is most of the time around here. Everybody lives right next to their parents. I know one of my friends just had a baby, and her mother keeps her baby while she works. A lot of them put their kids in day care. There's a day-care center in Lineville, and one in Ashland. And there are several ladies around that keep kids, too. So it's pretty easy.

I do just about anything. I've got a regular job, but I do nearly all the jobs in the parts section. I guess I do about fifteen jobs now. I work an automatic machine, that's my regular job. I sew extensions and flaps. And it just goes by itself. You just lay the stuff down and it goes right through. You deal with pieces and parts and it's not hard at all. Not really. What I do, there's nothing that you really have to have a lot of skills to do. But I think something like V-backing and taping, stuff like that is a real hard job. Most of the jobs in my section are just sew up one little place.

Jobs are a lot faster now. There've been a lot of newer machines, and a lot of automatic machines. They just got in some presses that are computerized. They set theirselves for the type of material that you're working on. When Mother and Wendell's mother started working, they did everything by hand. Well, they had tackers and things like that, but not anything like they have now. I think it's easier now. A lot easier. Older people have a lot more trouble. Like Mother and them got used to the machines, and now they're different and faster. It's a lot harder for them to pick it up than it is for younger people to. Because they've been doing it so long.

You know most all of the people. Before they put me on the regular job, I worked a good bit out in the plant. You see most everybody all the time. Most of them you know from around here, just living around here, too. Most of them live around here. You make a lot of friends.

Wendell: I work in the stockroom now. Packing pants in boxes to ship them out. It's pretty well straight time, because you're going to be there putting boxes out the door. Really, your pay, it might not seem no better. Because it's just straight—you get the same pay all the time. But you know you're going to get a week's work.

Jan: I make more than he does. The cutting table job's a good job, the men back there make good. But other than one or two jobs in there other than that, most of the women make more than the men do. Most of them.

Wendell: Overall, on production, she makes more than I do. But I still like my job.

Jan: I don't make millions more than he does. But I bring home about twenty, thirty dollars a week more than he does, sometimes. But then sometimes I don't. Sometimes it's about the same.

Wendell: What's good about mine, if they do get off a day or something out there, I know that I'm going be there.

Jan: I never really know. If I'm on my job, I can just about say how much I'm going to make in a week. Because I usually run about the same thing, if I don't have machine trouble or something like that. You get paid three thirty-five an hour while you're on machine delay. Most of the time I'll make about the same thing. I haven't had to go home—I asked to go home one day because my mother and Wendell's mother was going home and I didn't have a ride home. And that's been a long time ago. Two years ago, we were on short time for about three or four months. We worked every other week, something like that.

There's times where you think, "Well, we don't have anything to do." But it's not as bad with us over where I am, because most of us know how to do different jobs. Where like with Mother, if they get caught up, they have to go home. We can move around. I guess back in the summer they went home about every Friday, or were off on Friday.

That's just the kind of work where you don't get a raise very often. You don't go into there and they say I'll raise you up to so and so and then raise you on up. You start off—I guess you start off on base pay. And then if you're on a production job, you have to make production, you get off of base pay.

Everybody's tired after working all day. No matter what you do. I think as you get older, you get even tireder a lot quicker. It just depends on how your day has gone and what kind of work you've had. Like if Mother side-pockets or something like that, she's a lot tireder. Or plaid or something like that, she's a lot tireder after sewing that.

*   *   *

Wendell: A lot of people, they'll buy pants somewhere else, and buy our pants, and most people say they really like the way our pants fit.

Jan: You can tell a difference.

Wendell: I could go to the stores, and you could take the labels out of them, and I'd try on two different pair of pants, one from us and one from somebody else, and I pretty nearly know I could tell you which pair we made. The way it's made, and the way it fits. They're real particular on the way their pants fit. The material—they want to make the best pair of pants for the price possible. They're put together well enough that you can't just pull them and tear them apart. They're a real good pair of pants.

Jan: We make good pants. There's no doubt about that.

HAROLD HIGGINS
Fifty-nine, Higgins Company president, Lineville, white

We completed our first pair of pants on July the fourth, 1946. I have that first pair of pants ever made sealed up in a drawer in my office at home. I was seventeen years old at the time. July the first was about the first day. It took four days for that first pair of pants to make its way through the plant. I think it was just by accident it came out on July the fourth.

This was a fortunate time to go into business, just after World War II, because there was still a very large backlog of demand for clothes by returning veterans and people like that. And for people that had just been unable to obtain all the clothes they wanted during the war. And so it was a very propitious time to start, and this business prospered, and additional buildings were built, and expansions were made several times, and over a period of almost forty-two years the business has grown into a very substantial business. Starting out from just a very small production in the beginning to what we have now, I would hazard a guess that we have made at least fifteen million pairs by now.

*　　　*　　　*

We have a saying in my family—we always say when we cross the state line from Georgia into Alabama that you turn your clocks back an hour. And you turn your calendar back thirty years. And we don't mean that in a derogatory manner. We mean that some of the old values, and some of the traditional virtues that were present in the country thirty years ago are still present in Alabama. And we're proud of it.

We very much desire, then and now, to employ people who have the work ethic, and who have high moral standards, and who are friendly and courteous and disciplined. And these people all had those characteristics, and they still do, and we're very proud of them. It's a tradition in a state that is pretty cohesive as far as its ethnic makeup is concerned. That is, among the white population, you have a very strong northern European, Scotch-Irish type of heritage, and among the black population you have a very strong, work-oriented type people. And they blend well together, and we find that these people who live in this area have, generally speaking, very good work habits, very good attitudes when it comes to things like loyalty, and the desire to do good work, to take pride in what they do. And I think it's simply a tradition that's been passed down over hundreds of years here. I think the fact that they're not very many generations away from the soil has got a lot to do with that. The family-farm type of thing.

As far as being modern in a technological sense, we are very much up to date. We're perceived, in the country and the various markets, as being a very service-oriented, high-quality company. We are not a backwater little company in Alabama that sits on the back row and is allowed to exist. We're a very dynamic company in the marketplace. We're good old boys from Alabama, and we like to live that way. But we compete on a very aggressive scale throughout the country.

In a free society, in the capitalistic system of economics you compete, and then by competing you find yourself impelled toward doing things more efficiently. It's just been that way all along. I think in the late forties and fifties, up till maybe the mid-sixties, in that twenty-year period, I think we probably made our biggest strides. I think that the biggest moves toward efficiency took place before the imports became a problem.

Workers always resist change. But I think that here in Clay County that they're more willing than in most places to try to adjust, and they succeed very well. We have a very intelligent work force. There are companies in our business who can't say that. But our people are very quick to learn, generally speaking.

I think that if they needed a union they'd get one. I hope they feel—I think they feel they don't need it. Because there's completely open communication between me and the employees. Anybody who has a grievance is free to take it up to the very top with a minimum of effort. And they always receive a fair hearing, and we do our best not to do anything that is exploitative of the employees. We have been and still are nonunion. Naturally we hope to stay that way. We hope to be able to deserve to stay that way.

I wouldn't want to say they don't work hard. But it's not at all as hard a work as these people's ancestors had to do. When you're working on a subsistence farm, like previous generations have done, and chopping wood with an axe and drawing water out of the well and having to drive a horse and wagon a full day to get to the county seat. Plowing your fields with a mule and that sort of thing. People got old long before their time. And so these people that work for us come from a heritage of hard work. So I don't think they consider what we do here all that hard.

THE CHICKEN PLANT WAS HIRING

LILLIE TRAYLOR
Fifty-eight, Tyson chicken plant worker, Lineville, black

The plant had been running for about a year before I started working there. I had a sister work over there, and me and her's twins, and she told me to come on over there, that I probably could get a job over there too. So I went on over there, and they just hired me right off. Twenty-eight, twenty-nine years ago.

That whole year that I started, they began to hire blacks everywhere down in here. The rubber plant was hiring them, and Higgins Slacks went to hiring them, and the chicken plant was hiring them. That just broke the ice, and a lot of the plants just started hiring. Whoever come for a job, they just hired them. Gave Clay County a good start.

Back years ago, they didn't have a killing machine. There's a certain place in the neck you have to cut them. And they just had that knife, and they're just hanging on the line and you come by cutting them. I never did go back there too much because I couldn't stand it. You know they bleed, and I couldn't stand all that blood. Now they have a machine that kills them. And then they come through the scalder and they scald them, and then the ladies pick them.

And then they come on by, and they hang them out on a line—when they come out of the picker, they're just going over a belt, you see. And then they run onto a table. And then there's ladies back there to hang them over a line. And then they come on up, and you have to cut the oilbag off. And then they come by and you have to cut that tail open. And then you cut it open with the scissors. And then it goes to the inspector—U.S. inspector. And they look at it and see if there's anything wrong with it. And then it comes to me. I'm the helper. If they see anything wrong with it, I've got to try to make it right—take off a leg or a wing, or if it's got a bad bruised place on it trim that off. If it's more than I can handle I have to hang it back on a rack, for somebody else to come get it and get it in shape.

And then it goes through the drawing machine—that's to draw the liver and the gizzards, all that out of it. Then the next ladies up the line, they see to it that all gizzards and all livers are pulled off. Then it goes around to the necking machine. They got a machine that takes the neck off. And takes the skin off the neck, and them skins go way on out in another building—all that's done by machine, and belts and things—and they make dog food out of it.

Then it goes over in a great big old thing they call a washer. Oh honey, that thing's big as my house. With all that water in there. And it rotates. It turns round and round and round, they go on around through there and on around through there. And then they goes over on another line, and they falls out, and some old ladies hang them on that line. And then they go on through over in the deboning, they call it. And that's where they start deboning them. And one lady'll do this and one lady'll do that. Lord, I think they got about four or five lines of deboners in there.

I wish you could just come over there during the day. Because you could see it, and you could see more about it than what I'm trying to tell you. If you haven't ever been in that deboning part—it's a mystery to me how they take all that meat off them bones. And then it goes out—they send it over to Tennessee. And they grinds it up there, and that's where they send it out for chicken fingers and chicken nuggets and all that. That's what they end up making. We just started doing that for the last four or five years. We used to send them out whole. Well you know, these chicken nuggets and things is just come in.

We started off at a dollar an hour. Babysitting, housekeeping, you'd just get paid by the week, maybe fourteen dollars a week, fifteen dollars a week, something like that. Our children was already in school. We was trying to save for their college education, whatever they wanted to do. So I didn't throw away any money. Now, they usually hire them in at about four-fifty an hour. And you can go on up as high as six and eighty-five cents an hour.

Everything was done by hand. We didn't have no kind of machines. Now like, say, yesterday, we had seventy-four thousand chickens. And I'd say back when we started out, we wouldn't know what to do. It'd take us three days to run seventy-four thousand chickens. We'd have forty thousand, it'd take us all day long.

They used to cut themselves real bad. Somehow or other they got it where now we don't. They found how to use steel gloves. You put on a cloth glove, steel glove. Then the rubber glove. See if your knife hit it, it don't cut. So we hardly ever have anybody cut now.

It's something you have to get used to. If somebody was to go in new in the morning, they'd say, "How do y'all stand this? I don't think I can handle it." But if you want to work, you just have to stay there and get used to it. Because your fingers'll get sore, and your hands'll get sore, and if you handle the knife you might cut your hand or something like that. Your back gets sore, your legs get sore, your feet get sore. That kind of job, the longer you stay, the better it is. I know I said it was hard when I went there, because I was just like everybody else. But my sister told me, said, "Well, you just stay in it." And she said, "It won't be long, two or three days, you won't even know you're working." And she was right. I ain't going to say it's easy, but it just ain't real hard labor.

It's better now, because a lot of the machines is doing the jobs that we had to do by our hands. So it's much easier. We still have to use a knife, like we once did. And they use the scissors like we once did. But it's much easier, because somewhere down the line a machine is doing something that a person did have to do. They're working on a machine now that they say, they won't even need as many hands as they got now, if they can get all these machines to do what they want it to do. But I don't know what year that'll be.

$$* \qquad * \qquad *$$

We was on a five-month shutdown. It's been about seven or eight years ago, I think. The economy went bad. Looked like everything just went bankrupted. We had known it was bankrupted a long time before they shut down, because they was putting "bankrupted" on our checks. It was Spring Valley then. But they was still going through.

They just shut down all at once. We'd just come out of the plant that evening and they had a sign on the board that the plant was closed up. I think it was a Friday. And they had a letter on the board, said the plant's closed up. That's all we knowed. We didn't even try to go back over there that Monday.

Wasn't nice, but that's just what they done. Just said, "Well, the plant's going to be closed up," and that was it. So they let us sign up for unemployment, and we stayed about five months, and then they began to call us back. We all got back in there.

It was a shock to the whole town. A lot of these people around was depending on it. Everybody was just shocked. Because we had never experienced nothing like that around here, just a plant shut down like we see on television in the big city and all that. But I told them I'll be prepared now for anything. If the rumor gets out they'll shut down, I'll say, "Yeah, they'll shut down." Because they done it once before and they might do it again.

*   *   *

Most everybody belongs to the union. I'm a steward. Our headquarters is in Atlanta. The union's been in there now I'd say twelve or thirteen or fourteen years. Might have been longer than that. They come in—you know how they do—they come in and pick somebody out of the plant, and then they get folks in the plant to work inside the plant. So that's how they usually get that union in. Every year, if they bring in new folks, we'll contact them and say do you want to join the union and tell them what it'd do and all that. So that's how we keep enrollment.

You know no company don't want no union. They said when they first started trying to get a union, the company just didn't want it. But if you get enough folks to follow you, you can outvote the company. They'll have to accept it if they get enough votes. They didn't fire nobody. I never heard tell of nobody getting fired over there for trying to be in a union.

We come real close to a strike one time, but it didn't come off. I think it was something about the wages and the pay, or something like that. So we never have had a strike. But it usually helps out the people in holding their jobs—if somebody get fired or something, they'd bring them back to work. Because you know the company's got their rules, and sometimes the company'll edge off of their rules, just like anybody else. It's a good thing to have, I think.

If you feel like some of the supervisors or something is on your back too much, you know, ain't treating you right, well a person can file a grievance. And they'll get that problem straightened out. You know, sometimes the supervisor might get up and may not feel good when they leave home, and then when they get there they just—just nothing ain't going right, you see. The union leaders try to help, you know, not get on folks too bad. It's just a helping thing—it really helps. Things get better when you've got a union.

I told my husband I couldn't walk no picket line. You know a lot of times them picket-line people gets in fights and things, get hurt. You see a lot on the news. I'm kind of nervous. I don't want to get out there and somebody hit me—I know I'd have to hit them back, and we couldn't hit nobody back. You've got to be standing out there firm, not hit nobody back. So I hope we'll never have a strike.

*　　*　　*

I still eat them. I still love to have chicken in my freezer and all. A lot of folks think, I just couldn't stand it in there because I know it smells like the chicken do at home we used to clean. But it don't. You don't smell nothing. Because I'm weak stomached, and I was when I went there, and if I could smell all that I probably couldn't of stayed. And they keep the plant nice and clean.

THEY PUT MORE MILES NOW

By a corner of Ashland's courthouse square, near the shaded bench where old men congregate to talk and spit tobacco, the stream and racket of passing cars flows almost without break, a continual parade of rusting Detroit workhorses, late-model Japanese creations, one-owner forty-year-old gems, and even—every now and then—a battered hulk that has lost a tire and is riding on a rim.

The sudden opening of an isolated rural world could be marked at different moments—at the first crackle of a receiver headset picking up a far-off radio transmission, or on the magic night when Ashland residents screwed lightbulbs into newly installed fixtures, then sat and waited for the first surge of electric current to light the whole town all at once. But for a county set far from any major city, where a few thousand people lived scattered over six hundred square, hilly miles, the dust that trailed behind the first T-Model Ford augured perhaps the greatest change of all. As cars began to multiply, and the smell of heated tar that state road crews exude spread to more corners of the county, this influence expanded, altering the ways that crops were marketed and visits paid, as well as moving population from communities that relied on railroad depots to those located near the larger roads and—more important—closer to the jobs in other towns to which almost a third of county workers now commute each day.

The patterns traced by uncounted sets of rubber tires have defied all prediction, forming shifting, uncertain, and often paradoxical designs. The prospects for independent operations once eagerly seized on by would-be dealers and mechanics have fast been losing ground to outside competition and the centralizing power of large-scale dealers and advanced technology. The access to better jobs brings with it lengthy, tiring commutes and oft-performed repairs, and the promises of freedom cannot be wholly separated from its strains. Wrecks and deaths seem frighteningly common on the county's winding roads, so much so that some residents grow nervous and listen closer to their police scanners when a guest or relative is expected or overdue, and sometimes the crashes crowd so thick on one another—five deaths in as many weeks one summer— that timid drivers grow afraid to venture out at all.

WILLIS PADGETT
Seventy-four, car salesman, Mount Zion, white

The first automobile that I ever bought was a '27 T-model roadster. I give thirty-five dollars for it. I started selling cars back in the early forties, with T-Models, A-Models, old-model tractors. I just had that in my blood, I guess. In high school, in school, I was always trading. I traded on land, mules, cattle. Well, just about all my life I've been a trader.

I moved to Lineville and I went to work with the Ford Motor Company. One year I sold nine hundred and sixty-three automobiles, new and used. I was the highest in the Atlanta district. I've got a plaque right there, a ten-year plaque, that I was one of the highest ones in the United States.

The most cars I sold in any one day was seventeen. Back then on Saturday—now that was the day you sold the cars. They'd meet down there and they'd just buy them—you wouldn't have time to go to lunch. It was mostly repeat customers. I had customers that would trade with me every year, for a new car. They'd go up every year.

People quit trading so much in about '78. Now they're looking for a car that'll operate cheap. They're looking for one they can make the payments on. We have folks from here that works at Anniston, go every day. Then we have folks working in Atlanta and Birmingham. Back then, most of them wouldn't put over eighteen thousand a year. They put more miles now. Now it's not anything uncommon for them to put forty or fifty or sixty thousand on one in a year.

JERRY HOLMES
Thirty-two, construction worker, Delta, white

I work in Atlanta. I'm an equipment operator. I never have drove under about a hundred miles a day, one way. When I first started driving back and forth, we lived on the northwest side of Anniston. And I'd have to leave the house at about two-thirty in the morning. You have to go to bed when the chickens do. I get up at three-thirty now, and leave here by quarter to four.

In my opinion, most of the people in Clay County, they either drive out of town like I do, a long ways, or they're in business for themselves. You'd be surprised at the people right around here that drive to Atlanta. The guy that rides with me, his daddy hauls thirteen riders to Atlanta. He's got two uncles, they've got station wagons, they probably haul seven or eight apiece. Probably every other car you pass, headed to work, is an Alabama tag. I have worked on a job where ninety percent of the workers were from Alabama, driving.

It really pays a man to go on up there to work. When I tried to get a job around here, when I was making nine, ten dollars an hour in Atlanta, they were paying four or five dollars. I was making double what I could make around here. So I just started driving up there, and I've been driving ever since. Most of my driving's been around an hour and thirty minutes to an hour and fifty minutes. Hardly ever two hours riding.

My best friend in the morning is my cup of coffee. I drink about two or three of them on the way. And I listen to country music. That's it. Of course I do a lot of thinking. Most of the time it's thinking about doing something where I won't have to drive so far. What I could be doing for myself, making more money, staying here at the house. But just like anything else I guess it takes money to make money, and I just ain't got the money to put into it right now. I'd love to have a dump truck, is what I'd love to do. Drive a dump truck. If you've got your own rig it's decent money.

Driving back and forth ain't bad if you've got somebody to ride with you, or somebody that can swap out driving. Swap out driving's the best thing. If you've got somebody to ride with you and talk to you, it makes things go a lot better. When I first started driving, I fell asleep going up there one morning, run off the road—all four wheels. It was pouring down rain. I managed not to wreck that time. Then one weekend I stayed up pretty late the whole weekend, and I fell asleep a couple of times that morning, stayed on the road. Coming in that evening I fell asleep and kissed the back end of a dump truck. But after you drive it for a little while I guess your system gets used to it or something.

LARRY ROBERTSON

It's getting to be very expensive to run a garage. You see, we work on just domestic cars, but you got GM, you got Chrysler, and you got Ford. Well, all three of them are different. And it always takes three different types of equipment. You're having to put more in it. And therefore you're having to charge more. And it's going to make it much more difficult for an independent garage to make it because of the training aspect. An independent doesn't have the opportunity for training a dealer does. Because dealerships are trained—GM trains their dealerships, they have particular schools for them, which an independent can't get in. You have to be connected with a dealer. We've done our best, or tried to, and we've been able to get connected with some dealerships. Not locally, but some people that we know connected with some dealerships out of town let us go through their dealership and get some training—they've been nice enough to let us use their name.

It's a challenge, I think. It was for my father, too. Because ten years ago or fifteen years ago or twenty years ago, cars changed a lot. And twenty years before then, too. And the equipment that he used twenty years ago was twice as much equipment as it took twenty years before that. It was a challenge for him and it's a challenge for me to be able to finagle enough to figure it out, what things you've got to have, and what things you can't have. I'm afraid there's going to be some areas in which I'm going to make some decisions on, we're not going to be able to take this certain area any more.

The only thing I really worry about when Daddy retires is finding somebody to do what I do now. I pretty much do most of the work that takes a lot of time—something you've got to do where you've got to study a lot and you can't make a mistake on. Work where you're putting in five or six hundred dollars' worth of equipment and you can't make a mistake on it because you can't afford to lose that. It's hard for him to do that work because he's got to make bills and talk to customers and all. It's hard to do that type of work and have a lot of distractions. Another reason it'll be hard to find somebody to do that type of work is it's a skilled labor. But the trouble is, it's going to be hard to pay somebody. There's too many opportunities in other areas that can pay them more. A dealership's going to pay a person more.

My feeling has always been that you're going to have to have more and more education to become a mechanic, because everything's so high-tech. You have to have a good background in electronics, a good background in mathematics, a good background in English, because there's so much reading you have to do. If you're not able to comprehend a lot of material, you're not going to be able to cope. Because most of the material's not written on a first grade level. It uses quite a bit of pretty difficult language.

You've got to have a decent educational background. Even though you may have a good knack for fixing a lot of mechanical-type things, the trouble is electronics. You can't take electronic things and tear them apart and put them back together. It's changed. Most everything before worked on a mechanical-type basis, and most people could fix them. And even the electrical part of it was very simple. But now it's become so high-tech, you've got to be able to read. Most all your diagnosis for cars now is a situation where if this, then this, and you've got to go step by step, you've got to be able to read and follow. And you've got to be able to understand what you're reading. Or you're going to go this certain direction, it says buy this part. You buy an electrical part from a dealer, an independent does, when you buy it it's yours. So when you put it on and that didn't fix it, you got two hundred dollars sitting there, and there's not anything you can do with it. So it's gotten very difficult. Your guesses can't be guesses. They've got to have some evidence behind them.

LYNN SMITH
Twenty-five, tractor mechanic, Bluff Springs, white

I love mechanicking. I love to build engines. I've built a lot of engines for people around. I take pride in my work and all. I want it to be the best. I'm trying to sort of get people to know that. When you do something, you want to be the best at it. That's what I want to be about mechanicking. That's one reason I'm here working on tractors. When I first started there was an older fellow had done it all his life. In my opinion, he's the best tractor mechanic there is, on a certain brand. He quit us, and he went to work with a competitor of ours. And I want to be able to fill his shoes, and get the reputation that he's got.

I like being around the people, farmers and all. They're interesting people. They're out here working as hard as they can to make a living, and barely getting by. There's a lot of them come in here and need some work done on a tractor and I just hate to charge them for it. But I have to, to make a living. I do a lot of work on the side, just help people out. If they bring work up here, you're going to have to charge them for it. I go up and help a lot of people in the fields. Do a lot of work on people's in Ashland.

I've always wanted to be a mechanic. It don't pay all that great, but I'm making fair money, getting by pretty good. If you don't enjoy your work, you're not going to be good at it, and you're not going to want to do it. If you enjoy it, you'll try harder and do better.

I've always heard people talking, saying, "Well, I wished I could go back to school. Start over again and know what I know now." I used to think, "Well, that's crazy. I just want to get out of school and go to work and do what I want to do, be out on my own." But I know what they mean now. It's completely different when you've got to make a living for yourself. I still wish now that I'd went on to school. I graduated school, but I always took the basic and the easiest classes. The easiest way out.

If I had it to do over again, I would take every subject that I could, and learn everything I could. I'd still want to be a mechanic. But there's a lot of things that I don't know about mechanicking. They make these big computers and all, you just drive your car up there and you hook this wire here and hook all this stuff up, you punch in a number, crank the car up, and here it comes up and tells you exactly what's wrong with it, if it's a spark plug wire bad or if it's a valve bad it tells you. I can't run one of those machines. If I'd went on and learned more, I could. Now if somebody shows me something one time, I can usually do it. And tractors are basically the same thing. A 1965 model tractor is basically the exact same thing as the '85 model tractor. But it would help out.

I guess mainly math has a lot to do with it. You need a lot of math and algebra and all that stuff. You can take algebra and trigonometry and all that stuff, and get a plan of a car, and look at it, and tell exactly what it is. Where if you don't know that stuff, all you're looking at is a frame of a car. You don't know what dimensions and all this stuff means.

I don't think that would happen in my lifetime, as far as me getting out of a job on account of not knowing how to fix it. Because around '80 is when they really started getting complicated. And you've got people that can't afford to buy a car over 1980. And they're driving older model cars. And they're always going to be around. Somebody's got to fix them. I hate that I don't know it. But I've got to live with the fact that I don't. There's always going to be old cars around to work on.

I KNOW WHAT IT IS TO BE POOR

LEWEL SELLERS

I know what it is to be poor. There's nobody today as poor as we were. We were down there on the mercies of the world—we had no cow, no chickens, no nothing. And Mother cooked what we had. Well, Uncle William heard that we didn't have anything to eat. So he come down there and brought us a sack of meal and a five-gallon keg with syrup in it. And Mother opened up that keg of syrup—it wasn't full. They put their syrup in wooden kegs. Had a hole there where you could turn it over and the syrup'd come out. Well, when Mother did, there come an old dead rat out of it. You know what Mama done? She cooked that syrup over and we eat it. Now I know what it is to be poor.

L. D. LAMBERTH
Sixty-nine, retired postmaster, Cragford, white

These farmers, they'd rent on halves, you know what that is. Well, they'd rent from, say, my daddy one year. Wouldn't make nothing. Wouldn't even have a cow left. Rent from somebody else the next year. So they owed him twenty dollars in paid rent. And the next fellow. Around and around. Come back. Just a few years older. They just lived until they'd get old and die.

And there wasn't any money. You could work a whole year, and when the cotton crop was sold, you couldn't buy those shoes. Down there at the store they had plenty of them. They would of cost you a dollar back then.

These people with four or five kids. The daddy, he'd come in to Cragford. There were three or four stores there, but he wouldn't go in because he was barefoot. And he wouldn't take anything back home with him either. He just went to town.

I felt lucky. I've never moved. Not since we've been married. And like I said, a lot of people just had to. We had just a little bit. Really. If you had fifty dollars a month, you were just about rich.

Out on long dirt county roads, you can still come onto houses where people draw their water out of wells and springs, and where the only heat comes from the craggy depths of a mud-plastered fireplace. Many others, while they bear more traces of a modern world, are home to those quite thoroughly familiar with the plans and accommodations that being poor demands: patching your roof with uneven sheets of tin and figuring each mile of gas; planning errands with great care because your car's reverse gear no longer works; buying burial insurance for young children, because you never know.

Although most residents have left behind the days when everyone grew cotton and few had any money, many still live almost as though that era were not yet spent, leading lives that at times seem like stubborn memories of the older, harder time. While many county children are as pampered and prepared as any in the state, one teacher says, others come from homes where violence and deprivation raise obstacles almost impossible to overcome. When cheese and other government commodities are distributed at the county's Farmers' Market, the line of old and young, of black and white, stretches out the door and down the hill the building sits on. Poverty has no easy definition, but of forty-seven hundred households in the county, more than a thousand take in less than five thousand dollars a year, and many have incomes not far above that figure. The problem is compounded by the county's high number of people over sixty-five—well above state and national proportions—many of whom live alone on very few resources.

But if the marks of poverty are hard to miss—houses fashioned from a patchwork of materials; bare feet in summer and closed-off rooms in winter; eyes that cross, and crooked, broken, or decaying teeth—they do not always signal desperation or despondency. Poor people in Clay County live in the security of numbers, and although talk of public help can take on an uneasy air, the food-stamp office on distribution day draws women of both colors who wait, chat, sympathize about delays, and pass on family news. Many residents remember being poor, few families can afford much luxury, and even those with money often spend little on themselves. Neighbors and friends share with each other, almost everyone has land that in the summer will grow food, and communities do what they can when tragedy occurs. Warmth from the gay talk of children spreads through many homes where a year's income falls short of any poverty line, and strain is often softened by large amounts of love, by teasing laughter, and by country singing, all of which, although they cannot substitute for steady work, good heat, and health insurance, can offer happiness in unexpectedly generous supply.

I NEVER LET IT GET ME DOWN

The road before the small, red, tin-roofed house is full of turkeys, plump under swells of dappled feathers, their heads turned thin and comical toward the approaching car. They stroll slowly to the side, unhurried, unafraid. She doesn't worry for them much, says Lois Moore, watching from the cement slab that forms the house's well-used porch. Most passers-by know Ma Moore's turkeys, and they take care.

While so many county houses can surprise you with their starkness, with the sparseness of the furnishings and the bare whiteness of the walls, the Moores' burgeons close to overflowing with the contents of a lengthy life, and of four generations that still make it their home. Back rooms are crammed with several beds apiece, enough both for the numerous inhabitants and for a constant stream of visiting relations. Jars of the morning's milk and buckets of small green apples clutter the kitchen floor, and on the table rests an assortment of fresh tomatoes and cucumbers, glasses of homemade preserves, and gallon canning jars filled with beans and okra, peas and corn. Half-grown kittens tumble in and out a back screen door; a new-hatched set of ducks nestles in a box at the foot of the Moores' big bed; and out in front two little girls squeal as they chase each other along the road.

Seated at the kitchen table, surrounded by the clutter and the noise, Lois Moore relates a life of children, crops, and work. Her long, thick hair, once black and now approaching gray, twists round a mass of pins and combs, and still-white scars mottle up and down her heavy, deep-tanned legs. The wrinkles cutting through her skin can go rock hard when her voice tightens and her lips purse in disdain—usually at newfangled notions that offend a set of long and proudly held old-fashioned views of neighbors, church, and drink—but when her eyes begin to laugh, as she looks over at a pet or prepares to tell one of her many jokes, the furrows spread the signs of joy across all of her face.

LOIS MOORE
Seventy-three, retired farmer, Barfield, white

Back when we was raising up children, there wasn't no jobs but pulp-wooding and sawmilling. After crops were laid by, my husband would have to get out—you know, you'd borrow money to make a crop on—and he'd have to get out and get up jobs to support us till we got the crop gathered, and then the landlord would get the money again and he'd have to work in winters. Amen. Poor folks has their time, here on the earth.

This boy in here, his mother died. She was my stepdaughter. And I had raised her. And she died with these twins, they was twins. They was born Sunday night, and she died Tuesday morning. The last thing she told me, she said, "Mama," said, "I want you to keep my babies." Well I thought she was just scared, them being the first ones. And I'd say "Nah, you going to raise them there little boys, they going to be out here hunting," and talk to her like that. Well, after she got to where she wouldn't talk, she'd reach and pull me down to her, and try to tell me, but I don't know what she wanted.

I had a baby not a year old. I don't know, unless God was just with me, how I made it. I couldn't tell you how I made it. They both were premature. And this one in here wasn't stout enough, they had to take his blood and put more blood in. He looked like an old, rotten rubber doll, that's laid out. Well I went to the doctor and told him, "This baby can't nurse a bottle." I said, "Would it hurt him"—I hadn't weaned my baby—I said, "Would my milk hurt him." He said "No, don't think so." And that's what I did. I raised this one on the breast. And put my baby on a bottle.

I raised four of my other grandkids. One of them was here today. He's got a little boy now. And then this boy's twin brother, he married, and his wife went off and left him, and the baby, my great-grandbaby, was eight months old. They went and got them, and I've had him ever since he was eight months old. He's eleven. Well, they got it in court now. I don't know which way it's going to run. But I don't feel like I'll lose them. His sister's fourteen and he's eleven. And the mama never has been with them.

They all love me as a mother, and I love them as a mother. I'd fight for that one in there quick as I would my baby. Of course he drinks some. He's not a mean man. He's been married. But he married the wrong woman and she dumped him back here with me, and so I still got him.

It's pitiful to think about, the way things are nowdays. Like my niece up here. They're paying a hundred dollars a month for that house. And it out in the country. And it's just him to work. Well, they got a little four-months-old baby. And in debt, we know. So she went to work Monday. Had to leave that little baby.

People say, "Oh, how rough it was back yonder." No it wasn't. I had a whole lot more to eat—wasn't no such fine doings and things then, when we was bringing our oldest children up, as there are now. Our children was all at home. We all got out and played ball; we pitched horseshoes and we all worked together and we was all at home. And now parents work and anybody that comes along keeps the children.

*   *   *

We share. We have a garden, they don't have one, I divide with them. Of course my neighbors is back home, down in McCollum. They have anything down there, why they'll call Ma, and want to know if I need it. I'll say yeah, I'll take some of it. I call them, ask them how they is, and if they don't have something I send them some. Whatever I got.

It says, "Love thy neighbor as thyself." But who is our neighbor? You ever think about that? Some of them said, "Well, it's the ones closest to you." Well, that won't work. It's the one that shares with you. One who respects you as a neighbor. I've got some that lives way over here close to Morrison's Crossroads. There ain't a thing on their place—if they had two cups of milk, they'd give me one of them. Well, that's a neighbor.

*   *   *

Yes I've had a hard old time. But I never let it get me down. I've done everything but ditch, and I've cleaned out ditches. After my daddy got to where he couldn't work, I plowed. I'd go back to see about my daddy. Because Mother was going through change and all, and her mind got bad. And I'd have to watch after her. It was pretty hard for me to keep everything a-going, keep everything clean. So I'd have to go back, see about Mother and Daddy, and do the cooking part of the time when I was ten years old. And milking. My sister was three years younger. And of course my brother had to work at what he could, to help feed us.

The neighbor children, they'd stay with me. Round McCollum, all of them calls me Ma Moore. I just think God meant for me to raise children. Because when he married Adam and Eve, he told them to have sons and daughters, them to have sons and daughters and multiply the world. If you find a place in there where not to have, well, I'll eat it. I just believe in people living— they call it old times. Well, if it's old times, that's what I have. I just believe in everybody trying to love one another and help one another.

We've never asked for no food stamps. I've never asked for a penny welfare, to help me raise the children. And they volunteered these Medicaid cards. There ain't much to it, but it's a help. Proud of it.

With more money, I could probably get more proper food for them. Sometimes their shoes'd get bad, and I could keep them shoed and clothed better than what I did. I could help my neighbors that was unfortunate. I want to and it hurts because I can't. Because I done been through there. I know what it is. Especially where there's little children.

I'd want just enough to live on, and not have to worry today what I should eat tomorrow, and I never worried too much about that because He said, "How much better are you than the fowls of the air?" He feedeth the fowls of the air, and I always felt like He'd feed me. It might be a poor feed, but He'd give me knowledge that I would eat something. He'd feed me some way. That's the way I've been brought up.

No, I don't want no riches. Always wished I had a home, where I wouldn't have to move from pillar to post. Well, we was getting pretty old. Of course this ain't our home, this is our daughter's. But she bought it and she said, "Mama, this is your and Daddy's home, as long as you live." She was at home at that time. Of course we helped; we'd buy the groceries, and she'd make the payments on the home. And it's our home. We've been here fourteen years, will be fifteen in February.

I don't worry about money. Long as we got something to eat. I don't want to owe nobody. All that would worry me would be to get in debt. And have nothing to pay out with. As far as fine stocking-heel shoes and this eyelash doings and all, that don't worry me. Some people nowdays just have money and pride. I don't want it.

LINDA ROCHESTER
Thirty-three, director, Clay County Department of
Human Resources, Lineville, white

We have a large elderly population. We have had programs in the past that really were extra-large for a small county in the elderly population. Part of that I think is because people move away from here, and leave the elderly behind. And so our sup program—that's a supplemental assistance check to the elderly—is a real high one for a small county. Our elderly abuse and neglect population, we have a pretty high number. Because there'll be a lot of elderly left here.

Our ADC program, which is the check for mothers or fathers and their dependent children, that program is low. And always has been. I don't know why. We've thought a lot about that, and why it is, because we are poor. I guess—this is just off the cuff—but I think it's because a lot of families stay together, and the husband pulpwoods, or has some low-paying job. So we don't have that many people on the program. We have an average-sized food-stamp program. A lot of families live just below poverty level, just barely make enough to get by, and they're on food stamps. But it's the whole family, the intact family.

We have a real good child-support program. And that may be part of the reason that the ADC is low—we have a lot of people in the child support program. So in general we're poor, but we don't see many starving families. We're able to help people. People live on little money here. And it doesn't cost so much to live here, I think that's part of it.

They have gardens and there's a lot of jobs like at Tyson, and then there's pulpwooding. A lot of people that are unable to find any type of labor that's skilled work in pulpwooding. And so that provides a steady trickle of money. It's real unstable. It depends on the weather. In our Christmas program, we try to get a good amount of canned goods, to last through the two winter months, January and February. Because the pulpwooding people are down, and they're not able to get work. They really need help then. We're able to get support locally, from the churches and things, with clothes and different items. We have a little bit of local funds that we pay for medical bills, when people are in a real jam, just little things. Sometimes we'll get federal money in the county that will pay heating bills.

Many, many families get food stamps. There is not really a stigma that there might be other places because we have so many elderly families on. We just have a real good relationship with many, many of the families that come in here. Our kids are in school together, we attend church together— you know, everybody. And most of us have families on the programs. So we're just small and rural, and we're just right here together.

*   *   *

With the elderly, I think the very biggest thing is the fact that when they get in a jam, like one big bill or something, like a big medical expense, then it just wipes them out. And there is no service really to offer them. That's the area of biggest concern to me. Because we don't have many jobs for people, young people leave. I remember from my high school class about half of us stayed, half of us left. Most people try to go somewhere because there's just not much opportunity here. And then the elderly people of course don't want to leave a place they've lived their whole lives. So they remain.

Anywhere that there's not many family members, when there's not someone to take care of them, particularly with elderly people who don't have children, they're just kind of at the mercy of society. The problem is we find out about it after the money's gone. People go downhill gradually. And we don't get called until it's pretty bad. And naturally, elderly people have a lot of independence, and they want to be independent just as long as they can be. Which is what we want too, but sometimes it goes too far, and they've already been exploited by the time we get involved.

I will never forget a little man that saved his money all his life, never put it in the bank. Wound up with thirty thousand dollars. And he had lived in just real bare accommodations, real poor. And had saved and saved to keep that money. So he had to go into the nursing home. And then his money was gone in a very short period of time. It was just amazing how quick the nursing home ate up that. Before he got there, somebody had moved in and siphoned off some of it. Then it was down to the fifteen hundred they can have to go into the nursing home. And then that was gone, and now he's really short of money for cigarettes and little things. And there he was with this life's savings—he could have had some things—and now it's gone, and he's down to indigent status again. And that seems to happen to elderly, things like that. That's really a sad part of it to me. There just seems to be an area there in the elderly, that is really not what we want it to be. Not really fair.

*   *   *

The problems associated with divorce, they permeate all of our programs. Our sexual abuse cases, many times are broken families. Mother trying to manage, there might be a breakdown in supervision of the children, and we have the perpetrators that gain access to the children. I think divorce leaves people unstable, for a while at least. And that's where we become involved is when people are in crisis. So we see a good bit of that. I really doubt that it's any worse here than it is anywhere else. I don't know.

The thing that I'm most concerned about is the abuse of children, neglect of children. The culture of poverty that passes itself from one generation to the next. The child that doesn't get what he needs at those stages of development. And emotionally is unable to compete with the rest of society. So the fact that there's a large pocket of people that are not going along with the rest of society is my major concern. And we still have that.

Examples with our poverty families, I guess, are dropping out of school early. Having a baby, a family early, and then all the problems that go along with that from generation to generation. An even more concerning thing is sexual abuse of small children, who get up to fourteen or fifteen, and then you have those children sexually abusing little children, and it going on and on that way. Also in the divorce families, and families that fight—something we didn't mention, that's of real concern to me, is the gunplay at home. Heavy drinking in families, and the marital problems that follow, and all those sorts of things—definitely there's a pattern. We pick up a case record, and here's this child, grown up, that had the same kind of childhood. I know a lady said to me one time—we had to remove her children. It was a real bad neglect situation. The worst I've ever seen. It was so bad that one of the children was having just severe seizures, from not getting what he needed, and that sort of thing. Talking with her, she could not understand why we were removing her children. She didn't understand it. But when we got on the subject of her childhood—oh, what an awful childhood she had. She said, "They used to take me to school, and I would smell, and they would bathe me at the school and it was so embarrassing." She could not see that the same life she had had, her children were having, and that they were going to feel the same way. That it had happened just over again.

*   *   *

In a way, we've seen success. In the fact that the food stamp program really did do what it set out to do. Of course it set out to eliminate hunger. And of course it has not eliminated hunger, even in Clay County, because there's so many other reasons for it than just having that food available. But it does help.

I think we forget about the survivors out there. There's many, many families in the community that are able to rise above difficulties. We forget about them, and focus more on the ones that were unable to. But they're just all out there, and that's really a nice story. We've seen a lot of success here. Of course, we don't measure success probably at what some people measure success. But what we're aiming at here I think more, is that someone has a chance to compete for some of those quality things in life. And is able to obtain a pretty good feeling about themselves, and their ability. We sure don't measure it in terms of dollars and cents. So in those terms, we feel very good about some of the things we have seen.

KATHERINE EAST
Thirty, pulpwooder, Shady Grove, white

I went to work down at the egg plant back in January. Because me and Hubert couldn't make it just on that pulpwooding work. All our bills was getting behind and everything.

Rain and stuff like that will knock you out of work, and if the trucks is tore up, that knocks you out of work. You get sick, that knocks you out. It's a lot of things that keep you from working when you're pulpwooding. And it's getting where you can't hardly find wood. There's so many pulpwooders in Clay County, it's just hard to get out and find any.

When there's nobody out there with Hubert I like to go out there with him. I can do just about anything out there. I've helped him a good bit. He don't need to be out there by hisself either. My cousin got hurt out there in the woods a couple of weeks back. His brother was with him, and he was so scared he couldn't even drive the truck out. And my cousin said he don't remember how he drove it out. It busted his skull up pretty bad. Mother and them said that he had to go back in a few weeks to have a steel plate put in his head.

It's just all the time something. Trees fall or saws cut them. Gaither Mitchell took a load of logs up there to the yard, and they fell off—fell on him off of the log truck. Killed him.

*   *   *

We don't get any kind of welfare or anything. We get food stamps. And they go by how much income we get a month. Here lately, we've got them pretty regular. We've been getting them off and on for about twelve, thirteen years. A lot of times we'll get out here, when it's pretty and all, we'll make two or three hundred dollars a week or more. And we just go over there and tell them we'll just do it on our own till we can't. Then we can go back, and it ain't no trouble. They help out a lot.

A lot of people say that they ought to have some kind of Medicaid or something for families that have kids and don't get much income and all. It would be a big help, but I don't look forward to nothing like that ever taking place.

*   *   *

I've worked at different places off and on. I guess the longest I've ever been on one job was out at the chicken plant. I stayed out there about three or four years. But I had been out quite a bit with the kids, and they didn't like any of us being out so much, so they fired me on account of that.

Kay's twelve. Christy's nine—she'll be ten the first of this month. Kevin's eight, and Donald will be six in March. The kids helped up until the time Kevin got hurt. They haven't been back out there since.

It was back in the summer. I was gone in the truck, but Hubert was cutting. One of the other kids stayed there with Kevin, and I took two of them with me in the truck. I wouldn't let them all go with me, because you pull it a long ways down a dirt road, and I wasn't all that much familiar with it. I wouldn't let them all go because I was afraid the truck might get in trouble.

I got to Lineville, got unloaded, and I was filling up with gas. And this guy come by, and he told me come straight home. And I thought it was the truck or the saw, something like that. But when I met the rescue squad, I knew it had to be one of them got hurt.

They said a tree had lodged—that's where a tree falls over on your other trees, and it doesn't completely crash. And nobody was paying much attention to Kevin. He was trying to work too, helping them pile wood, and they couldn't get him in time. The tree hit him on the back of the head and knocked him to the ground, fractured his skull. But other than that, he was lucky. There has been so many people getting killed out there in the woods.

We've still got a pretty good bill. We haven't paid it yet. He stayed overnight in the ICU. The rescue squad came and picked him up. Took him to the hospital and then from there he went on the helicopter to Birmingham. That was his second ride on that helicopter. It come to over three thousand dollars. I had already owed the University of Alabama up there over a thousand dollars from when he got a nail in his eye. He's not but eight years old, but he's been around.

If there's nobody to keep them now, I'll stay at home. And then when they get the trucks loaded—they let me know what time they're going to be loaded—and I'll take them with me to the yard or something like that. I don't never leave them at home by theirselves because there's so much meanness going on, you know. I'm afraid they'll be out in the yard playing or something, and somebody could stop. I just don't leave them by theirselves.

Lord, the way that boy goes, when he gets up where I won't be able to be there with him and watch after him, it's going to be rough. I guess he's just accident-prone. I don't know what it is. I try to keep their burial paid up.

KARIN CHRISTOPHERSON
Forty, coordinator, Clay County Mental Health Center, Lineville, white

Most of our people work real hard here, and they get tired physically and mentally. Piecework. That's a hard thing to deal with, piecework.

We have many tree accidents. We've lost several people in tree accidents. It's scary. And that's another thing. They put them in cars here, because there's no phone to get the rescue squad, they bring them to the hospital, they're near death, they get the helicopter here. And they have to go by helicopter to Birmingham. Look at the time lapse. We're in the woods, we're in a car, we've been moved incorrectly, we get to the hospital, we're moved again, we're ready to be put on a helicopter. Most of the pulpwood families don't have phones in their homes. It's a time thing.

And it's always, "I don't know how to pay for it." The University of Alabama isn't cheap. This hospital here's real inexpensive, but big city places aren't. I have clients with ten thousand dollars', twenty thousand dollars' worth of medical bills. They don't make twenty thousand in five years. And they want to pay the bill.

I have one, she's been trying to pay bills on her three-hundred-dollar check forever. Three hundred a month. She sends everybody two dollars a month. She doesn't even understand it. She doesn't read or write. See, our illiteracy rate's high. Many of my clients can't read or write. She doesn't know that Lawyer So-and-So says that she hasn't paid her medical bill. She didn't understand that. She'd been paying two dollars.

It's economic stress because they want to pay their bills. If they didn't want to pay their bills they'd all have phones in their houses and get them disconnected and all this. These people live on what they make. They might have a house paid for and a car paid for, but no health insurance, a four-thousand-dollar income, seven thousand with food stamps and all, and they don't know how they're going to pay that bill.

We don't refuse services. We request money, but we don't refuse services. But you know what? Almost all my indigent patients pay. Six dollars. There's a few that ride it, but I've had many people pay bills. Long after they're done here. Two dollars, three dollars. These are proud people up here. They're not seeing what they can get.

They can accept being poor and live with it. It's just they don't handle tragedy well. Big bills, treatment centers. They don't handle things that we handle every day. Things that you and I will take for granted is a crisis for them. We spend a lot of our time going through little logistics. Just drive the person to the treatment center, and it'll all be taken care of. But they don't know. I do a lot with education. And explaining. Because they don't know. They don't know their options in life.

KAY'S PRETTY SMART

Kay East, twelve years old, has about her some of the poise of maturity as she stands on her front porch in jeans and a striped shirt with a monogram that did not come from her name. Her thick gold hair, unlike most county girls', bears no mark of a permanent wave, and she speaks with the assurance of someone used to handling family affairs.

Inside the house, as her father and mother talk, as a younger sister and brother chime in and a small dog and half-grown kitten wrestle on the living room floor, she picks up a mop and scrubs at the Coca-Cola spilled a night or so before. When questions turn to the children, sister Christy talks with giggles and glee, delighted by the attention. Kay looks at the floor, and answers only briefly.

What are you going to do when you grow up?

Christy: Nothing. *All laugh.* Lay around in bed.
Hubert: She's told the honest truth right there now.
Katherine: Christy has a lazy streak in her. You have to make her get up and do something. Kay's pretty smart.

What do you want to do?

Kay: I want to leave Clay County.
Christy: She's going to marry Chuck.
Kay: Go to work. And have no brats.
Christy: When you marry Chuck, you're going to have five brats. *She is laughing again.*
Katherine: What kind of work are you going to do, Kay? You going to work in the sewing plant, egg plant, chicken plant? *Pause.* She's interested in computers.
Christy: I don't do my work. I'm going to go home and lay down in bed.

Let your parents take care of you all your life?

Christy: They'll be dead and gone before I get big enough.

Katherine: Well if you think Kay'll put up with you when you're grown, you'd better think again.

Kay: Oh, no—I'll leave. I'll leave Clay County before she'll live with me. Go to Africa.

Christy: She's going to live with Chucky-boy. Kay's going to live with Chucky-boy. Get married. Chucky, Chucky, Chuck.

In the Black Community

Preceding page: Mary V. Adair

On the west side of Ashland, years ago, the First Avenue paving gave way to dusty red-dirt road, and the water lines ran out, and even with no one on the streets, the clusters of small, ramshackle homes signaled your arrival in what polite folks would have called the colored part of town. That neighborhood, with those in Lineville, was called by black and white the Quarters, some-times the Jones or the Collier Quarters, after the main landowners, or even, for a rough section during the Korean War, the Korean Quarters, but all with that lingering plantation ring, suggesting the past of servants, vast lands, and patrician ease that remains one of the region's most persistent dreams.

Those blacks who did not live in town were scattered through the country— a tenant or a field hand here or there, an enclave of railroad workers by the tracks at Cragford, a group of small farmers in the part of Millerville that bore the timeless name The Glades. As elsewhere in the South, black lives wove through white in close and intricate design, crossing in the homes they cleaned, the fields they worked, the stores they patronized, and sometimes on the ground of friendship. But in a county of poor whites, blacks were usually poorer still— his family was well off, one man recalls, because his father had work pressing pants, and got a nickel for every pair of shoes he shined. And most blacks lived encompassed by bounds tighter even than those around the county's whites, in a world where a few visits between churches could keep almost everyone in touch, where the single black high school had only three instructors, and where, for many years, the classroom and the pulpit were the only sites of status to which bright children could aspire.

Stories of the past, told by both blacks and whites, spin the county's varia-tions on familiar figures and events, some near-lost in distant time, others more recent than a listener might imagine: stories of hiding corn in mattresses, to keep it from a landlord's greedy eyes; of midnight flights from the bondage sharecropping could so easily become; of bodies buried deep beneath one rail-road bed, belonging to blacks who spoke back to white workmen, and were shot and buried on the spot.

Still, recollection can also bear the flavor of nostalgia, felt for overflowing churches, for neighbors of both colors who knew when you needed help before *you asked, and perhaps most of all for youth, for a time when, despite the hard work and hot sun, you could race someone all day to put one, two, or maybe three hundred pounds of cotton in the sack that trailed behind you. And they hint of hope and growing promise, of study in a school where teachers who had finished college lavished all their strength on their black pupils, of distant places where there might be jobs, of a wider, better world from which, despite the isolation that the hills around enforced, flashes of heartening news at times would come. In the battered Quarters homes blacks followed the exploits of Joe Louis, and of other heroes, even though it would be decades later, and years after marches and protest began in other Southern towns, that they would really start believing they might live long enough to see things change, and that events would finally bring what both black and white called "trouble" home.*

IT'S SOMETHING LIVING IN THIS WORLD

The red mud left by early winter rain cakes fast onto your tires as the long dirt road that leads to Mary Adair's house plunges into a sea of pines that has no end in sight. The receding cluster of trailers and small houses is swallowed quickly up, and close on a mile of silent space will pass before a near-ageless wooden house, topped by a deep red-rusted roof and a tower of mud-plastered stones, comes into view.

The stretch of porch across the front has been patched with so many layers of mesh screening that at first the figures it conceals seem like the shades and voices of householders long since fled. But smoke rises from the chimney into the cold December air, and in the front room, where bed and chairs jostle for space with a scattering of purses, brooms, and other artifacts of daily life, the pictures on the walls are full of children.

Mary Adair, sitting near the open fire, talks with a mix of slow reflection and not-quite-suppressed amusement about the way things used to be. Her voice sounds deep and soft in the still-chilly room, until the sudden moments when it rises, grows louder, and then breaks into laughter, usually at questions— about cotton, work, or money—to which everyone once knew answers that now must be explained. But there are also times when she herself appears to marvel at the childhood she recalls, and the far-off world her words describe can seem as elusive and fantastic as a dream.

MARY V. ADAIR
Seventy-six, retired farmer, Millerville, black

I've been working all my life, since I got big enough. I reckon I was doing something when I was five. Mostly tote water and get in wood, something like that. We had our own land. I've forgot now—it wasn't too big. I married my husband, and we farmed. He was on his daddy's farm. We'd start the last of March. We'd plant corn, maybe, and then wait a while and plant cotton, when it got warmer. I didn't never plow, but when he got it in shape to plant, I dropped the corn.

Yes ma'am, it was hard. It was. The cotton when it grew up. You'd chop it. It'd grow up sometimes, and that was some hard work. Sometimes we had to chop the corn. We pulled lots of fodder.

I guess I picked a little over two hundred pounds a day. We used to go off. We'd work here, try to catch up, and then go somewhere else and work. Sometimes it'd be turning cold when we finished. Sometimes it'd be weeks, and then sometimes you'd just get through with it pretty well. Didn't make too much. Sometimes we'd make two or three bales, something like that. We took it to Ashland. It'd take you a long time—had to carry it in a wagon [laughs].

We'd buy us something to eat, that'd be the first thing. I don't know what all we bought now. I know it was something to eat.

Down at Millerville, that was the closest store. And them days, we used to get out and walk to the store. It was far, but we had to do it. I didn't mind it then. But Lord, I couldn't walk to Millerville now. I tell the kids I walked down there many a hot day, but I had to go. And then I didn't get much. You know I didn't, when I had to tote it. A long walk for nothing much, but it was the best I could do. They don't believe it. They couldn't do that.

It's near about the same way now. Can't hardly get nowhere. I ain't got no way myself of going, and I still have a time. I get out sometimes to church. Used to get out and walk to church. Didn't think nothing about it. Day and night. They walked then. Nobody walks now.

Just here recently, my husband had one of his legs cut off. And so we can't farm now. We quit growing cotton a long time ago. It got to where we just couldn't make no cotton worth planting it, and we just quit. Everybody quit about the same time. I don't know whether they just wanted to quit or what it was. I know I got tired of it. You had to work so hard in that cotton. I was glad to be shed of that. It didn't pay off, hard as I worked, looked like enough. You'd make some some years, and sometimes it just didn't look like worth planting. That's when I fell out with cotton.

I cook and clean up. First one thing then another, in the house. Wait on him. We get a check. Sometimes we do pretty well, sometimes I can't hardly get along. Time I pay my policies and the light bill and the phone bill, I don't have nothing much.

This house has been here a long time. His parents had it. His brother was here, but he passed. We put this stuff up side of the house, the metal stuff. Tin roof. Just the fireplace for heat. It was after I married we got electricity.

When we moved down here we dug a well out back of the house. We ain't got no water in the house. We have to draw it and tote it in here. We just never could get it fixed. Have to heat it on the stove or on the fireplace.

I don't know if things are better now. Maybe it's a little bit; I don't know. But I know it ain't with me. Because I miss that farm. I could go out in the field and get what I wanted. And it didn't cost me. I sure miss that. We had chickens. We didn't have to worry about eggs. I've still got seven. I've got them fastened up. I used to raise them, kill them and eat them. Never had to buy no chickens.

*   *   *

I sit down here and think about it a lot. I think about how we come up and all, and didn't have nothing much. Didn't have nothing much at all. It was tough back yonder, I'm telling you the truth. Had to eat cornbread for breakfast. That's all we had then. We had a hard time.

My daddy used to ditch all the time. Just different places. Some weeks he'd go off to ditch and have to stay till the weekend. We'd be so glad to see Papa coming in—we knowed we was going to get a sack of flour. We made bread with it. It'd rest us from that cornbread till it give out. Mama used to take a handful of meal and sprinkle in that flour, to make it go further. It'd be gritty, but we ate it. He done a lot of hard work, ditching. That was hard work.

I think about how I worked, and my friends, and what all we did, and everything sometimes. When the children's around, I'll be telling them about it. And they don't believe me. They'll sit and listen at me, but they don't believe the stuff. I tell them about how y'all have anything you want now, and we didn't.

I had a little boy to spend the night with me last night, and he asked me did Santy Claus come see me. I said yes. He said, "What did you get?" I said, "An apple and an orange, a few sticks of candy. And raisins on the stem." He said "Is that all?" I said, "Yes, that's all." I said, "We thought we had something. You couldn't tell us we didn't have nothing." I said, "Now y'all eat apples all the time, when you get ready for them. And it won't seem like Christmas like it did when we was coming up. It seemed like Christmas then."

We'd get us an old stocking, and tie a string on it, hang it on that chair.

I think about all that stuff a lots of times. And another thing, they kept us fooled a long time about Santy Claus. They'd even make marks in the ashes, show us where he'd been. We just knowed there was a Santy Claus. Children now, you can't fool them. We were great big old children before we knowed there wasn't no Santy Claus. Grown nearly.

She tried picking cotton one time in her life, Amanda Scott says, sitting amid silk flowers and stuffed chairs in a room marked by the same elaborate care as the braids and curls in her upswept black hair and the clear enunciation in her teacher's voice. Her husband's students planted a cotton patch one year, she continues, and when harvest season came she offered to help out. "I put on my jacket and I got out there and I picked. I started about eight o'clock. Picked until about twelve or one. And I said, 'I'm going to get a hundred pounds today.' After dinner I went back. So when I looked out there I think I had about forty-six pounds, and I said, 'No more for me. I'll have to do another job. I'll cook for them, I'll do anything,' I said. 'But I can't get that cotton.'"

AMANDA SCOTT
Sixty-eight, retired teacher, Lineville, black

I came for a weekend in 1938. I was born in Birmingham. My sister and I came here, to this house. And we visited. My fiancé, David Scott, had his mother living here. And I said to myself, "I don't know whether I'll be able to adjust there or not." But later on, I saw there were some of the same people right down here as you find in the cities. But to just come in, and sit around, and go to church and all, you wouldn't know it. You just have to visit around. You study. Learn each other. You can pick up quite a bit.

When I came here, these kids had to stay out of school for a while, to pick cotton. In Birmingham we had a chance to go straight through because we didn't have that cotton to pick. So it made these kids here longer finishing sometimes. Sometimes, when we'd start school, they'd get out in October, September, pick the cotton. Get out so many weeks. Then they'd come back. I think they stopped that in '59.

When I first came, some of the white people used to see me, and I'd smile and speak to them. Some would stop me on the street and say, "We're look-ing for a girl to come in our home and stay and help us." I didn't tell them I was married, working. I said, "I'm sorry, but I wouldn't be able to help you. But maybe I could help you find somebody." So later on they learned who I was [laughs]. But I didn't tell them.

For a while I taught the high school kids. I was tickled to teach geometry. I was crazy about that in high school. So I taught that, and some of the kids said, "You know, Mrs. Scott, we don't need all of these different terms and everything." I said, "But you're not going to stay here all the time. You're going to leave, go all over the world. Different states, different countries." And I said, "We're going to have to learn to cope with the situation." They said, "We don't want to do it." I said, "But let's try it anyway."

So they studied, and I had one particular student who went in the service. In the forties or fifties, something like that. He brought his family when he came back. He said, "I told my wife and my kids that you were my teacher, and that you insisted that we take the math and everything and do our best." So he said, "I had to come back and tell you you were right." And said, "I was in this math class. My instructor came around, he noticed I could do the work, and he said, 'Who taught you?' And so I told him. He said, 'Well, you know more about it than I do,' said, 'teach the class.'" And so I say whatever you're going to do, do your best.

The majority of the students left. We have quite a few here, but it seems as if more left. I have some in California—all the states. And some still in Germany.

Many parents thought they'd just finish up, get them a job. And maybe marry, have their kids. And stay around. But I didn't see it that way. I knew they'd be going places. And I said, "As you go different places, learn to do something worthwhile. To bring credit to yourself, your family, your people, and everybody."

We enlightened the parents too. So that they could help talk to the kids. We had PTA meetings, so they could come in and give their input. Activi-ties: first one, then another. And they enjoyed it to the highest.

We had assembly programs every Friday. Different groups would take charge. And we tried to instill in the kids to be somebody. If you're not going to be in a profession, whatever. Be good at that. Get along. Make a decent living. Be honest. Faithful. Truthful. What have you. If you can learn to live with yourself, you won't have too many problems. We got up different poems. And we read stories. Autobiographies of outstanding people. We read the lives of the presidents, and studied that.

It's something living in this world, and so we talked to them about it. Encouraged them. You see, you want to live peaceably with everyone. But you have to have peace with yourself first. And we talked about the Bible. I know they didn't want too much of it. But you'll find some of everything you want in the Bible. So we encouraged them to read it, and think about it, and see what part they can use. And it helped quite a bit.

I had to pray a lot. Some people didn't have time to read to the kids and talk to them very much. So I had a lot of work to do. My husband said, "You're just worried about those children." I would try to get them to write in the second grade. He said, "Well, they're going to learn." I said, "But I want it done now." So when they did get it, you couldn't take it away from them. They said, "We're proud." So I was proud for them. And some, when they married, and had kids, I'd have to be the godmother.

I said, "With God all things are possible." I just believe that. And so when we had little problems, turn it over to Him and go out with a smile. Come out all right, too.

WALTER FARR, JR.

You know when I first became aware that blacks could not do everything that white people could do? It must have been the summer of 1944 or '45. I had been in South Carolina. I rode the bus to Anniston, and met a good black friend of mine. And we got to talking, we were there on Noble Street, and he said, "Hey, man, let's do something together. Let's go to a movie. There's a good one now on Noble Street here."

And we got down there, and it dawned on me that I would be sitting down on the bottom floor and he'd be upstairs. And of course we just decided not to go. And that was just—it was a shock. I knew it. I had been going to Lineville all of my life. And the white folks sat on the main floor, and black folks were upstairs in the balcony. But when this black friend and I started to go to a movie together, and we got to the ticket office, it hit us both about the same time. Wouldn't be much fun. I hadn't seen him in a long time, three or four years. I've always thought about that; it's always stuck in my mind.

But I had been a segregationist. Not a racist, because I grew up with black people. But it was just accepted. We played with them and even I socialized with them to a point, but when it came to eating with them or sitting down, you just didn't do. Looking back I can see that I discriminated against those people, but it was out of ignorance. I just can't stand the thought of people being in bondage, one person or one people being over another. Master and slave—it's so repelling to think. But yet I grew up under that, and I didn't think anything about it. It was just something that you just took for granted, I guess.

JUST LIKE STIRRING UP A POT

In its early days, the fight for civil rights reached Clay County mainly as a feeling in the air, a sort of tension, and perhaps anticipation, as the ripples from Montgomery and Anniston, from Birmingham and Selma, moved across the county like the warning tremors of a not-so-distant quake. The movement was not a subject talked about in public, some establishments banned the topic from the workplace, and its goals were commonly dismissed as dreams that no one then alive would ever see. Clay County, with few blacks and fewer institutions to wield discrimination's sting, edged through those first hard years without disruption, and residents felt proud that at least at home the races lived in peace.

But within their household walls blacks kept close watch on the events, and even now the images tumble from firm-fixed places in their minds: the dogs, the school door, the flames from a Freedom Rider bus barely fifty miles away. Words like "overcome" still resound with tones of reverence, and you will sometimes see, among photos of family, of grand and great-grandchildren, the likenesses of Martin Luther King and of the Kennedys, John and Robert, in the clean, earnest poses of dreamers and martyrs.

Still, although the movement's brave young leaders became a new set of black heroes, a new example for black youths, in a county where you learned to bypass conflict, a place where, even now, most blacks speak of prejudice in tones of tactful moderation, it was hard to know just what to do. The violence that had torn at so many other towns and cities could prove a powerful deterrent, and the benefits of integration were far from wholly clear to everyone. When county schools entered the brief era known as freedom of school choice, few challenged the order that had stood so long. And on the morning when a young man walked a single black girl to Clay County High's first day of integrated education, the air rang with the screams of two black women, who begged in fear for him to turn away.

AMANDA SCOTT

In '69 we finished up here. The fall term of '70, we crossed over. Before we integrated, about '68, '70, some of the people started talking that it might be trouble if some of the kids would come over and enter before the law was passed. That in 1970 they would integrate. But afterwards they accepted it.

I was the type that could mix and mingle with all of them. Because all my life I had been with the others. My great-grandparents and some grandparents were white. Didn't make too much difference with me. My husband was dark. But his mother was half white because her people, some of them were white too. So it didn't make too much difference.

You would find some people with a little different attitudes. But you handle it tactfully. I heard some kids talking on the playground. See, we had duties on the playground. And one parent I know of had told the kids that "I don't want you playing with these nigger children." And so I noticed the kids out playing. The mother had come down. And so then I went over to talk to her with a smile. And so I told her, I said, "We have to remember that niggers come in all colors." I said, "When you act ugly to me, that's nigger." I said, "Now we have to treat people like we want to be treated." And I said, "You're such a nice person yourself, I just don't believe you said that." Didn't have any trouble; she's one of my best friends today. And her kids are real sweet. So I learned how to kind of smooth it out.

You could feel a tenseness up there sometimes. Not too much. But as we stayed, things got better and better. We had a beautiful relationship. A lot of people have trouble because they don't know how to get along with people. But we didn't have any.

RUBY KING
Seventy-one, retired teacher, Ashland, black

I hadn't thought about integration too much, but along with the rest of the teachers, I couldn't help but realize the difference. Because just before integration I had children that was in school. And you just reach a certain point where it's so obvious. Where all of the books—after they began to even furnish books, the new books would never come to us. And the books would all be torn. There was so much disparity there. And so you couldn't help but notice. I didn't have any idea when integration would take place, or if it would. But it was just obvious that you were just second class. It really was.

My daughter was the first—before it was the law—my daughter was the first to integrate the school here in Ashland. It was her own idea. She was in the eleventh grade. She wanted to go. And then at that time, they had started something—it wasn't mandatory that all the kids would go, but they had something like freedom of choice. And you could choose the school you wanted to go to. You had to go through a lot of signing papers and all of that. But it was just something she wanted to do—I guess because at this age she could see that there would be better opportunities. And my children were just like I am, it had been instilled in them that it would be nothing else but for them to go on to college. She thought she'd have more opportunities.

It was terrible. It was just terrible. Those were some of the worst days of my life. We had bomb threats. We had a cross burned. We had groups of— I guess it was Ku Klux—just cars ride up and down through here. We had telephone calls all through the night. We were harassed. And this started before she even went to school.

We expected some reaction, but we didn't expect some of the things that happened. My husband, fact about it, his patronage at the dry cleaners was white, mostly. And then it began to drop off. People who we thought were our friends. It was a difficult time. As you think back over it, it's just really hard to even talk about it sometimes.

I didn't pay attention but one time. This was the year that my son was getting ready to go to college. At the same time that my daughter was preparing to go to school over there. One day somebody called and asked, "Where is Robert?" My husband. I said, "He's not here right now." He said, "You will never see him again," said, "he's so many feet underground, out at the graphite place." Used to be a graphite mine out there. Said, "You'll never see him again." So I called the cleaners, and sure enough he wasn't out there. And it disturbed me. Because those threats—it was just so violent till you didn't know what was going to happen. So I called Bobby, my son. I said we've got to find your dad. So he got in the car and he rode around and couldn't find him noplace. And I really did get disturbed about it. And so when he came, I said, "Where have you been?" That was my most anxious moment.

And they would throw these cherry bombs. All through the night be throwing these things in your yard. I feel that it was a lot of people doing that. And they were people who were hiding, who didn't want us to know who they were. People, so-called, who've been your friends. I think it was a lot of people.

But I tell you what, a lot of black people became involved. There was a group of black men who had started an organization, something like a league. The Better Citizens' Club, I think that was the name of it. Anyway, the president was the one who went to school with her that first day. Because we had had threats. They had called and they had said if she went to school that first day the cleaners was going to be burned down, the school was going to be burned down. We had every kind of threat you could have mentioned. And that morning this young man came by and picked her up and they went.

Out here, across the street, there was a big tree—the tree is still out there. And black men started coming over at night, climbing in that tree, to watch our house. Because they had threatened to burn it down. They would come with guns, and they would climb that tree, and watch this house, and take turns all night. Oh, it was terrible.

*   *   *

You know, after it was over I just forgot about it. And I have some very good friends, white friends. I have worked with some. In a sense, unless you just really sit down and begin to think about it—it brings back a lot of bitterness for that particular time. But I have no hard feelings.

My daughter doesn't like to talk about it. I imagine she has some bitterness. Some of those people who was nice to her, she likes to talk about them. I just don't know how to explain. It's just one of the phenomenons in life. Just what happens when you change. And that's a big change. I think one reason I don't have any bitterness about it now—it's just a matter of understanding. You can understand why people would be like that. It's fear, it's prejudice, it's racism and all of that, and you can just understand why people would react like that. It was hard for everybody to understand back then. It was just a whole turning over. Not only in the South. Just like stirring up a pot or something.

WALTER FARR, JR.

I became principal of the Lineville Elementary School in the fall of 1964. I was an administrator. In '69 the Clay County Board of Education had a plan, the federal government plan, and I had to make it work. I believed in it, but there were many people who were against it, and I had many soul-searching thoughts on that. What bothered me was some of my good friends who turned out to be just total racists. They were just against a child because of his color. That was all it could be.

I did all I could to make sure that we had an equal number of blacks in every class. I even got down to the point where we had the same equal number of females and males and all this, but I still got a lot of criticism. Because their child was in a black woman's class, this type thing. I had calls from black people, "Don't put my child in a white woman's room." They were proud of their school just as we were proud of ours.

The summer prior to, I say, quote, "total integration," I taught a summer school over at the, quote, "Clay County Training School." A PE class. And we had a good time. I had those black children and they came up and they put their arms around me, and three or four would take each hand as we went out to the playground. Of course I've got to admit I looked around to see if any white folks were looking at me, because this was uncultivated territory. But I liked it. I said, "These people are human beings too. I just don't know them."

Things worked out all right. We had problems. We had problems with the older people. But I don't know how you can work with people, and young people especially, and be prejudiced. I just don't see how you can. They become family. They're just a part of you. That summer I taught summer school, I came in contact with them daily. I was surprised that they were so much like our own kids. They were just black in color. I don't really know why.

FLOSSIE MAE WOOD
Sixty-two, nursing-home worker, Delta, black

Here out in the country, people has always been nice to us. But back in town, they didn't want to live beside the blacks, the blacks live in a small place in town, they didn't want to live beside them. But out here they do, they're real nice, you can live where you want to.

And our children, growing up. All the children played together, like they was sisters and brothers. It didn't make no difference to them. Not out here in the country they didn't. Now my children, they didn't go to school with white children, they went to black schools, because all this hadn't passed, it hadn't happened. All my children was through school when that happened.

At first I thought integration wasn't too good because I thought that it was going to be a lot of pressure on the children. But since it all happened, I guess it did ought to happen, because now they all seem real happy with it. But you know then a lot of people had a lot of madness in their hearts, and I thought it was going to be just a big mess, and I really thought everything would change. We were afraid that it would make some people mad. I thought they were really going to get mad at me. They didn't, though, everybody was just calm and suffered it out. [Laughs.]

I guess it just come a time that—things aren't going to be the same always, it just was change. So to me that was really a big change. And I felt like there was going to be a lot of trouble, but it wasn't, everybody just calmed down, and it was still the same way. But you know in places they did have a lot of trouble.

You know what I like about it? When my children went to school, they didn't use the same kind of books that the white children used. You know, I didn't realize that until afterward. And my grandchildren, well the books are a lot different than they were with my children's books. You know what I like to say, when these white children come out, they could be highway patrol, they could be law enforcement, take on most anything. And our children's books, they wasn't saying anything like that. It really wasn't doing us no good—they learned to read and all, but it really wasn't doing us good. But now my grandchildren have it, and they have to study hard, and when they come out, if they want to, they can be anything they want to be.

We hadn't ever thought about anything like the schools being different. Well, we all came up the same, and so we didn't think anything about it, and then there was all this stuff, and I wanted to know, "Why do you want the children to go to school together like that?" and I thought, "Forget about all this rumor stuff," you know, all this jealousy stuff, in your heart, you know what I mean. Anyway, in your heart. And I didn't know, why would they want to start something like that? But since it all happened, I realized that there was so much difference. And I said to myself, I said, "Now I see why white children were so far advanced over the colored, because their books were different. And when they finished they knowed something. And our children, when they finished, they knowed what little they knowed, but it wasn't really much good."

Now that the white children and the black children are going together, it's just all around different. Now if they want to when they come out they can have a job. So I'm glad that everything worked out to get everybody together. I just don't like all this hatred stuff, you know.

PEOPLE HAVE GOTTEN USED TO IT

The road through Ashland's west side has by now been built into four lanes of state highway. To one side, several blocks that once were filled with the substandard houses where black families had grown used to living, now sport the red brick of a federally funded project, with water, and indoor plumbing, and doors and windows that keep out cold and wind with considerably more effect than those that they replaced.

Old people with long memories never seem to tire of talking, amazement still in their voices, about how much things have changed, how they can turn on the television set and see black boys competing with, and often beating, white ones, how they can sit so many places and do so many things that at one time, not really all that long ago, would have drawn the full and heavy weight of Caucasian wrath. Those a generation younger, who still remember how things used to be, seem proud and almost satisfied with the distance that they've come, although younger ones, with less span and drama in their recollections, can be impatient with all that's left to do.

With the passing of the fields of corn and cotton, most of the county's blacks now live in town, with only a few settlements left scattered here and there across the countryside. Old bonds still run with lasting force through these communities, where church and kinship ties still form the centers of activity, and where children from fragmented homes, and old people left to manage on their own, can often find refuge and help more easily than whites. But past troubles hold to their grip as well—black students both touch the top and crowd the bottom of many county classes, black leaders direct poverty programs for which their neighbors are among the major clients, and in black neighborhoods comfortable, well-kept homes sit often only steps from patched constructions of tar paper, half-mended supports, and shiny glints of metal siding. Poverty rates run twice as high for black families as white, and the narrow range of prospects the county has to offer—where success in a well-paid profession often seems reserved for those who follow in their parents' footsteps—has sparked precipitous erosion in a community placed always at the margins of economic life. While parents tell proud stories of the success ambitious children have achieved in far-off homes, local leaders break into frustration when they talk about how hard it is to get those who remain to press for goals that blacks in nearby counties have already reached.

Integration has spread in patchwork pattern through the county, holding firm in schools, in some jobs, and in many public places, but stretching to near-invisibility elsewhere, just as in conversation tones of friendship and satisfaction can suddenly give way to the silence, reservation, or at times open hostility with which people express views on a still-touchy situation. While blacks stand out in the melee of the football field, in loud, confident, and laughing groups along the sidelines, patronizing Lineville stores and parking on the Ashland square, they can be just as clearly absent—no black has ever worked inside a county bank, behind a courthouse desk, or, until a recent lawsuit, in elected office. Most still earn their living at the chicken or the rubber-tire plant, workplaces which, despite gains won by the county's lone two unions, many whites still shun. Black activities take place in largely isolated neighborhoods—strung out along dirt country roads, tucked into secluded parts of town—through which few whites have cause to pass, and white talk of race relations, shot through with the resentment left by the flood of civil rights publicity, still mixes fond accounts of personal relations with sharper, less specific, and often mistaken words—on unwed mothers, welfare checks, and a lack of proper manners—that point toward persisting gaps in culture and experience.

And although formal segregation lies far enough away that young people have trouble even imagining what it was like, blacks still pour their energies into their own community. Old instincts still lead many to distrust the sheriff, and the courts, and it is not always easy, even when whites try, to get blacks to join in county projects. When one black woman who speaks with passion about the benefits of integration describes the senior citizens' center she would like her community to have, she adds that, for the sake of many members, this one institution would be better off without it. And when local leaders talk about community advancement, they concentrate less on their hopes for whites than on endeavors blacks can undertake themselves.

HORACE SIMS
*Fifty-two, deputy director, Talladega-Clay-Randolph
Community Action Agency, Ashland, black*

I have seen where the inferiority built. You're living in a better home than I'm living in. You're wearing better clothes. You're having access to the things that I haven't had access to. The type of homes and cars. It makes a person feel inferior to another person when they get in those type things like that. It's hard for a person to come out of a low-income, poverty area, and go in places and hold your chest up. It's just an instinct that I think had built it in me. There was a time, you had to say yes, sir. You had to say no, sir. You couldn't go up and talk to a man or a lady without saying yes, sir or no, sir if they were white. Any time you're riding on the back of something, and have to go there and be on the back, it's making you look little. That was some things that had been through the years, and that built. That type thing stays in a person's blood until his generation wears it out.

I had to overcome some portions. But it didn't tie in as tight with me as it did a lot of people. The biggest thing was like cafes. When I started first going in the first cafe, I was as inferior as the devil. I felt funny. When I walked in for the first time, and I never had been in a cafe where the whites were sitting, I felt funny. I felt funny when I got on a bus to ride, where I had been going all the way to the back, and sit anywhere I wanted. Although I could do it, I felt funny. You had inferiority; you just felt different. There'd been a system that people had to live by. All those type things made you feel funny the first time you did them.

There may be some barriers now. Like even our banks. We've had some qualified people go to a bank for a job. And we don't have any blacks in the banks in the entire county. That's an improvement I'd like to see; that's one piece of crust I'd like to see cracked one day. Things like that I'd like to see. I'd like to see some black people working in the courthouse, like they have in Anniston, and in Talladega and Randolph counties. We don't have any. That's county money, their own money going there. I don't know why. It's a hard thing to say why. We have not knocked down the barricades in this county, as far as some jobs. But I think in the future those things will happen.

When you think of this thing, see how you're living today, you can see how God has been able to work these people's hearts, and make the changes in life. It makes you appreciate life more. You'd be surprised, how things were. Things that I have experienced in my little short time at my age. It makes you feel good.

I don't think nothing at all now. It's just like it's been all my life now. It's like it never existed. I don't believe I have any of that inside now. I don't believe I have any.

OTIS HIGGINS, JR.
Thirty-three, state trooper, Lineville, black

I'm sure a lot of things went on in the sixties, fifties, and forties. But since I've been on I haven't encountered any departmental racism or anything like that. It may exist, but I've been always treated just like anybody else. You're kind of your own boss out here. If you do right, and do what you're supposed to, they leave you alone. It's just when you go to messing up they get on you.

I stayed in a rural area. My closest neighbor was about a mile away. Nobody bothered us, and we didn't bother anyone. I think most of my neighbors may have been white. People just respected troopers, I guess. You never did hardly see any state troopers. It was always nice to see their car go by, because it was just so exciting. Played baseball in the road. That's about how much traffic we had.

I think that probably the best thing would be to talk to the first black trooper there's ever been in the county. Because the first black troopers only came on—I guess the most they could have is fifteen or sixteen years on. There was a time where there was not any black troopers. I'm sure that was something to see when they first came in the county. It's been four or five or six of them. People have gotten used to it now.

Of course you have black people stay on one side, white people stay on the other side. Then you got white and black people staying in certain sections. I stay between all white people. I don't think about it. I'm here to do a job. And I don't think about belonging to maybe a black community or belonging to a white community. I do my job; they don't bother me, and I don't bother them. That's just the way it is. That's the way I feel about it. I don't feel more strongly towards one than I do towards the other. I know I'm between a white section. I know I'm the first black to probably ever get in this section. Nobody bothers me, and I've been here almost two or three years. Nobody's ever bothered me on anything.

RICKY BURNEY
Thirty-three, security guard, Lineville, black

About eleven years ago I went to work as a security guard. At the time, I was in construction security here in the county. And then I knew when the work was finished, I was going to have to go somewhere, so I bidded into production security.

I would say at this time right there was the first time that I ever thought that I'd encountered a lot of racism. Because I had a lot more seniority than the most of the people that was there. Matter of fact it was three of us, three black guys, that had the most seniority. When the work was finished, I felt like the normal procedure was if you was the last hired, you were the first fired. But they did it backwards, and they went and got the ones that had the most seniority and was going to not let them stay. They decided they was going to get the people that they wanted, which didn't have the seniority.

The other two guys at that time decided they wasn't going to fight it. But I had just built this home, and I wasn't going to leave it to go work somewhere else. So I fought it, and finally got the job. I fought it through company procedures. I went to the equal opportunity department and talked with those guys and they finally realized I guess that I was right. Because the people they had hired had a whole lot less seniority. I had trained these people that they hired. I had trained them to do the job, and taught them more about security. As far as education-wise, I had more education than any of them. So I had them beat as far as education goes, and I had them beat as far as seniority goes. And experience. And so I think they kind of saw that it was a losing battle. I got the job.

See, in my life I'd always had harmony in this area as far as racism goes, as far as black and white issues. But after encountering that problem with the company, I saw the strikes against me.

AIN'T NOBODY GOING
TO GIVE YOU NOTHING

Lisa Hardy is trying to keep her voice to the calm, explanatory tone so many of her elders seem to have perfected, where words rise and fall like water working slowly on a rock, and waiting doesn't seem so large a task. But the tension of the subject, of tactfully sidestepping harsher words, and of holding back the drive that lies behind her community involvement proves to be too great, and now and then the stream of patient intonation breaks, falling hard on a single word, or on a sudden deep quick-spoken phrase, or cracking in a burst of not-quite-easy laughter. Such moments are brief at first, the even rhythm rapidly recovered, but as the conversation lengthens the balance starts to tip, and her words take on more life, if also much more pain. Discussion of white prejudice or weakness, harsh as it has often been, is not the problem. It is when she turns to friends and neighbors that the emotion comes, pouring out in joyous relief over stories about her Sunday school students or her beloved grandmother, but rising to highest pitch of passion and frustration when she talks about the trials so patiently endured by county blacks, for whom she wants so much, but who often seem to settle for so very little.

LISA HARDY
Twenty-seven, wood-products plant worker, Ashland, black

I think black people feel like if I have anything to say, I might can't stay in my apartment. I might can't go uptown and borrow money like I've been borrowing. They're going to run everything anyways, so why should I go over there and be bothered?

Most of your old people that you talk to, you can tell they remember. Because it's about the first thing they say. "When we were young, we had to work, like all day and night to make a good fifty cents. And then we had to pay it to the man uptown, or we didn't have no flour." I hear that told a lot. And I guess they never forget.

*   *   *

Earlier, you asked me do parents push their kids. We might have about one percent of black parents that go to PTA. Well to me, that's not pushing your kids. Even when I got out of school, my mom wasn't leaning on me—you should go on to college. It was just go with the flow. If you want to go, you go, if you don't, you don't. Nor was she leaning on me to make good grades. I try to push my baby sister. I've got two sisters that didn't finish. So now it's instilled in her, that she should get good grades. But at the beginning, it was like, I don't care. I feel like black people need to get out of that rut that they're in. Because ain't nobody going to give you nothing. You have to at least let them know that you want it.

In '76 the first black girl went out for varsity cheerleader. And they gave it to her. But then they took it away. So we weren't going to class the next day. So we asked all our parents to come over there and stand with us. That this wasn't fair; that we wanted a black cheerleader. I mean, they had eight. They could have at least given us one. We had two black teachers, couldn't even get them to stand with us. Nobody but us. And my preacher, Reverend Johnson, was the only one showed up over there at that school. And I told my mama—I was really hurt that my mom didn't care enough to come over there. You ain't got to say nothing, just come over there and say, "Hey, we're one hundred percent behind our kids." What's one cheerleader? Because most of the football team was black boys. So give them one. The football team boys walked off, basketball. Everybody walked off. But the teachers wouldn't stand with us and the parents wouldn't stand with us.

So I came home and told my mom, I said, "It's terrible that you didn't even care enough. You've got three kids in high school, and you didn't even care enough to come over there and stand up. You didn't have to say anything, Mama," I said, "you just could have come."

And then—I was so glad it happened, and it's terrible to say—they gave us the cheerleader. Just to get us to go to class, because we didn't go for two days. They had the cops over there and everything. That's when a lot of teachers told us they were prejudiced. They admitted it. And they didn't think we needed a black cheerleader.

When they gave us that cheerleader, and got us to go to class, that next day all of the white students walked out. And all of the white teachers walked out. And all of the white parents came over there—I bet ninety percent. And they had to get two more white cheerleaders. And that's how they got ten cheerleaders. So black folks I guess just haven't ever stood up for anything.

At first I was angry. Especially not going to parents' meetings, PTA. And when that incident happened. Because I thought it was terrible. We need to stand together. Not only was I angry at my mother, but I was angry at all black parents. And I don't think I was the only one. It still bothers me a lot.

But I love Clay County—don't get me wrong. It's a fine place to live. But it has its problems, I guess you could say.

RICKY BURNEY

When you work at the rubber plant, you're something. You got a decent job. I'm working as a security guard at Alabama Power Company. And believe me—and it's not a pat on the back for myself. Because they say, "Hey, I would like to have a job like yours." These people are looking at a security guard as an outstanding job. I'm fortunate to be making what I'm making. But it's nothing to look forward to. I know it's got to be better.

One day, in the middle of the ball park, myself and about three or four other guys got to talking. And I was telling them that the employment situation in this town is poor. The banks especially, they would not hire a black as a teller. We saw that need, and we just kept talking about it, and then I said, "Look, why don't we just form a corporation here?" We said, "Hey look, we can combine our money and maybe found our own business. If not, we will have the money to work toward a business." I cannot afford to go out and buy a two-hundred-and-fifty-thousand-dollar business. But if we got two hundred and fifty people that's willing to put up a thousand dollars, in this county, we can come up with the money. So this is what we did.

Some of the guys, about five of us, said, "Hey let's not waste no time; let's start it right now." So two years ago, in March, we decided we'll try it. We come up with the name, Men Doing Things. I proposed the name, because that's exactly what I wanted it to be—men doing things. I said first of all we'll make it up in our minds, to join the club you're going to be a man. What we mean by being a man, that you're going to live up to your responsibilities as a man. You're going to act as a man, and we were going to do things to upbuild the community.

There hasn't been that much done here. I think there was a lack of leadership that the young people could look up to. They were just carrying the attitude that it's nothing here, and nothing's going to be nothing, so I might as well not be nothing. But my daughter in there, my four- or five-year-old daughter can tell you about Men Doing Things. Because that's one of our jobs—we wanted everybody to know about Men Doing Things. Especially in the black community.

We had a beauty pageant not long ago. It was the first black beauty pageant that had ever been through this county. We come up with the idea because every time that a black would participate in the other ones, they'd always lose. We had a few winners—in the span of maybe five years, or something like that, you might get one. So we decided we was going to have a Miss MDT contest. And we had it and it was very successful. We chose our first black beauty queen. And the people saw what we were doing, and everybody participated, and we had a large turnout. And we fixed a float and put her in the Christmas parade. After that, after we crowned her, I felt like the people saw "Hey, we're going to start looking a little bit closer at these girls." Because we have some very beautiful girls in here. I don't say they should win every time, but I thought some of the judges wasn't looking hard enough. And after that, they chose a black as the winner. And then the one after that, they chose a black as the winner. We feel that we made an impression that we'll start taking the girls out of every one that they give and give our own. They chose several of them to be winners after we had ours.

It made me feel good to know that when these girls won, that they walked down that aisle and they smiled and to see my people—when I say "my people" I mean the black people—standing up and applauding this girl. Because this was the first time that this happened. It was a very good feeling to see. I was definitely proud that the thing turned out the way that it did, to be a great big success. And not only that, after that finished, everybody was asking, "When is the next one? When is the next one?" See, all it took was just a little bit of effort, to try to let the people see that this can be done. Everybody wants to do. It's just going to take somebody to step forward and start it.

*   *   *

I'm looking for that day when we can put that building out there. I'm not talking about a recreation building. We're talking about a sewing plant. I'm talking about something where we can say, "Hey look, we can hire our own people." I tell this example, and I mean this from the bottom of my heart. I feel that if I own the business, like the white man owns the business, and my brother or my sister is out of a job, I'm going to hire my brother and sister. If my cousin's out of a job, I'm going to hire my cousin. You have to call it the way it is. If that white is out of a job, he's going to hire that white. So I say, "Why can't we do it?" That way we'll hire our own people. I don't want to sound racist in this statement, but the thing is, it's a fact. I'm saying that when it comes to jobs and things, the situation speaks for itself. If the blacks wants to rise, they're going to have to do what they've got to do. This is what I'm looking toward the future for, is seeing this happen right here in Lineville. I think that we do have the people here that want to do it. They're standing out there alone right now. It's just going to take some type of effort to get them together to see that this can be done.

I think that once a black group, or a black community, opens themselves up and says, "This is what we've done, we've started our own business," that will be the biggest boost that could ever happen in this area. I was talking to a guy the other day. Prime basketball player. Could probably play college ball. But he taken the attitude, "I know where I'm going to work. At the rubber plant." Only because he don't see anything else. He knows that ain't no black going to be president of the bank downtown. He knows that ain't no blacks going to sit in the front office of Higgins, Amerace. So he taken the attitude that "I'm going to be a laborer just like my daddy." They don't see no way for an education to help. But once this thing is built, and you see blacks in the front office down there, this might give them an opportunity to say, "Look. If I go to college for computer programming, this may get me a job out here in this plant. This is a black plant here. This will give me an opportunity."

I feel that the blacks are going to have to take the initiative upon themselves to help themselves. Not only here in the city of Lineville, but they're going to have to do it in Calhoun County, Cleburne, and every other county surrounding. We're going to have to be the ones that start it. I can't wait until my daughter is the one to do it. Because I have waited. This is one of the reasons why I work so hard. I use that as an example, that it should have been done years ago. If I mess around and die and let it go, then it's not going to get done.

My five-year-old daughter cannot see an influence downtown. Because there's no black stores downtown. And I feel that she will take this attitude that I had when I was coming up. Nothing there. And there never will be anything. I felt that way. So this is another reason I say, "Hey, we can change this thing." You hear people come back from other counties and say, "I saw this black girl working at a bank down there." That's a big thing; that's about like seeing Santa Claus. This is what I'm talking about. In my personal opinion, hiring a black in that bank down there is not going to help the black person that goes down there, because the job don't pay enough. But it would give the community an idea that Lineville is growing. When I walk in this bank right here now, I can pass my money over to a black person. All my life, I've put it in the hands of a white person. I think that will make a change.

That's Politics
in Clay County

Preceding page: Judge Johnny Rochester

Judge George Simpson
WELCOMES YOU TO
CLAY COUNTY
HOME OF *FRIENDLY* PEOPLE

*A picture of Clay County that left the politicians out would probably seem as
incomplete as a portrait of a stretch of county road without the kudzu painted
in along the sides. It requires skill to dodge, at almost any public gathering,
the handshakes and smiles of those whose jobs depend on votes, most of whom,
despite the absence of a local TV station, look always ready for the cameras to
come in. When election time swings round, candidates' combs, nail files, and
matchbooks bathe the countryside, and when a man says he came home one
day to find the dirt road that he lives on neatly scraped, and his commissioner's
re-election card at his door, he isn't joking.*

*Surviving the rough and sometimes bitter tumult of a countywide election
has always called for skills of formidable scope, and Clay County has produced, as well as scores of local and state officeholders, the senator turned
Supreme Court justice Hugo Black, a head of Alabama's Populists in their
turn-of-the-century glory days, and an imperial wizard of the Ku Klux Klan.
So few inhabitants felt surprised or mystified when the billboards exhibiting
Judge Simpson's great esteem for county residents appeared, one facing each
direction, on the road between Ashland and Lineville, where any strangers
who might be in need of welcome to Clay County would reach the greeting only
after they were halfway through.*

*Most times, Clay County voters have shown the kind of loyalty that politi-
cians dream of, standing constant by the leaders they have chosen to support, by
the Democratic party and by their own group of generally conservative ideals.
United States Senator Howell Heflin, in the county on an annual trip through
his constituency, seemed right at home delivering a straight, unabashed anti-
Communist pitch (although most of the listeners' questions dealt with Social
Security and the financial status of the local hospital). In wet-dry elections,*

held with great fanfare each few years, the count on each side is almost the same from vote to vote. And Clay County, along with much of rural Alabama, stuck with George Wallace even in his final governor's campaign, when he was in a wheelchair and almost constant pain.

But even tradition—or consistency—will only go so far. In the 1986 governor's runoff primary, when Democratic party leaders declared the winner gained his edge through illegally cast votes and made the runner-up the party nominee, angry voters in the county and the state responded by electing the first Republican since Reconstruction.

One of the county's judges, who must run for re-election, has two signed pictures on his courthouse office wall. One is of George Wallace. The other is of Senator Ted Kennedy, to many local conservatives the ultimate symbol of political and moral degradation. They're both good Democrats, the judge says with a smile. He doesn't think the voters will hold it against him.

PEOPLE'S BLOOD PRESSURE GETS UP

Rising a grand four stories from Ashland's central square, the tan bricks and silver dome of the Clay County courthouse dominate the view in all directions. It's not quite clear where a poor county found money for such a stately structure, a local historian says, but someone did, and columns, balconies, and garlands grace the building's walls, ceiling fans turn in its old courtroom, and screen doors slap to and fro all summer long.

Inside, amid the tag sales and the tax assessments, around the white-coveralled state prisoners whose renovation work has filled the space with scaffolding and plaster dust and the sounds of hammers hitting nails, a quiet but persistent sense of old and new campaigns hangs in the air. No matter what your business, the courtly, white-haired probate judge, the tall, good-looking sheriff, and the circuit clerk called Shotgun are waiting with smiles and assistance, ready to assure you that if you ever have a problem, you should simply let them know.

Red-headed Circuit Court Judge Johnny Rochester, who occupies a second-story office, is young, new at the job, and looking at his first election. But the easy confidence that marks his speech, and the energy with which he tackles strategy-planning phone calls that interrupt his conversation, suggest that the campaigning brought on by his appointment to the vacant seat will not prove too great a challenge. The fine furniture in his office, the certificate from the United States Supreme Court on the wall, and a certain distance in his overview of local matters, suggest interests and perhaps ambitions that have reached well beyond the county lines. And already his voice could go up against the best, as he professes admiration for democracy, for the voters who participate, and for the leaders it has anointed in his small corner of the world with the soft tones of sincere conviction that perhaps only a true deep-Southern sound can muster to perfection.

JOHN ROCHESTER
Thirty-two, circuit-court judge, Lineville, white

Some people would like to say the creek which divides Ashland and Lineville, that side's going to vote one way and the other side's going to vote the other way, but that doesn't happen. I guess the closest thing we have to a division with regard to forces, or even people interested in something, is when we have a wet-dry referendum. Then we have the wets and then we have the drys. As far as classifying or grouping, we just don't have that in Clay County. Someone, if they're popular, they can get elected, and it doesn't really matter what business or trade they're in, or where they're from.

The first thing you'd want to do is to visit country stores. And then I think you'd probably want to visit other goings-on, whether it's a sale for the fire department or whether it's a rescue squad dinner or something like that. You'll want to become involved in those type things. Then of course I think you need to be involved with community activities as well, not just somebody who drops in around election time, but someone who's truly involved and gives of themself to the community because they expect to take a little back out. I would think whether it's on a county scale, or even a local scale, it's people that are willing to give that are going to be elected. That's where I would start. In a community this small, it's mainly who has had the past experiences of treating someone decently, and who you know that's going to be honest. Things like that more than looking at your background, what grade did you go to in school, things like that. Because most people, if they do elect to run for something, they're going to be known by at least half the voters there.

With county government, they're looking at taxes. Looking at how quickly they can get the tags. When they come over to get their driver's license, they just want somebody here. If they want to look up a land record, they want somebody to be able to help them, or if they're wanting to research their ancestry, they want to know if they can go in the vault and do that. Have somebody to speak to. Those are the main things.

It's not predictable at all. A lot of times a certain area, if there's a candidate from that area, they will do well. But on a particular issue, you can't know. We have a referendum coming up on the tax issue for the hospital. And I could honestly not tell you within thirty or forty percent which way it's going to go, and which section of the county's going to vote which way. People around here are pretty personal about their politics. Private and personal and it's kind of like when they walk into the voting booth, then they're going to vote and that's their affair and their business. The right to vote is just a precious right that we enjoy, and most people want to keep that as their private right. I certainly respect that.

*   *   *

They'll have shootings and cuttings over elections here. Even now. People's blood pressure gets up, and it goes out of the top of their head. They have fighting, and family feuds, and it's just awful.

I think they get excited because someone's maybe taking a different point of view, and it's just—you know, that's politics. That's politics in Clay County. You have one view, and you're willing to express it, and someone has another view, and they're willing to express it. Then you meet head-on, and it's fun. Then a month after the election, you go and you start getting cranked up for the next one, and you start fussing a little bit more. It's just fun around here, and it's something for people to do. It beats soap operas.

We had a referendum, or it may just have been a straw poll—do you favor deer hunting with dogs. I think the Department of Conservation was talking about banning it in certain areas of the state. And I'd say it's the most excitement any election has drawn in thirty years around here. Except for wet-dry. People really got up in arms about it, and they did battle. I don't think there were many long-term enemies over it, but people got out and they felt one way or the other.

On wet-dry, there's a ministers' association, I believe, that generally takes the side of the drys. I don't know who leads the wet forces. I really can't even name you any names on the dry, I just know that they're always out there. There's always going to be a referendum; they can always get signatures for it. And once they have them, there's going to be a battle. I would say three to four in the last twenty years. Maybe five. Maybe one every four years. Pretty regularly. It's really a pretty equal split. Just about the same—the drys win out by I forget how many percentage points. Not a whole lot.

When Carter was running there were some local people that worked, and when Reagan won his first term, there were a lot of people working for him.

So there are some candidates who will light up the local folks and they'll get on the bandwagon and really do some legwork. But I think when it comes down to it, they're really going to get more excited about the local races. They might talk about the president because they're on the news more, and things of that sort. But when it comes down to local races, people get excited.

*   *   *

I grew up just off the square, coming up here to listen to trials. Sitting under the bench, shining shoes, under the big old tree down there, and they'd talk politics. That's what I heard, growing up, and I think it really interested me—not so much that I wanted to be a politician, but that it was just interesting, I thought. I think that's the way everyone grows up around here. That's a good source of an education. In politics you learn a little bit about everything. You learn about people—you learn about what to look for in a person, what not to look for in a person. You learn good character traits—who is going to be honest, in my opinion, and who's not going to be honest. You learn a lot of lessons that way. Keeping up with who has done what they said they would and who has not done what they said they would and that sort of thing. It's just interesting. You can keep up with what's going on if you'll put your ear to the grapevine.

One of the strongest political storms in memory is raging across the Alabama countryside, the swells and flashes of anger, indignation, and unadulterated rage threatening, for the first time in a century, the Democratic party's right to run the state. The man who got the most votes in the governor's primary did not get the nomination, and the voters do not much care to hear the reasons.

But inside the Bluff Springs country store, where the hum of the ancient soda cooler set against the wall is all you hear, the two old men sitting near the stove have the patient air of those who know that if they wait, the gale will pass. Aubrey Patterson, who remembers when election day meant fights and knives, and who, in 1965, stood in his state trooper's uniform on the bridge leading out of Selma, has seen his share of trouble. A firmness in his features hints at a handsome youth, and the traces of deference that waft in his direction suggest a position and an influence some cut above the norm. The Democrats will lose this one, he says, almost as proud of a correct prediction as a victory, but next year always comes. When he questions store patrons about election day intentions, his words tease more than urge, and his eyes betray less worry than amusement.

AUBREY PATTERSON
Seventy, retired state trooper, Bluff Springs, white

I've been a Democrat all my life. I was born and raised a Democrat. O. D. Sparks got me started into politics. He used to be tax collector and tax assessor. And he was one of the best politicians I ever knew. He just knew everybody. He knew everybody that would take money. And he knew everybody that would take whisky.

I got started working some for him, he'd want me to go see certain people for him, and he'd tell me what to say. And it worked. He'd tell me how to talk to them, things that would work. That's the way I got started. Of course things has changed now, it's not like it used to be. They let everybody vote now. Everything's changed.

There was some people wouldn't take money at all. Some of them vote like they want. I didn't fool with them much. But there was people who would. Some people wouldn't vote if you didn't give them some whisky or give them some money one. If you didn't do it, somebody else did it. You had to. You just almost had to. There was a certain class of people that you could handle. There was enough of them to swing an election sometimes.

Sparks would be involved in other politics. We was trying to help get somebody else elected. Say somebody was running for sheriff that he was interested in. He'd call me and furnish me a car to go somewhere for him. I used to know everybody in this country; my daddy did too. My daddy owned a good bit of land, had a good many tenant farmers.

He'd have political pull with them, you know. That's what he was after. There'd be different things. Like maybe somebody'd go to him, they'd have trouble getting the sheriff to do something for them, you know. They'd go to him, and he'd go to the sheriff and help them, or the probate judge or something. He was a powerful man in Clay County back in his day. He never did get beat. He got elected when Hoover and Al Smith was running for president. And Clay County went what they call Liberty Bell ticket. Same thing as Republican. All the Democrats got beat. But him, he got elected. He was the only one that got elected.

You didn't exactly buy their vote. You had to work around and get them in the notion of working for a certain fellow. Put them some money to work for somebody, you know. You didn't just come out and tell them you'd give them so much to vote for somebody. You didn't do that. Some people'd have to have more than others if they was going to get out and help you. And some—some people they'd get fifty cents back when money was hard to get ahold of. Of course they still put out a lot of money in politics. I don't have anything to do with it, but you can't fool me—they still put it out to people.

I wasn't getting any money out of it. I just enjoyed it. I always enjoyed meeting people and talking to people. I always thought I could talk to you and I could figure out pretty well what kind of a person you was. The FBI says you can't do it. But I don't agree with them. Like Mr. Sparks said—he always said somebody can handle you. When we was politicking, say somebody couldn't be changed. If I could do it, if I could figure out some way to do it, I got the most kick out of that. Just like when I was law enforcement, when there was some case you couldn't solve, and if I could solve it—I done that a few times—I just got a kick out of it. I enjoy doing what somebody says you can't.

I know we had a fellow down here in the low end of the beat. He married some of my kinfolk. He always went along with my daddy. But one time he wouldn't do it. Just wouldn't. And me and him was close friends. And O. D. Sparks told me what to go down there and tell him one morning. That morning I went at three o'clock. The day of the election. And I done it. My daddy said, "It won't work." Says, "I've done everything," says, "It's the first time we've never been together." And he says, "It just won't work." And I says, "Well, it won't hurt to try." I says, "I'm going to try." And I went down there and got him up out of the bed. I got him up and we got out there and sat down in the car. And I done what Sparks told me. He could handle about fifteen votes. And he brought them all up here and voted. I'd better not tell what he told me to tell him. He's dead now. He was deacon of the church down there. But he was a good fellow. There was something he was going to need. And Sparks could get it for him. So we got it worked out.

*   *   *

There've been some crooks got elected. I think I'd better not talk too much—there've been a good many crooks got elected. You just can't be honest and straight I believe and get elected. Now we've had some to do that, but they're not many of them. We've had some, but they're mighty few.

Fact of the business—I ought not to say this—we had a lot of good sheriffs way back yonder. But we had a lot of crooked ones too. You know they used to be on the fee system. And they couldn't hardly make a living if they didn't sell out to somebody. Some of them'd get well off in that sheriff's office. But now they get a big salary, you know.

*   *   *

I've still got some good friends in this district. But most of them that I used to deal with's died out. Lots of them'll tell you one thing, and they'll go right and do another one. They're bad at that.

The people, it seems like they just lost interest in politics. Since I've been back here, we had one commissioner's race was a pretty hot race. But outside of that, down in this part of the country they just don't seem to be interested in it. The trouble of it, they'll talk one way and vote another one. I used to could predict the vote. I could guarantee you I could predict who was going to be the high man in this box. But I can't do it no more.

Now it used to be maybe one or two people would control these boxes pretty well. But that's not thataway any more. It's changed. Most people now in this beat's young people. Not many people's got any age on them. It's hard. You just can't figure out lots of them. All this young generation's growed up and these people voted that never did vote before and you can't predict any more. I liked it better before. Yes I did. I could guarantee you, I could tell you how this box was going. Whether it was going to go like I wanted it to or not, I could tell you.

I never have voted anything but a Democratic ticket. Like I told you before, I've got too old to change now. I went through the Depression. And it was just awful. And every time I think about it—I've seen some times I didn't want to vote for the Democratic ticket. But I'd go ahead and vote. It was rough back yonder. The Hoover days. People don't have any idea how rough it was, that didn't go through it.

Now I might get involved in some of it this next race. We're going to have a probate's race next year. We'll have a probate judge, and we'll have a clerk's race. In my opinion neither one of them's going to get defeated. But I'm sure they're going to have a hot race. A lot of people's got it in for them. But they're good politicians, both of them's good politicians. It's going to be mighty hard to beat them. But they've got some bad enemies. They've got some bad enemies that's good politicians too. I'd like to stay out of it, if I can. But I might get in it head over heels.

HE DIDN'T WANT THAT SEGREGATION

The most important man ever to come from Clay County—some say from all of Alabama—is also the one that, through the years, residents have been the most reluctant to acknowledge. Supreme Court Justice Hugo Black may have been one of this century's more influential thinkers, but to many of his former friends and neighbors, he had, on reaching greatness, done worse than just forgetting where he came from—he had turned on his old home, lashing out at the one issue where his fellow Southerners had invested so much of their sectional self-image and their pride.

Clay County was—and to some extent still is—a place that puts high value on consistency, where many have been proud to call themselves yellow-dog Democrats (meaning they'd vote for a yellow dog if it were on the Democratic ticket) and where, even now, you sometimes can hear those who switch their vote called pollywogs. When Justice Black, a Clay Countian, a Southerner, and a former member of the Ku Klux Klan who won his first Senate seat with Klan votes, voted for school desegregation, it seemed to many that the enemy they had for so long placed in the remote Northeast had instead grown up among them. When, later, he decided to forbid school prayer, that did little to improve his reputation.

Feelings have for the most part softened in the more than thirty years since the Brown case was decided, and the few staunch Black supporters, along with the younger people who know anything about him, talk about the late justice with the calm confidence of those riding out the last winds of a shrinking storm, certain that Black will, in the end, get the recognition he deserves. But attempts to build a Black memorial have proved unsuccessful, and when, two years ago, people elsewhere in the country commemorated Black's centennial, they held no celebration in Ashland, his home town. The mouths of many older residents still tighten when they speak of Hugo Black, and on all the monuments in all the county's six hundred and three square miles, the name of its most famous son is nowhere mentioned.

MORLAND FLEGEL
Sixty-one, owner, Sunshine Cleaners, Ashland, white

A cousin of Justice Black's was probate judge back in the early seventies. He and a gentleman that worked with Auburn Extension Service as a rural resource development person were considering the possibility of a museum. And a cousin of Barney Watley, here in Ashland, received a letter from Mr. Barney Watley of Denver, Colorado, that he thought that we should place a memorial in Clay County of the late Justice Hugo Black. He had sent a check for three hundred and fifty dollars. And Mrs. Zola Riley was the person that received this letter and check, and she came to me and asked me, as I remember, would I present it to the Rotary Club.

And here was the catalyst, in my mind. Now he was thinking kind of along the lines of a statue or something on the courthouse lawn. And I felt that if you're really going to have a memorial to somebody, why not make it something really worthwhile. I was thinking along the lines of a library—a general public library, not a research type of library—that would really benefit the county and benefit the children. Then we only had a small building that was called the Hut that a group of ladies had supported and maintained as a library.

We arranged a meeting and invited a lot of people. There was a large number of people present. I don't recall the number right off, but it was a large number. Many, many more than I'd expected. It seemed to be the general consensus of everyone there that this was a good thing to do. And so then we formed a nonprofit corporation, and got up our bylaws and all of the requirements, and had an election of officers and directors, and started to work on it. I was elected chairman of the board. And we talked to Mrs. Black by phone, and it seems as though we may have written some letters to family members. And they were delighted, those that we talked to. They thought it was real good.

Then of course, when you're talking about bricks and mortar, building something, you're talking about money. And of course money had to come from donations, or possibly come from grants. You have your peaks and your valleys in life, and you also have your peaks and your valleys in trying to raise money. There were many times when it looked real good, even in the way of grants, but there was always something that kept us from getting those grants. I couldn't say for fact, and I don't think that all of them were waylaid because of someone that just didn't like Justice Black's decisions. But I honestly do feel that one or two of them were probably pigeonholed because of someone's dislike for his decisions. In fact we had a request considered in committee, in the state legislature, and it didn't last two or three minutes in the committee. And if a request doesn't last two or three minutes in a committee, it doesn't look like someone in there, or several in there, is very enthusiastic about who this is for.

As far as I was concerned when it was impossible to create a general public library as such and a museum in conjunction with it was when the county and the city of Ashland took over the Clay County Library Board and disbanded it and absorbed their assets—books, tables, and a small amount of money. This had nothing to do with the Hugo Black library assets, as far as that's concerned. But still a library is a library. And we were building two different ways, you might say, for one goal. Until this occurred. But then this meeting was held, and the county officials and the city officials relieved the Clay County Library Board of their duties, and they assumed and then renamed the board, and then the town of Ashland used grant money to build a library, more or less in spite of what we had planned, rather than incorporate and work together. This really killed the library and museum project, as I see it.

It's not really a hundred percent lost yet, as far as a memorial to Justice Black is concerned. There is money on hand. We can still create a memorial. But it wouldn't be what was originally planned by any means.

LEWEL SELLERS

I was out in Kansas City at one time. And a bunch of us were standing in the lobby, talking there, and one old fellow says, "Where're you from?" I said, "Alabama." And he said, "What county're you from?" I said, "Clay." He said, "Good Lord, that's where that damn Hugo Black's from." He'd learned about him; he kept up with what was going on.

He let his own people down. His own folks, he let them down. By that decision that he made. I still think it's a mistake. For both races. The black man's way down behind us in civilization. I had an anthropologist to tell me one time, he says if you want to make a scale of civilization, our American nigger would be a thousand years below the Caucasian, the white people.

I'd say it's true with seventy-five percent of them. Their culture and ours are a long ways apart. And our mannerisms and all is so different. We can't relate to them; they can't relate to us. And what it done, it set us back, set the whites down to the level with them, in our school system.

Our morals are way, way gone.

JOHN ROCHESTER

I think that he's someone that I look up to, and I know I can never attain what he attained. But as far as a role model, I suppose he's not. He started out as a lawyer and then a prosecutor in Birmingham—of course he started out in Clay County, and then when his office burned he moved to Birmingham. And my avenue's sort of a little bit different. I've done basically general law practice here, and then I was on the district bench doing traffic and misdemeanors, and now I'm on the circuit bench doing other things.

I guess maybe it's because he left here so long ago. It was back in the twenties when he left. And then when I was growing up, all you ever heard about him was bad, so how could someone like that be a role model? I have role models—I can honestly say that as a judge, my role model would be Judge Kenneth Ingram, whose place I took, rather than Hugo Black, who preceded me. I'm trying to think—that may be a little egotistical, even if I thought he was, to say that I thought he was. But I think I'm being candid.

WILLIAM CARTER
Sixty-three, retired chicken-plant worker, Lineville, black

I remember Hugo Black. I was a little bitty kid. He used to be a Ku Klux, they say. I heard my daddy and them talking about it. My mama used to wash for him. Then he died a couple of years ago. He didn't want that segregation. I didn't know too much about it. I thought he was dead for a long time; I never did hear nothing about it. He went on to be Supreme Court justice in Washington. That's where he died at. He was an old man, he was eighty-four years old when he died, I think. He used to live right there in Ashland.

They say he used to put the Ku Klux on. That he was one too, they say. I don't know. I heard a lot of them say that was way older than I was.

RUBY KING

I didn't know too much about Hugo Black. But we were friends with his sister. His sister lived right out here. And I knew her brother was Hugo Black. But it wasn't until way later that I began to read and really find out about his positions or things like that. I read enough about it to be informed, but as far as any feelings, I didn't have any feelings about it one way or another.

As far as I can see it, the blacks here really don't know too much about him. Hugo Black just doesn't mean too much to them, period. Where blacks would have to get that would be in the schools. Or people that they come in contact with. Now if his birthday had been observed, and a lot had been written in the paper about him, and a lot of things, then that would have been informing everybody. They're just not informed.

MORLAND FLEGEL

Had Justice Black not been a controversial person, there would have been no one that would have cared to see another old house or care whether Ashland, Alabama, was his birthplace or not. And it was because he was such a controversial person that made all of this a tangible project. Something worthwhile. If you have somebody that'll yes-no every question, yes-no every opinion, who really would care one way or another where he came from or where he went, really? And Justice Black wasn't a yes-no person. It was either yes or it was no. And this is why. And whether it were controversial or whether it were not controversial.

I believe very sincerely that he was an independent person, that he thought independently. He was a person that gave everything adequate consideration before a decision, in his own mind, and I think that he was sworn to uphold the Constitution of the United States. He was. So he had really more of a responsibility of doing so than just his individual convictions. And all of these admirable traits that you like to see in a youngster, or see in an individual. Everybody doesn't possess them. I think he demonstrated very very good intelligence during his tenure on the court. What are our privileges as citizens? It brought the people that were on the outside looking in, brought them to the inside where they could look out like the rest of us.

And the issues were not just Brown versus the Board of Education. It was many, many more decisions that were rendered. His stand on gun control. He was for the American citizen allowed to have a weapon. And frankly I believe that this is our heritage and I don't see anything wrong with it. Just like our president was shot. And so many people talked about why wouldn't you be for gun control, and I said, "Well, he was shot in an area that had the strictest gun controls of any place in the United States. It didn't work, did it? So what really good is it? All you're doing is taking away privileges and more privileges and more privileges." Here again is an example of people, in my opinion, that are—well what would you really call them—anti. Anti-gun, anti-hunting, anti-everything.

I like to think of people to be kind of like John Wayne [laughs]. I don't think it's as hard to live your convictions as it is to be somebody else and decide whether they're right or not. Now being convinced of something for my own well-being, knowing myself and so forth, knowing my God and what I believe in, these things make up a person's . . . philosophy. Whether someone disagrees with me or not, that's not really here nor there. Because that's not my decision. That's his decision. And I think it's the same way with Justice Black. The simple fact that he had to do what the Constitution told him. As well, if he could influence his personal convictions, and they did coincide with all of this other that was required, he really didn't have anything to worry about. That's what allows a person to be able to lay down and sleep at night. And if something's been done wrong and it comes to your attention and you realize it's wrong, then I think you should be man enough—or individual enough—to say, "I sure did, I messed up, it's my mistake." I try to be like that. I'm very much of a person that has an opinion of things. Right or wrong. I will yield if I'm wrong and someone proves I'm wrong. But they're going to have to prove where I am wrong before I will accept that I'm wrong. And I have been occasionally wrong, believe it or not. But I'd rather be wrong than not have any opinion of any kind.

*   *   *

I remember when this elderly individual—not old by any means, but older than I was—came to me and wanted to learn the dry-cleaning business. And he had already applied for a correspondence course, and he was willing to work for free if I would allow him to come into my establishment and work. And he would also appreciate any information or whatever I could impart to him to help him learn the business. And he was going to really work on that correspondence course and try to become one hundred percent professional. I agreed to allow him to do this, only I didn't agree to let him work for free. I told him I would pay him a figure—it may have been a nominal sum, but it wasn't all that much of a nominal sum at that time. Because at that time the wage and hour scale was very low. Nevertheless he was there every day, just like he was on the job, being paid. And a very dedicated person.

And then it was learned in the community that his son had jumped the draft registration requirement and went to Canada and chose not to go to Vietnam. And there were a number of people that set out to persecute him—the father, you might say, because of what his son had done. They threw cherry bombs and shot, I think, at his house, and different things that I'd heard, and upset him, he and his wife, something fierce.

And I had two people one day, two men come by and ask me if he were employed by me, and I said yes he was. And they asked me if I didn't think I should get rid of him. And I told them no, I didn't think that I should get rid of him. And I didn't think there was anybody that should imply such a thing, that as far as I was concerned, as long as he wished to continue with our agreement, and he conducted himself satisfactorily, why our agreement would stand, and that was it. And they were making a very serious mistake if they considered any way of destruction or harm or what have you towards me about it. And I felt that if they were causing any disturbance towards him it'd be best if they'd discontinue that.

He was forced, you might say forced, to leave town. Through mischievous and undesirable actions of people. Now I'm not saying that at the time I would condone what his son did, or that I condone what his son did today. And I'm not saying that he condoned what his son did as right. I never did discuss it with him; I didn't think it was any of my business. It wasn't his decision. It was his son that did that. And frankly any harm that anyone intended to bring to this man and his wife, I feel was horribly unjust.

And I feel personally that it was a tragedy that this unjust action was taken towards them.

They didn't say just what they were going to do. They told me they didn't think that he should be there. And I wouldn't consider running him off or getting rid of him. That would be his decision, not my decision. And stood my ground. And nothing was ever said again to me. Evidently they felt that I was probably right.

THEY'VE GOT AWAY
WITH TOO MUCH ALREADY

*Along a road deep in the hills, the scrubby growth of winter gives way to a
small clearing. At one edge sits the burnt-out shell of a house built out of rock,
on the other a small home with a cluttered porch. A stretch of bare-dirt yard
lies flat between them, filled with the assorted dogs and rusting cars found in
front of many of the county's poorer homes.*

*A woman separates herself from a group of children in the house and comes
out to inquire about a visitor's business. She disappears again inside, and a few
minutes later out comes Alvin Horn, retired electrician, sometime preacher,
stalwart member and once grand dragon of the Alabama Ku Klux Klan—a
tall, old man with some missing teeth and a bad heart who is, he says, just
waiting out the days until he goes to be with his old friends.*

*The rock house burned, he says, so he and his family have moved into the
small one. Fire seems to haunt him, as does death—an earlier blaze in a different house killed a wife and children, and two other wives were apparent
suicides.*

*At first he is suspicious—he has, he says, been lied about so many times.
But when he settles in the front seat of a son's compact car, and starts to talk,
he delivers two straight hours of stories and opinions, the old scorn and pride
and passion still in his voice, clearly delighted to have someone who will listen.*

ALVIN HORN
Seventy-four, former Ku Klux Klan grand dragon, Idaho, white

My first interest in the Klan happened when I was very young. I'd say
ten or twelve years old. My late father-in-law was initiated in East Lake
Park, in Birmingham. And I just can't say how many, but there was a world
of people that was initiated that day. And that was the day that the Klan
gave Colonel Bibb Graves and Hugo Black a lifetime gold card. And Hugo
Black, you know, was from Clay County. And I'll never forget Hugo Black's
remarks. He said our boys is just come back from France, fighting a bloody
war, making the world free for democracy, only to come back home and find

that we had another battle here. Making America free for Americans. And when Oscar Underwood died, Bibb Graves was governor, and he appointed Hugo Black to the Senate, and following that, Franklin Delano Roosevelt measured Hugo up to fit his program, and he was loyal to it the rest of his life. When I was grand dragon, I would have banished Hugo Black from the organization, but I couldn't, because he was given a lifetime membership.

Now you take the old Klan, shucks, Ashland was a wheeler-dealer. The people that was involved in it was the very best. All of the preachers and everything. Clay County, we had one imperial wizard, which was Dr. Hiram Evans. He was from Lineville. I don't remember the years, but it was back in the late twenties. Hiram Evans was the imperial wizard when it was at its peak. When we had over twelve million members.

It was in the forties when I became involved in the Klan. I was in my thirties. And this Henry Wallace was running on the Progressive ticket. When I first joined, it was lodge work, just like the Masonic Lodge or the Odd Fellows. The rituals of the organization—go in, open, close. Discuss the issues that was at hand. And I tell you, the ladies' auxiliary played a great part in the organization. They'd get the lowdown on what was taking place and what needed to be done, and turn that bunch of women loose on those politicians and shoot, they'd make it so hot for them that they'd get things done. And they didn't go representing the Klan or nothing, they just took it on themselves to go.

The biggest thing the Klan had to do at the regular meetings was to see if these Klan members was living a life that was becoming a Klanman. Going to church and—you take an alcoholic or a drunk, well shoot, he was unloaded in a hurry. You just couldn't have that. If they was tangled up in court, especially beating just and honest debts, they had to toe the line or else kick them out. Help to be better people—not just us but everyone else. We was obligated to that. And for the protection of white womanhood. Now that was one thing that was in our obligation. In some cases the organization made up big grocery lists and lots of money for widow women that was having it rough. We would take care of matters like that.

*   *   *

You could usually tell the ones that had wandering eyes. Like that daggone nigger over at Lineville—I forget now what his name was. When

Higgins first came into Lineville, their first sewing room was in an old store building. And that nigger worked down there at the Ford place across the street from the old bank. Well in place of getting back there and eating lunch, he'd come up there and sit down out there and lean up against that bank building as them girls would get off from work. And that nigger, he'd sit out there: "Hey you, you just started here, ain't you?" He'd sit there looking at them women and try to wage a conversation with them.

Well, one night they went and got that son of a gun. He was took out to one of them pulpwood roads and they gave him a few lessons in common ethics, I think, and the mayor was the one that owned that Ford place there, he said that nigger'd eat his lunch in there then, and look out that window down south like he was looking way off somewhere. He didn't come up there any more. I don't know what they done, but whatever they did, it worked.

*   *   *

Our message to the Klanmen, when I was grand dragon, it wasn't to strap. That that was the thing of the past. Forget it. That we had to do ours at the ballot box. It was '52 or '53, when I became grand dragon. Speaking of it politically, I was governor of the state of Alabama, and the panhandle of Florida. Each state would have a grand dragon. And the imperial wizard, he was over all of it.

In the fifties, Clay County was strong. It was really strong. Shoot, they come in just like the first day of school. The ones that had never been members, they all just about it came in at once. We had some good men that took care of Clay County. Clay County didn't have a bunch of riffraff in the organization. They didn't give not a minute's trouble.

I believed in it. From the very start. That was inbred in me. I believed in it and I believe in it now. But it's got to be disciplined. You can't let them run wild. Can't do that. Better off without an organization than to have one that is irresponsible. Yes, I believe in it. Because I believe that God Almighty in his selection of white Protestant people gave them certain rights and obligations to God, and to their fellow man. Not for self, but for others. If you could only one time get it across that it wasn't a leather-strap organization, but that it was strictly one of obedience to the law. That our power's not in the strap, it's in the ballot box. And that'll get it too. That would get it then; it'll still get it now. Get people together.

I've heard that there's a bunch of Clay Countians that belongs to a chapter down at Roanoke. But I don't know. I do just what I'm doing now. Nothing. Well, I'm waiting on open heart surgery. I've made a few speeches, just on invitation. Went down to Mobile about twenty years ago, and I guess that was the last invitation that I accepted to speak at a Klan rally.

Clay County, they're in better shape than they have been. But we've got an element that we're having some trouble with, that interracial dating and so on, which it's ungodly, it's disgraceful and shouldn't be. But it's going to take more than just a few to stop that. I've said this, that it's got to get a whole lot worse before it gets any better. When it gets bad enough, all the white people'll get together and demand something be done about it. It hasn't got that far yet, it's just enough to be irritating and aggravating. They've got away with too much already.

*   *   *

Well, God had a purpose for this civil rights stuff. It's just like this dag-gone AIDS. You see where it originated. In Africa. They say ten years, there won't be a nigger in Africa. And the way that people and the politicians is backing up and giving ground and saying that they have their rights, this dag-gone bunch of gay rights and homosexuals. That they're looked on today as just another way of life. There's a lot of things got to happen before the end of the world. The churches will be raptured first—Christ will come and get the living and the dead. And the rest of the world will go into a period of great tribulation for seven years. I wouldn't be surprised at any moment. I sure wouldn't. Because the world has got in the same shape that Sodom and Gomorrah was. I see nothing now that hasn't been fulfilled concerning that. And looks to me like the timetable is set.

I thank God for letting me live. Because I enjoyed every minute of it. My people, all except my daddy, they backed me up. Now my daddy didn't. He sent word, when I was in jail over in Sinclair County, by Mama. Said, "Tell Alvin that I'll help him to get out of this, but I'm expecting him to get out of the Klan." But when Mama told me what he said, I said, "Mama, will you do something for me?" She said yes. I said, "You go back and tell Daddy that I love him, that I appreciate all that he ever did for me, but if it takes me coming out of the Klan and vowing that I'll never be back in it, for him to be in good grace with me, tell him that I thank him a lots, but tell him I said bye. I'm through with him." I felt that strong about it. Because I'll tell you. If I hadn't of believed in it, I wouldn't of been in it. He apologized. He said he was sorry. He said, "There's so many people that could get you in trouble." And I said, "Well, that's true too." But I said, "On the other hand, I'd rather be in there doing what I could for the cause than be outside and not doing nothing."

WE ARE ALL RESPONSIBLE

MIRA CARMICHAEL
Eighty-nine, retired air-force procurement officer, Brownville, white

I have a very strong sense of family. We had horse conveyances, horse and mules, in my growing-up days. And with the horse and buggy you couldn't get around in Clay County. It was just your small group here. Uncle Bud had about nine of his children before Father's began to come along, and then there came along the eight of us. And there were enough of us, you see, to have a social gathering whenever we would want to. So as a family we were nearly self-sufficient. With the result that we didn't develop the interest in all people in the county that a lot of other people did.

I was an unalterable snob. I was just sure that we were better than anybody else in the world. And that the Carmichaels, and a few of the cousins, and probably Uncle John McPhail, who was superintendent of the Sunday school, were going to make up Heaven. And the rest of the world just wasn't in it. I had to grow out of all of that. I remember talking to a cousin of mine, a boy a year older than I was. And he said, "Mira, I don't think you're right."

LISA HARDY

For me, just about everybody over here is kinpeople. Because my grandmama's maiden name was Sims, and she married a Ballard. On my mom's side it's Fords and Ballards. And every time you go back a generation, you'll find a Sims or a Ballard. The Sims and the Ballards is kin to everybody. And then you go back and you get my grandmama's mama, and she was a Russell. And that gets you on the Heard side and the Street side. And so by the time you go back to her mama, that gets you on the other side, and they just keep going on back. Everybody over here, I'd say, except for maybe four percent is kinfolks.

I had a lady that was at my mom's house. And I walked in. I knew her name. And she said, "Hello, honey, I'm your aunt." And I was thinking, "Aunt?" And she said, "I used to be married to your uncle, Joe Bob." And I thought, "Oh God, I'm twenty-seven years old and I never knew that." You don't never know who you're kin to. We have these family reunions, and you walk and talk with some people daily, and you don't even know you're kin to them until you get to the reunion. And my mom'll say, oh yeah, that's your fourth or fifth cousin. I don't count that far back. I stop most times at second. They go on past fourth and fifth and sixth. They claim everybody.

I can remember one time I wanted to go on a date with this guy that was a Crawford. And to me, he was only like my fifth cousin. And Grandmama was: "No. That's your fifth cousin—you don't go out with kinfolk." And I was like, "Fifth cousin! I guess y'all count sixth and seventh too." They don't care how far down the line, if they're a blood relation, you don't go out. Everybody I used to bring to the house—"No!" And I even went to Lineville. "No!" Finally I met my husband. And I asked, "Are we kin to him?" My grandmama said, "I don't *think* we're kin to him." And she started asking questions. She said, "Now wait a minute, you say your grandmama was a Burney." I said, "But Grandmama, that's way on down the line." "Well, he might be about your seventh or your eighth, but I guess you can go out with him." My aunt, her mom, they all think the same way. Most of these folks around here I believe married cousins, though. Because they ran out of men that weren't kin.

The fund-raising radio campaign for the Clay County Learning Center has swung into its final day, and the parking lot beside the new-built Farmers' Market, now the center for most large-scale county events, is filling rapidly with cars. Inside, workers dish out Sunday chicken dinner to the people thronging through the spacious, modern structure, while on the temporary stage speakers and performers appeal for aid in tones that mix enthusiasm with an edge of desperation. The center, which offers classes and activities for residents with mental handicaps, has failed this year to match the state grants that pay most of its expenses. The six staff members have received their notice, the director has announced the center's closing, and the people who said Clay County was too poor to maintain the institution seem to have in the end been right. Supporters have rallied round the center and organized the radio project to give it one last chance. But the shortfall comes close to twenty thousand dollars—the kind of sum a county with so few inhabitants can hope to raise only if almost everyone contributes.

When local leaders talk about Clay County's future, they almost always emphasize the need for countywide cooperation, envisioning joint efforts to search for industry and jobs, to maintain local services, and to help improve the lives of less fortunate inhabitants. But finding ways to gather and direct the widely dispersed energies of county citizens can prove a delicate, complex, teeth-pulling kind of task. Despite breaks in the isolation that once bound residents' affections to small portions of the county—to families and communities whose disputes burned hot enough to flare in violence—attempts at large-scale ventures still run up against persisting patterns of power and influence, compounded now by the larger paychecks, longer-hour jobs, and out-of-county entertainment that leave often little time for community affairs.

A lingering sense of social stasis hangs over many conversations, evident not only in frustrated words from those who work for change, but also in less direct remarks, as when a judge's son recalls he was astonished to find most of his law school classmates were not, like him, continuing a family tradition. Altering county institutions has often proved a slow and painful process—it took a statewide lawsuit to create the city-council districts that made it possible for blacks to win elected office, and even a project like the Farmers' Market, strategically located midway between Ashland and Lineville, and paid for out of earmarked state funds, required a lengthy process of coalition-building before work could begin.

In other places, though, people talk more of change, of the ways that cars and radios, well-paved roads and television sets, have cut into ties once tightly drawn by the work rhythms and mutual dependence of small-scale farming operations. Scattered monuments and relics left by such shifting loyalties lie all across the landscape—unlighted country stores whose customers now go to town, shuttered schools lost to consolidation, church buildings only used on rare occasions. Less visible landmarks lie etched in people's minds, with the excitement felt at broadening horizons, when pathways opened up to better jobs and bigger towns, contrasting with the sorrow—often felt most keenly by those used to directing community affairs—brought on by the closing of a locally controlled school, by watching a once-thriving business district fade away.

Still in many spots hard work and common feeling have helped residents to overcome division and indifference, and grasp the benefits of coordinated effort. A blueberry cooperative organized some years ago now has members all across the state, local picking and processing jobs, and good prospects for profits. Residents of Delta have turned their closed school building into a thriving community club, with turkey shoots, programs for children, and monthly potluck suppers that fill the main hall with plans and conversation. A dozen more communities now focus energies on recently organized volunteer fire departments, whose spotless buildings and well-cared-for equipment show what people can accomplish when they try. And when sometimes a cause fires people's hearts, results have been spectacular enough to earn the county's generosity a measure of statewide renown.

As the final hours of the Learning Center campaign wear away, the urgent tone slips from the on-air voices, leaving in its place the ring of pride. Organizers have auctioned everything that anyone would donate—an old car, a week-old calf, even a twenty-pound-weight snapping turtle—and in the program's closing minutes, they put leftover hotdog buns up on the block as well, with the near-tipsy delight of people who have cause to celebrate. As the center's clients jump up and down with unconcealed excitement, organizers proudly chalk the totals on a huge blackboard, and pose with it for a picture. Most of the donations have come in small amounts, but together they far surpass the needed figure—more than thirty thousand dollars raised from a county with fewer than fourteen thousand residents—and such results, the center's director later says, make you feel humble, grateful, and very, very proud of where you live.

CALVIN COOLIDGE SIMS
Sixty-five, owner, Ashland Pharmacy, white

We had our biggest change right after World War II. Your changes made during the war and immediately after were rather drastic everywhere. I don't think maybe it changed here as much as it did some places. Of course the big change was where we did have all of our interest centered in the little town here, our interest had branched out into going to Anniston, or to Talladega, or Alexander City, to skating rinks, skating parties. We didn't do this before. Going to the theater more. Maybe broadening our horizon a little more. We had just been kind of here at the foothills, kind of isolated and living our own lives in a quiet way. Maybe we modernized a little—I don't know whether that's the term I'm looking for or not.

Before I left here to go in service, we were typical teenagers. Well, in the military you grow up faster than you do in most places, especially during wartime. Most of us had served overseas, and had various degrees of combat duties, and grew up. And when we came back, we seemed to have more of a grown-up attitude. Things had broadened out—maybe we saw some more of the world outside our little circle. Saw how other people lived and made acquaintances in other areas. I guess that's just natural. I guess if the war had not come along we'd have still had this effect, but it did come along at that time, and that's why it reflects on my thinking maybe that we grew up faster during this process. I guess I'm talking too much about war years, but there's so much involved in it, you see. We had a lot of people who left the county to go to defense plants, and go to the military, and go to jobs other than right here. We converted from a farming community to more of an industrial community. I think there was quite a revolution in the whole country, not just in Clay County.

*   *   *

Social life here for me has been basically in your civic organizations— Jaycees, Rotary—and church. At the time I came back to Ashland, in 1949, I joined the Jaycees—we had a real active Jaycee chapter here at that time. And I also joined the Rotary International. I had a lot of civic pride, and I just wanted to be a part of the community as it was developing, growing. The Jaycees had projects that we worked on. One of the things that we did that I can remember in particular was we built a baseball field for the high school. We built the stands—dug the bank and built concrete steps there. We built a concession stand at the high school. We helped with the lighting of the field. Just several kinds of projects like this.

We have to pitch in and all help to have the things that we want like this. The school didn't have the money. They had the land, but they didn't have the money to develop a baseball field, and the stands, and so forth. They didn't have the money to build the concession stand. So just as a project we would take these things on. I think it's good. And it made all of us feel a part of the community, I think. I mean, you can stand back years later and say, "We built this during the time I was in there."

Rotary was established in 1937, it was chartered in '37, and it was active until just three or four years ago. But it just dwindled in membership to the point that it couldn't support itself, so it just disbanded.

I think it was because of the turnover in management of businesses and ownership of businesses that some interest was lost. I think we had so many of our—I don't know hardly how to say it—but our old, established family people who were in business here had gone out of business for various reasons—death, retirement, and what have you. Then you have other businesses coming in, maybe associated with a chain, that's not as much a part of the community as your old, established home businessmen were. And it lost some interest in this respect.

The Jaycees folded for a while, then it was reorganized. In fact it kind of slowed down, and reorganized, and went for a few years, and then got slow again, and then another group of young men got interested. Now I understand they have a pretty good chapter going. Pretty active. I hope they can keep a good active Jaycee going.

I hated to see Rotary fold up. And I think it's left a certain gap, yes. Because it was here so long. And I thought it did so much good. We supported a lot of projects.

We lived on this four-way test up there on the wall [reading]. "The four-way test of the things we think, say, and do. First, is it the truth? Second, is it fair to all concerned? Third, will it build good will and better fellowship? Fourth, will it be beneficial to all concerned?" There's our creed, so to speak. About every meeting, see, this was mentioned. It means a lot to me today. And I look at it a lot. I still try to live by it.

Young people now in small towns are just not going into business much. Because the opportunities are so limited there, and the future is not too bright for them in a small, rural area like this. It wasn't all that bright when I came back, but it was brighter than it is now. I can understand the trend. Wal-Mart, K mart, places like this, your general-merchandise store cannot compete with them. We're having a hard time in the drug business doing the same thing. We've had to change our operation considerably. The clothing business, they can't compete, I'm sure. Because people have the means of transportation now. Twenty or thirty minutes, they can be anywhere they want to be, get a better selection, and possibly a little better price. So that's what they do. It has gotten to the point, sadly—to me, that is—that we have placed price ahead of loyalty, maybe, and convenience. I think it's nationwide as far as that. I think in small towns now you don't have this loyalty to you that you once had.

People just don't know how important it is to have these small communities. I wouldn't take anything in the world for having raised my children in a community like this. They're sheltered to an extent, but to me that's good. I intended to shelter them. Because I think they needed sheltering at tender ages. They need to be sheltered and guided, and you need to come up in a community that's I think conservative. I wouldn't take anything in the world for having raised my children here. You might not have as many picture shows to go to. You may not get to go to the skating rink every day. But right now, if some of our kids at the First Baptist Church want to skate, we have a skating rink in our Christian Life Center. Of course that's not as much fun as going where there's music and lights flashing and all this. But they can have fellowship there if they want to—good, Christian fellowship. And I think that's good. I may be an old fogey, but that's the way I feel.

RICKY BURNEY

I feel that one of the reasons why the area is not as big as it should be is because we don't put out as much as we should to draw the industry in here. We've got people here that love this town the way it is. You take a husband and wife, family with two kids, the kids is already grown, gone, making it good. Husband and wife is doing fairly well. We don't need no business. Everything's fine. I own the business, so why bring another business here? I believe that. I've seen things that could have happened, and a lot of people just didn't want it to happen.

I've been in meetings where these people would say, "We're going to do this. We're going to come into this town and we're going to do this right here." And we're thinking then, "Tomorrow we're going to have a business out there." And the next thing you know, this business is no longer there. I've seen one business that was in Calhoun County. It's doing very good in Calhoun County now. They had already bought the land here. But still, that business is in Calhoun County. Lineville didn't get the business.

You hear rumors stating that this business will interfere with this business. So we don't want to kick our home guy out here right now. We want the money to stay here. Still, if this business came, it would create a lot more jobs. And I think that is a problem. We sell the city to things that we want it to have. Something that might create a little bit different atmosphere, a little bit different thing than what we're used to, we're not going to follow up on that. Which might be good to some extent, but overall I think it's bad. You don't want anything that's going to be bad for the community, but if it's going to create a job that's not going to be anything derogatory, or physically harmful to somebody, then that business should come here.

These plants here peak and they fall. Up, down. Today we're hiring everybody that comes off the street and tomorrow everybody's laid off. But if another industry was here, it might take up some of the slack. And probably would help the wages around here also, when you've got competition.

People really don't want Lineville and Ashland to join together and try to make a county. Power people, I'll put it like that. They'll fight that. If you're from Ashland, you're from Ashland. And if you're from Lineville, you're from Lineville. There are times when the county needs to get together and say this is what we're going to do to try to bring this business here. If it's going to happen anyway, then they say, "Well, we'll work together on that." This is an individual who's going to buy regardless of what the situation is. Then they work together. But I've also seen situations where they say, "That Ashland bunch over there, we just need to keep them out of it." Or that Lineville bunch. That's true. They have a county industrial board. I think they just met to form it, to say we got one. But other than that, Lineville's going to pull everything they can to Lineville. If that business is going to go to Ashland, or can go to Ashland, we'd just better shut up about it. Let it go on to Talladega.

I heard a guy one time that served on one of the boards, said we don't need no industry here. He worked every day out of town. He's got a business of his own. So why should he want a business? But he's serving on a board down there, that's supposed to be trying to help the city. If I have all the money that's necessary for my family to live, then I don't need a business. Unless I'm concerned about the people. I think that hurts the city. Because those people are the ones that got the power. Those people are the ones that say "Hey, this goes," and "This don't go." They put those people on those boards and different things, and those people say, "I don't like this one." "OK, we'll let this one come in." It's a little business. It's not going to do much. As long as it's like that. But if it's going to hire a lot of people, and it's going to bring a lot of people in this town, that's not good for this area. That's the attitude I think those people take. It's just not the right job. Bring in sorry people. People'd be worth a little more, they might be able to buy a little bit more, but still they think it might create a whole lot more ruckus because of the people they're bringing in. And they're afraid the city might get too big.

Even when Harris Dam was being built—that was one of the biggest things that ever come through this county. It had like eight hundred and something people working on that dam. And the biggest proportion of people here, your pulpwooders, they got to go make seven dollars an hour on a job. And then when that job left here, people were going back to doing the same old thing. And everybody's hurting. They didn't like these people coming in here. Some of them were real rough. Traffic was a little bit more congested than normal. So everybody was glad it left, brought it back to normal. But people that went to work, made that seven dollars, eight dollars an hour, they done a whole lot better, and now they're a whole lot worse off.

That's why they come here. Most of them has left and made the money anyway, and they come back here and so now they don't want this thing to change. This is why they came back, because it was a quiet, rural place, and let's keep it like that. Let's just keep it the way it is.

JIMMY WILLIAMSON
Forty-four, Clay County Rescue Squad member, High Pine, white

The rescue squad got started in 1969, January the twenty-ninth. There'd been some lost people in the county—most of them in the national forest— and nobody really to hunt them other than the sheriff's auxiliary. That's really the main reason that we organized. For search and rescue. The day after that, we went around both of the towns, Ashland and Lineville, and made up something like twelve hundred dollars, and gave a man fifty dollars for a Corvair van. And the county donated a '59 Ford station wagon. That was the only equipment we had at the time.

In 1971 we were asked to take the ambulance service at night, because the local funeral homes couldn't handle it. We started with that, and that same year we had a couple of local boys that drownded on Lake Martin, and we stayed down there for about fourteen days, looking. While we were down there the people of the county got together and made up some money, and that helped us to buy a '72 model Chevrolet van, which we used for an ambulance. Then in the last of '72 we were told that the funeral homes were going to drop ambulance service altogether. So we agreed to take it over until the county could do better, and this is 1988 and we're still running it. We've bought I don't know how many ambulances over the years—we bought one last year at the approximate cost of thirty-five thousand dollars. The people of the county paid for it by donations. And the two towns and the county have helped us. We've got I believe eleven paramedics, and probably nine intermediate and approximately twenty EMT-one level.

When we organized, we decided to be a volunteer organization, and of course we don't charge for anything that we do. We never have, and we never will. I guess it's the only volunteer, nonpaying rescue squad in the South. No ambulance service is free in the state, other than this one, and we don't know of any states around us that has a free ambulance service. As far as actual calls, there's sick calls, on ambulance runs, and of course there's automobile accidents and so forth, lost children around the towns. Whatever comes to mind. The most trips right now being made is ambulance trips which involve sick people. Bring them to the hospital or transferring them back and forth. Last year we made twelve hundred and forty-one calls—we had something in the neighborhood of fifteen thousand man-hours spent. Out of that there was something like ninety trips to other hospitals, which is Birmingham, Anniston, Opelika, Montgomery, or wherever.

We have some mighty good people—I think they're fine as they come. And they give of their time and money and efforts. Take a lot of time away from their families, take a lot of time away from their jobs, just to help people. It's just something that they feel like they need to do. I don't guess we've got any two people in the squad that do the same thing. We've got everything from plumbers to electricians, mechanics, truck drivers, car salesmen—you name it. We've got people from all walks of life. We've got a few retired people, and we certainly keep them busy.

We don't have a lot of new members because nobody hardly ever gets out, unless they move away or something. We bring applicants up before the squad, and it's voted on, and if they're accepted, they're a member, and if they're not they're not. We always have a backlog of applications. At the present time, we're carrying fifty members.

Just keep it going, that's about all I want. Sometimes that seems tough. Times have changed, and things are getting harder every day, seems like. Seems like twenty years ago, people could get off a job easier to spend time with volunteer services. It's not that easy any more.

We feel like maybe it has helped pull the county together. Because we feel like people are proud of the squad, and of course the squad's proud of the county. There's not many places in Clay County now that I haven't been. Not many dirt roads I haven't been over.

EMMA JEAN MCKINNEY
Sixty-one, founder, Clay County Learning Center, Ashland, white

I have a Down's Syndrome daughter, and I was a home economics teacher before I had children—taught twelve years—and with the child-development training I had, I realized that Billie could learn. My husband and myself carried her to Birmingham, Montgomery, any place we thought that could help. And there was a man from Decatur, around Decatur, that came to my house one time, and he had this armful of material telling how to organize an Association for Retarded Citizens. He told me if I'd organize, I could help the retarded in Clay County. And he was a very convincing fellow. I believe he's a retired veteran, a lieutenant colonel, and he had a retarded daughter. This was in '70 or '71.

So I began to talk to people, and put pieces in the paper saying I was a parent of a retarded child and I was wanting to help all that needed help. I began to drive all over the county, and my phone rung day and night at home, giving me names. In six weeks I had a hundred and two names. And they began to give us donations, and anybody that I thought would help write a grant, I got. In '74, in June I believe, we got the gearup grant to organize. And then we opened the school in September of '74.

*　　　*　　　*

I had read where there's an average of three percent born retarded, but Clay County's about five percent, because there's a lot of relatives, and we have several communities where cousins will marry cousins, and our percentage is higher.

The children were just staying at home. They'd try to send them to school, one or two years, and they'd see that they couldn't function. Or they didn't send them to school at all. And of course they didn't function well—we're just beginning to have a special education class. The first class I saw Billie was in, it was an old storage room, and there was fifteen students when six or seven ought to be. I was horrified at what I saw. And I got her back home. That's the year I started carrying her to different places.

When we started we was still in the ages where sometimes people would call and say, "I have a cousin, I have a neighbor, that has them but don't give my name." And I would go to the house. But they're beginning now to come to us. It's been a slow thing.

There's a lot of places the insurance people would comment, they would see them there at home. They would have them in a back room somewhere. Well, as they say, they was trying to protect them, but it was—having a handicapped child is kind of like accepting a death. I've had both—my husband died, and my parents more recently. You've got to accept it and then do something about it. The parents didn't realize what they was doing, but it was a lot for their own sake. And so many of them, they just couldn't believe what they're doing, since they got here. One little blind girl that we have, she was just laying and listening to music, showed no emotion, mad or joyful. Now she uses a cane, she goes to the bathroom here, finds her way, and she takes a shower here.

The difference in I think the very rural people and the urban people: the urban more or less accept the fact they have to form a second family—they just put them away, they call it, in an institution—whereas the rural people in Clay County had their faith, and they just felt like this was something brought on to them, that God meant for them to be born, and they had just to accept it and bear it, as they said, and take care of them. They just didn't think they could function outside. A lot of parents, they didn't want them to be mistreated, afraid somebody'd laugh at them. It took us a year sometimes—they was so protective of them it was hard to get them out of their sight. At one time, we even had one of the sisters—we looked out the window, and she was peeping in the window, to see if we were taking good care of her sister.

*   *   *

After I got back home from the hospital, and I got the birth certificate back, and I saw what he had written on it, I cried. But then I said it was meant for her to be born, and for her to live, and there was a purpose for it. The county says if it hadn't been for Billie McKinney, Clay County Learning Center would not have been, so maybe that was the purpose for her life. Maybe I've helped lives—I hope I have—by having lived myself.

I do try to stress that God created everything and everybody, and God created the handicapped just as well as he did the others. It's not for us to say why, but we are all responsible for the way that we treat them and feel toward them. And that's the main thing I've done all these years is try to change the attitude. Clay County was just like the others; they thought it was something that should not be talked about, or when the families— nearly every family I had to deal with, they had to go through a period of still crying. And when they once got through that then I'd tell them what they could do and every time they did something at home that they hadn't done they'd report that. All the parents now, they just laugh and joke about it, if they make a mistake, or what they'll come home and say, and right now I think we've come a long way.

Pretty Good Entertainment

Preceding page: Paul Shelnutt

C. P. HORN
Seventy, medical doctor, Ashland, white

Anybody that comes in here sick, we never do ask them about the money. They get served. One woman, she had so many children. I said, "You're just going to break me up. I've delivered eleven kids for you, and you haven't paid me a cent. You're breaking me up. Would you take some of these birth-control pills for me?" No, no, no. Afraid of them. I said, "Well, looks like there's something I could do." She said, "No, that's the only entertainment we have." I said, "How about I'll buy you a television?" Didn't want that. So I just waited.

WOODROW FETNER
Seventy-four, retired school-bus driver, Cragford, white

I remember when we used to have a circus. They used to go around the country, with the camels and elephants and animals. Walking. They came down by here one time, and set up over there on the hill from Cragford. I was just small. They had some, I guess they was giraffes, that'd reach up in the old tree up there and just bite leaves off them. Maybe they had some zebras too, striped zebras. I don't know whether they had any caged animals, lions or anything. I've seen them since, but I don't know whether they had them then or not. They drove them down the road. Those elephants was really big.

I guess the giraffes, I guess that was the biggest impression. That's the ones that reaches way up yonder, ain't it? Reaching up and biting those leaves off of the old tree out there. I never will forget it.

Even when most Clay County folks lived on the farm, when they got up before dawn and worked until the sun slid down to the horizon, they made time and found energy for fun, not just the constant teasing that still goes on today, but activities that required more strenuous exertion—the square dance sets danced all across the countryside, the practical jokes that could require elaborate preparation, the long hours spent alone in the woods, stalking for miles the traces of a trail.

Though people now have access to more forms of entertainment—TV, of course, has made its mark, as have video recorders, and satellite transmission, and the money to spend on motorboats and trips—many fill their spare time with the old activities, changed little by the advent of electric instruments, stocked catfish lakes, and four-wheel drives. The county remains a place where storytelling is an art, because there's so much time to practice, where the crackle of police scanners breaks into homes all over, and where two dozen onlookers can beat the ambulance to an accident scene. And perhaps in part because the county's poor, since many jobs are hard and full of repetition, a fund of pent-up passion still often seems to pour into spare-time activities, transforming them into something more than just a way to pass your time.

Such emotions can run in some disturbing channels. Families no longer fight in front of church on Sunday morning, and most men no longer think it's fun to put a raccoon on a log and float it to the center of a lake to see whose dog has guts enough to swim out there and kill it. But even though the county's dry, you can always find the liquor that offers an escape from work, from troubles, or from boredom, and even now, in some parts of the county, there are fights, and wrecks, and people talk about bootleggers bringing their customers to the bank, to cash their paychecks and redeem their liquor debts. A few men guard their hunting rights with the ferocity of some of the prey that they pursue, and when a piece of land they've always hunted on is for some reason posted, or if a timber company raises its hunting fees, a grudge fire may well sweep through the property one fine, dry day.

But strong feelings more often lead to levels of enviable skill. Arrow-straight rows of garden corn and lush tomato plants reveal talents once needed to nurture a vital source of food. Musicians' fingers conjure up the swift and polished sounds that come only after lengthy hours of concentration, and some high school football stars throw blocks they know could mean the difference between a college scholarship and a life of heavy labor. To see such efforts as purely entertainment would be to miss the point entirely.

ZENUS WINDSOR
Fifty-two, Baptist preacher, Corinth, white

A great portion of our humor is practical jokes that people pull on one another. What we call good, clean fun. I guess they've got away from that a lot all over our country, because they don't have the time. But over here, for instance, there was a man that would walk and see his girlfriend—that was back before everybody had automobiles. He passed away some eight or ten years ago. But he walked to see his girlfriend, and people'd try to run him in. That used to be one of the big things, to run boys in at night, when they'd been out—the old saying was gallivanting around. And they couldn't; he just wasn't very scary.

But over here at his uncle's place on the creek, there was a shop where people worked on their plows and things. Had an anvil in there. And so two boys got together, and they put a wire around that anvil, like a clothesline, a slick clothesline. And they laid it across this little bottom, and there was a tree on the other side of that bottom, and they climbed up in that tree and tied that wire up at the top. They knew what time he'd come in, so that night just before he was to come down the road, these two boys went down there to where they had their device fixed. One of them got in the shop, and the other one climbed up in that tree and took a lantern.

When that fellow got about even with there, he lit that lantern, and let out a scream and turned it loose, and it went sliding down that wire and went in that shop and the other man caught it and blew it out. And I don't know whether it's true, but they said that man actually ran past his house, he was so scared, and he had a bad story to tell how this big ball of fire came out of the elements and went in his Uncle John's shop and all that.

But that's the type of thing that people used to do. Hide in the bushes next to the field and scare the livestock; take a man's wagon apart and put it up on top of the barn and assemble it back, and it'd be sitting up on top of the barn the next day. Lot of things that people did around here that I've heard about, from the past, all through just fun. That's more or less the way they entertained themselves. They didn't have televisions back then, and people basically had to create their own entertainment.

One of the big things in my time has been calling people on the telephone and fooling them. That's been probably one of the best-used pranks in this country. You know when people are sincere with you over the telephone, it's hard to not be sincere back, and naturally you want to help if there's something to do, and a lot of times you're caught off guard. And this man told me his sister called him and told him she was with the telephone company. And that there was water in the lines—had gotten in the telephone lines and caused some problems. And she wanted him to help her if he would. And of course he was wanting to cooperate—he didn't catch his sister's voice, you see.

And so she got him to back away ten steps from the telephone and holler "Hello" at it. And he did. And so she finally got him in the closet. He was closed in the closet hollering hello. And you can imagine how hilarious that had to be to his sister. To realize she had her brother walking all over the house, hollering "Hello." Trying to discover the water in the lines.

I know a friend of mine over here, he had a colored lady keeping his kids, seeing after them. And he called her and told her he was somebody with the telephone company. He says, "I'm so-and-so with the telephone company," and said, "We're fixing to blow the soot out of the lines." And says, "Take whatever precautions you can to keep from getting the soot in your house." So he goes on up to the house—he was only down at the country store—he goes on up to the house, walks in there to use the phone, and the colored lady says, "No, no, no!" She had quilts over it. She says, "I don't want to sweep all this soot up out of the room." But things like that have been a big part of what people pull pranks on folks about.

One of my cousins had a swimming hole, and they had a big tree blown over beside that, had what we call a clay root, an old tree laying there. And these boys had an old billy goat. And they'd get behind that clay root, and the old billy goat out here on the log, and they would shake their head at him. Well the old billy goat would come a-charging to hit them, and of course just before he hit them, when he made the lunge, they just dropped down behind the clay root, and the old goat would go in the creek. They liked that. And my uncle caught them doing it. And of course, he whipped them and sent them home. Shamed them, you know, for what they had done. But after he whipped them and sent them home he got to studying about that was pretty good entertainment. And he got back there and got behind the old stump and waved his hat, but age had kind of worked on him, he wasn't as fast as the kids was, and the goat knocked him in the creek.

MARK CARTER
Seventeen, bass drummer, Lineville High School band, Lineville, black

There's not too many things to do around this place. I just sit around with my friends and talk a lot. Talk about the drum. About different bands, what theirs are like, and how we should do ours. They tell me what they did Friday night. What they did on the weekend. Some of them just tells they just got drunk on the weekend, and they traveled all over, to other counties. They went to talk to people; they went to the dance; they went and saw the other football game, and all that stuff. How the game went, what the band sounded like. Just talk.

When I was about thirteen, fourteen, they did have a theater here, but they closed it down. I don't know why. It would be a lot of people there, if they had a real good movie there. It'd be full up Friday, so a lot of those that wanted to see it, they had to go Saturday night, and if it was full Saturday night, they had to go Sunday night. If it was full those whole three nights, they would let it be extended.

I've traveled to Georgia two times. That was back years ago. I'd like to go off and do something different. Eventually, a lot of my friends want to leave Clay County and do other different things. They all have different ideas, different places where they want to go. Different kinds of jobs. Some want to go to Alabama State, some want to go to Tennessee, some want to go to Mississippi or Georgia or Florida. Most want to go to college. It's kind of hard to find a job, and then they're kind of tired of staying around in Clay County.

Not too many want to stay. All I heard them say, they want to go far away from here as they can. Because it's poor—well, it's not poor, but it's not a lot of stuff around you can do. You have to go to Anniston or Oxford or Talladega just to see a movie. You have to go to Talladega or Wedowee to go to the skating rink. No way to have fun.

I TELL YOU, IT'S WORKING QUILTING

Suspended from the ceiling in Allie Mae Ragland's near-ageless country house hang four slender, straight-planed boards nailed in a square almost as large as her living room itself. They get in the way sometimes, she says, because when she lets them down to work on a quilt, which she does much of the time, you can barely squeeze between them and the wall.

Allie Mae, who is black and sixty-nine, is sitting by the fireplace that provides the room's only heat, and as she talks she often leans forward, puts her fingers to her mouth, and spits into the flames. The chimney has been built from unshaped stones, and the clay on the fireplace walls has eroded in craggy, irregular design. Behind her, a door fastened by a wooden peg shows large cracks of the cold daylight, and from across the room, you hear her granddaughters playing beneath the tin roof of a somewhat unstable porch.

Annie Pearl Harris, sixty-nine, and Sarah Simmons, sixty-seven, nearby neighbors and longtime friends, join in with talk about quilts that they have pieced or sewn—more, they say, than they would ever want to count. After a while, Allie goes to get the one she has just finished, and proudly she displays the pattern of squares and colored ships, as bright and neat and up-to-date as you could want to see.

Allie: My mother learnt me how to quilt. I had to.

Annie: Mine did too.

Allie: She didn't make us, we just had to quilt.

Annie: To have some covers, to cover up with. It'd be cold.

Allie: We used little old pieces.

Sarah: Piece them on paper sometimes, just strings.

Allie: Piece them up and then put them together and then tear that paper off and then quilt.

Annie: A peddler man'd come around.

Sarah: And an old candy man, you could sell candy. You'd get cloth for so many boxes of candy you'd sell, and the scraps'd make quilts and things.

Annie: Mama had a book of quilt patterns. I don't know where she got them.

Allie: You used to order them.

Annie: I know *Progressive Farmer* had books like that.

Sarah: I had a few after so long, you know. I got a Gentleman Bow Tie and a ship and a tree. I had a star. I gave it to Annie Sailor before she died. I had it in yellow and navy blue. I don't know what they ever did with it.

Allie: It was fun. I liked it so well till I still do it. I need them to stay warm.

Sarah: I'd rather have a quilt anytime than a blanket.

Allie: When you went to quilting, there'd be two or three of you around there, and that's when it'd be fun.

Sarah: Mostly there'd be four, one on each corner. One on each side, one on each end. Just laughing and talking and enjoying yourself.

Allie: You didn't take no time in getting it out.

Annie: No telling what all we'd be talking about. [All laugh.] First one thing then another.

Sarah: I used to just sit up and piece all the time. In the wintertime, when I couldn't get out and my children was little. That was mostly the reason I did it. Wasn't doing nothing but sitting around. That's when you'd do that, in wintertime. Because summertime, you'd be out doing something else. In your garden or something like that. Picking berries. Canning and stuff like that. You'd just have to piece those quilts and things in the wintertime, when you couldn't get outside.

*   *   *

Sarah: I have daughters, I've got five, but nary one's of them pieced a quilt. They don't even hardly have quilts; they've got blankets. Most of them've got electric blankets, and that's something I ain't never cared nothing about.

Allie: Annie has them.

Annie: Mine, she do all sorts of work. She take in sewing. Got a sewing shop onto her house.

Sarah: They just don't be interested in nothing like that.

Allie: They didn't have it to do, and it was easier.

Sarah: They didn't have to, and so they don't do it. Maybe somebody'll give them a quilt or two. I know when Kaye got married Aunt Bea give her a whole lot of quilts.

Allie: I keep Annie in quilts. That's what I give her at Christmas, a quilt.

Sarah: Well you can give me one for my birthday, that's January the ninth.

I'll be sixty-eight years old [laughs]. I'm asking for it now. I'm going to buy me some if I ever get a little spare money, but you know how it is, you just don't have nothing, I'm telling you.

Allie: Annie, you could put your frames up in the basement there. When it got cold, make some fire down there, and it'll be good and warm in there.

Annie: Went down there looking for my frames. Ain't got but three frames. I know them children done away with that frame. Them was Grandma Sallie's quilting frames.

Allie: They was probably easy broke, and somebody probably broke one of them.

Annie: Throwed it away or something. My grandma was a hundred and six years old when she died. I know I won't get old as my mother.

Allie: You don't know. We don't know how long we going to live.

Annie: I don't feel like I will.

Sarah: I won't get old as my grandma did either. She was ninety-eight when she died.

Annie: My mama was ninety-eight too. Miss Shirley was a hundred and six.

Allie: I don't think Granny was quite that old. She was in her nineties, though. She wasn't no hundred and six.

Sarah: Grandma Alice would have been ninety-nine if she'd lived to February, I think. But she died in November. I always heard a lot of folks say if you pass seventy-five you're living on someone else's time, but that's not so. You're living on your own time. I don't feel like that. When the Lord gets ready for you He's going to take you, if you're ten or twelve or whatever, that's your time. I don't believe you be living on nobody else's time.

Annie: My time come, I don't want them to be trying to keep me here, suffering.

Sarah: I don't either. I don't want them to put no kind of machine on me.

*　　　*　　　*

Allie: I tell you, it's working quilting. It's not entertaining, I wouldn't think. Because you've got to work to get it done. If it's entertaining, you'd just be sitting down and talking.

I'VE PICKED FOR MANY A SET

They call it "the music," as though the sweet, lively warmth of the sounds they love so well lived of itself, inhabited a place you might pass on your way to Heaven, until a songwriter, and afterwards a fiddler or a deep-throated country woman singer, reading carefully copied lyrics from a perforated notebook page, should call them forth. The music came here, they will say, or went over there, or will be at someone else's house tonight, bearing with it the near-magic atmosphere that makes people break into delighted smiles when they see a fiddler come unexpected in.

The book of Sacred Harp religious songs was once second only to the Bible—and perhaps the catalog from Sears—in distribution, and in the few, brief summer weeks between laying by and harvest, singing schools drew pupils by the hundreds. For a time, church songs were almost all you heard, and people still tell tales of fiddles found tucked in attic corners, put away when years ago revival preachers spoke of Satan's music, and uncounted instruments were smashed or burned. But now you find few, no matter of what age, who will not set their feet to tapping at the sound of a good, fast hoedown, who cannot mouth the words of an old Hank Williams standard, who are not ready to relate their memories of the Grand Old Opry's Saturday-night broadcast, to the sound of which children all across the South once went to sleep.

Now, old and young will often play together, relying on each others' ears and on a common fund of country songs, and sounds from ancient banjos and guitars, with spots rubbed bare from years of strumming, blend with the twang of newer strings, plucked by fingers with the strength and quickness needed to pick the harder tunes. A house with well-worn bare wood floors, and boxes that once held government commodities along the wall, fills with words of thanks to God, sung by a group of friends who smile even when some notes sound out of tune. In the front room of a cement-block home up in the hills, a young man who does not even own a car takes out his fiddle and plays an impossibly lovely tune, even though he protests that he is not in practice. And an old banjo player, who once called his band the Happy Hill Billies, sits on his slick parlor floor, arms clasped around his long, thin legs, listening. He has set his tape player in the middle of the room, plugged it into the bare-bulb socket that dangles from the ceiling, and his lips are moving to the song he's heard a thousand times, utterly alone, wholly and completely happy.

LOIS MOORE

We just kind of come from a music family. When I was twelve, my brother was fourteen, and I can't remember who give my brother the guitar, but anyway he had a guitar and there was one of our friends come across this banjo. Well he kept fooling with it, never could do nothing with it, and I just took it up. I just learnt myself.

After we growed up, there used to be dances. Of course we couldn't have them nowadays, too much drinking and rough stuff in the world, but people enjoyed that. Old people went same as the young. And we got to going out and picking for dances. It'd be four o'clock next morning we'd get in. We had to work. And Mother would get us up; we'd have to work all day. We'd be so sleepy. And the last few years that we played together, this drinking and carousing started, and I quit. My brother, they'd get him drinking, you see, and he'd pick all night and never get tired. And I'd have to drag him home. I got tired of that. So that broke it up.

I guess one thing, you see us kids was just left with Mother. And we was poor folks and didn't have no way of going and we just learned to entertain one another at home. We'd pick at home and people got to coming in and hearing us pick, neighbors and kids, you know how it is. And they got to inviting us to come and make music. I've picked for many a set.

Us women used to buck dance. I used to could. But when I was little I had—used to call it infantile paralysis back then, but it's the same thing as polio now. And I never did have much use of my legs and hands and arms. I didn't have a severe case, but it crippled me till I couldn't walk only on crutches till I was about ten, eleven years old. And I crawled most of the time. You can see the scars on my legs where I crawled on the rocks, kid-like—wanted to be where the others was. I tried to play a little ball and junk like that. But I never could get out like other children. And I'd just sit around and thump on my old banjo.

I used to pick, but I couldn't keep up with picking because my hands was stiff. So I learned to do like Grandpa Jones, I learned to rap. And keep up.

I like old-time. I don't mess with this new-time frolic. I don't like this old pop music, and I don't like this old jazz mess.

Some people have criticized me about making music and going to dances. These here good Christian folks. And you know what I'd tell them? I'd say the Bible says there shall be music and dancing in Heaven. I may not get there. I'm going to get my part here.

JOHNNY RAY WATTS
Twenty, fiddler, Shinbone, white

I was two years old when Daddy saw I had an interest. He had a fiddle here at the house, and I drug it around for about a year and a half. Then he bought me a cheap fiddle. A little bitty thing. And he started teaching me to play little chords and stuff like that. I was about four years old when I learnt my first song. And I just went on from there. Him teaching me up till I was about nine or ten and then I started on my own because I'd done learnt everything he knew. From there I was by myself.

If Daddy went somewhere to play, I was ready to go. I was always with my daddy. I mean if he went somewhere to a friend's house to play, he didn't have to ask me if I wanted to go; I was ready to go. I just wanted to play. A lot of friends used to come down here, or we'd go up to their house, and we'd play until twelve or one o'clock. That's basically what I wanted to do when I was little, just hang around with people that wanted to play the kind of music I wanted to play. If you was hunting me, that's where I was at.

The first contest I ever went to I was six years old. We went to Athens, Alabama, up to the college. They had a fiddle convention there, and I still go to it. And I won it that year. Every year I went to Athens I won it. In the beginners. I won first prize every time I went.

*   *   *

When I was twelve and thirteen years old I knowed a lot more songs than what I know now. I done forgot a lot of them. Right off hand, I'd say maybe about forty or fifty, something like that. I remember writing down in a book, I'd written down the name of all the songs that I knew, and I think it was about a hundred and twenty-six. I think Mother throwed the book away.

Every song I played I liked. I didn't have any particular one I liked better. Now I do. I like waltzes. I like slow songs. You can add those double notes to it. Six-chords and stuff like that. You can add a lot more to it. I mean a hoe-down's fast and it's just—it ain't got that slow drag. To me, there's nothing better than a waltz. Every time I pick it up, the first thing I want to do is play a waltz. Later on I might play a fast song or two, but that's all.

I used to practice every day. Between work and everything else, I don't get to do it like I want to now. I don't do it like I should. I mean, if I'm going to go to a contest, or something like that, I might start, maybe three or four months before the contest. And I'll practice. I'll dig out my records, and run over my tunes, whatever I want to play.

And after I run over them, I'll sit there by myself. I don't want nobody else around. I don't even want nobody in the house. I'll just sit down by myself, and I'll figure it out. I mean, you run a song through your head and think of things that you want to do to it. You'll be playing a song, and you'll hit a note that you didn't know was on there. A different kind of note, like a six-chord. I don't tell nobody to leave the house, but I just wait till they're gone. And I'll just dig it out.

My daddy says it's a God-given talent. It was God's will. That's the way I look at it. Everybody thinks, "Well, if it's a God-given talent, why don't he play church music?" Well, I do. I don't go to church. I believe in the Lord Jesus Christ, but He gave you the freedom to do what you want to. I think if you're not going to use a talent, He'll take it away from you. And my daddy, he laid it down for about four or five years, never picked it up. Of course he can play simple tunes. But he can't make the notes. But if you're going to play it, I don't think He'll take it away from you. I think that if He was going to give it to somebody, He'd give it to somebody that He knowed would use it, or try to use it.

I want to learn all there is to know about music. I've got a friend that lives in Nashville. He's a recording artist. And he told me that after I learnt what I want to learn down here, for me to come and stay with him, and he would teach me everything I needed to know. That's what I want to do.

*   *   *

Older folks play a lot of songs differently from what I would. I mean back then, like my daddy says, they had the radios, and they got to listen to the

Grand Old Opry on Saturday nights a little bit. And if you didn't get it the first time, you didn't get it. You didn't learn it. And they learnt what they learnt the best they knew how because they didn't have the stuff we have now. They didn't have tape recorders they could tape and if they didn't catch that part they could rewind it and stuff like that. That's the advantage of growing up now.

I like being around people that's up in their fifties and sixties and sit down and listen to them talk about how they used to do things, and where they played at. Now a bow, it's got horsehair on it. I have heard them talk about they didn't have no horsehair and they had to rosin the stick and play the stick. I wouldn't want to go back to those days where I had to do that. Not knowing that the future held better things. I mean that would be rough.

You can always learn something off somebody. I don't care how long they've been playing. You might run across somebody that's been playing a year, and you've been playing twenty years, and you can still learn something off them. But it's all the same music. I don't care where you go— Texas, Georgia, it's all the same stuff. It's old-time music.

*   *   *

There's still a lot of people around here that plays. My friend Randy still comes over here all the time, and we'll sit down and we'll play. And every now and then Daddy, if he's not tired, he'll sit down and play the guitar with us. And we got some friends up the road, they still play a little bit. I know two or three guys that's my age that plays. And both of them are good.

There's nothing like it. When we get together, we all make recordings of it, or somebody makes a recording of it, where when we get old, we can go back and say, "Hey that's us playing." The good old days. I mean when you get old, and you start getting arthritis, you slow down. You can't do all the things you want to do. Just like my daddy. I've got tapes of him put up that were made back when he played. And it's hard to believe that my daddy now, from what I've heard him play now, it's hard to believe he could play that good. But my daddy was good.

I'm going to play till the day I die. That's what I plan on doing. Old-timey music.

I LIKE A STILL NIGHT

As people have retreated from Clay County, the woodlands have advanced, retaking land once laboriously cleared for crops, and giving the hillsides something of the feel of frontier wilderness, with relics, and maybe ghosts, from Indian wanderings and battles, with the abandoned shafts left from gold, graphite, and mica mines, with coons, and white-tailed fawns, and possums with their young, who die by scores along the roads, but in the woods take work to catch.

Although the land is no longer all your sustenance, and even if it fails you still can eat, it surrounds you always, fading at winter into bare-branch hardwood and brown, close-eaten pastures that stretch tight over every hilly undulation, then breaking green again in spring, with the spangled lace of dogwoods, and the sound of hungry bees. You venture out for the logs that fuel wood-fired heaters, for game, or just to walk and be alone. Clear land is often sowed in pasture grass, and filled with cows of all descriptions, some for profit, some as a hobby that offers the excuse to ride a tractor, to make hay and tramp around, a farmer on your own piece of ground. Garden patches, and even tethered mules, lie within a block or two of Ashland's city square, and many women can and dry the way their mothers did, as much from habit as necessity.

The day deer season opens, rifles suddenly appear in all the gun racks of all the pickup trucks in sight, and you often come on empty vehicles parked and waiting for their hopeful owners, who stalk and dream of many-pointed bucks. Among them you find those after rabbit and wild turkey by day, and coon at night, listening for the voice of hounds, trained and cared for and valuable enough to steal, and even now, a local lawyer says, land-line and dog disputes should be avoided at all costs.

When people move away, the land is often what they miss the most, a place not only where you can step outside your door and yell anything you want without offending neighbors, but where you can watch the hawks, and study catfish habits, and hear bullfrogs at night. This longing seems to tug with special force at men, and it would be hard to count the couples who moved out from the city because the husband wanted, and asked, and sometimes begged to come, and the wives, although they preferred the comforts of an urban life, gave in and let them have their way.

MORLAND FLEGEL

The big thing is letting the hound know what you want. Their trailing instincts could be used to trail any animal. Or person, for that matter. My pleasure really comes from working with the dogs. And I have to admire their strength, their courage, their determination. Then too, they do love to do this, this is their thing, but at the same time, they're also wanting to do this to please me. They could quit any time they want to.

Each one has their own personality, just like people. They have their own ways about them. Some are just hustlers, just going; some are regular comedians, they're into something all the time. They're having a good time all the time, and nothing bothers them, seemingly. Really hard for them to get serious with what they're doing.

There are certain things I look for in a hound, and that is the desire to get out there and hunt, the desire and the determination to when they take a track to be smart enough to be able to know that they can finish it, and then put the pressure on it and make them go up. Make them climb a tree. I don't want one to run a coon all night long. Or half the night, for that matter.

Normally a hound, when it opens, it'll let you know what it has. If you really pay attention. And you'll know whether it has a good track or a bad track, a cold track. Now every hound has its own way of doing this. Also you can tell, if you know the hound, by its voice and how often it uses it in different situations, how fast it's moving and really what the situation is all through the race. If you can hear all of it. A lot of times they'll get over a ridge or two, and you don't hear them for a while, and then you'll get to hear them again—you'll have to move to hear them or something. All I do is enjoy the hound and the race and everything that's done, and then see what he's accomplished.

*   *   *

When you stop and think about it, a raccoon, this is where he makes his living, and this is where he's survived by what he knows and what he can do. And there isn't a tree or a rock or a hole or a crevice or a branch or anything else, whether it's a muscadine vine or a grape vine or what have you, that he doesn't know where it's at, and what to expect when. In fact, some raccoons I believe honestly enjoy the race, up to a point. They'll pull their tricks, and if these tricks don't fool them, then of course they'll have to climb a tree to get away.

The cutovers and beaver swamps and heavy growth are places that a coon will hit real quick to buy time, so he has an opportunity to get ahead. The beaver swamp slows a hound down, because they have to swim, and they have to climb out on mud banks and then maybe they're able to trot along in the water for a little bit and then all of a sudden fall into the deep water. In the cutovers, usually you have brush that's thick, and treetops— they'll run those treetops. Especially after an ice storm, when it's laid the small pine over—four inches in diameter, or six inches even, laid over like a rainbow—a coon can jump on one of those and run to the top and usually cross into another one, and just keep a-going.

You shine the light up in the tree, and you get a reflection from their eyes, if they'll look at you. Now when there aren't any leaves, you can pick him out, normally. You can find him in the tree even though he won't look. But with leaves on a tree in summertime, they have to look in order for you to ever see them.

You can squall. Make a noise that sounds like a coon would make if he were fighting a hound or fighting whatever there is on the ground. Most occasions, they'll look. And many occasions, they will come down the tree— walk down the tree headfirst and run to create a diversion, thinking that this other coon was fighting the hounds. And then others will come down a tree for no other purpose than to fight the hounds. One night I squalled, and the coon was up a tree probably thirty-five feet tall. There were a lot of grape vines in the tree, and that rascal came down probably five feet and then just jumped down, bailed out of that tree just like a flying squirrel. And when he hit the ground, he didn't get up to run. The hounds were on the other side of the tree, probably twelve feet from him or more. And he went and hunted something to fight.

*   *   *

You're away from everything. But airplanes. I like to get back away from housedogs. I want to hear my dog; I don't want to hear somebody's housedog barking because they hear my hound opening. I don't care for cars. I don't like to hear the interference. I like the crickets and whatever. Tree frogs and other frogs. Now I'll have to admit that sometimes the katydids can stir up a racket that you wish there weren't so many, and you can't hear your hound because of the blasted katydids. But it's all part of it. I like a still night, one that's not real windy.

The opportunity just to get out and be away from everybody and everything except God's earth as He created it, you might say to me is beautiful. The things that you come across even at night. Being on the west side of Cheaha with nearly a full moon, and seeing the mountain silhouetted by the moon. It's a sight to behold, really. Now here it'd be rare to ever see the northern lights, but the northern lights at night are something to behold. Here, the stars, the clouds, of course the moon. Now I did say I like to hunt on a dark night, which I do. And one that's not real windy, so I can hear what's going on. I like cooler weather over hot weather, and of course cool weather over cold weather. You can't have everything.

For seven years, I probably averaged four nights a week. My wife doesn't mind. She has things she enjoys doing, so there's really not a conflict. That still leaves three nights.

WINNING MEANS IT ALL

All over Alabama, on autumn Friday nights, the football floodlights shine. Clustering round the bright, vaporous intensity come countless residents of countless towns, drawn to the high point in most small-town weeks. Above the crossing lines of loyalties stretch feelings for the big-time teams, for the Tigers of Auburn and the Crimson Tide of Alabama, which inspire pride, devotion, and in many cases a self-image that with some people never seems too far from conversation. "Alabama," one young man answers when a guide on a Tennessee tour asks him where he's from. "Roll Tide."

But even in the flood of feeling all around, Clay County can more than hold its own, as a place where the Ashland-Lineville game sets off emotions unusual even for the state and region, where fathers watch their sons on the fields where they once locked in battle, where, say loyal fans, their teams draw strength from all the winners that have come before them, making them not only good players, but also able bearers of tradition. When people talk about how much they love the county, they often mention playing on or rooting for the football team. He's always found it hard, one staunch fan remarks, to understand how anyone could stay home on the night of a big game.

In such an atmosphere, the game becomes a metaphor at least as large as, if not surpassing, life, as the boys press against each other in an ideal world of courage and endurance, dreams and heroes. And, in a sense, reality holds much of legend's promise, if only for a brief handful of bright years. A young black boy can dream of football glory in a way that he cannot aspire to someday direct a county plant, or run for probate judge, because the grassy fields, scored with painstaking lines of chalk, are among the very few places, in all the county, where ability is all that matters, and where your color, your family's money, who your daddy was and who you know, count for almost nothing.

ARNOLD CLARK
Seventy-four, former Lineville High School football player, Bellview, white

Winning means it all. When I went to school, we had pride. They even painted the football white, and we played at night with that football. That was before they had lights. After I was seven, every day in school they'd turn the kids out, and they'd go down and pick up brickbats, to build a football stadium down behind the grammar school. And from that time on, Lineville had a desire to win, win, win. They wouldn't give up. Win. Win. Every time you'd meet somebody it'd be "Beat Ashland." "Beat Sylacauga." We played Anniston one time. We beat Anniston. They wouldn't play us no more. Said it was a disgrace to get beat by as small a school as we were.

And I'll tell you another thing. They didn't go by age then. When you went to school, when you got up about the seventh grade, they'd run your age back if you looked like you was going to be a pretty good prospect. You'd go to school, play football in the fall of the year, till Christmas, then you'd quit and come back next year and play. All right, this is just something I'm going to throw in. This kid was going to school down here—he wasn't no kid, he was a grown man. They found out that he was twenty-six years old and they throwed him off our team.

Winning is one thing that they just dwelled on. Johnny Ingram's daddy, and Hill McCrary and Coach Garrett, they'd get on top of you, and they'd just beat you with that winning, winning, winning, winning. You've got to fight; you've got to fight; you've got to go. And we went. There's no question about it.

I want to show you how dedicated those kids were. Doug Hunt's daddy was laying a corpse, up here at Delta. He was playing center for Lineville. And he came down here and dressed out, and the coach wanted to send him home. He said, "No, sir," said, "I'm going to play this football game." His daddy was laying a corpse. There was five of those Carroll boys. All five of them boys had to run away from home and stay with some relatives to play football. Their daddy would not let them stay at home and play football. Now they had a desire to play. They had a desire to win, and every one of them has done good—I'm talking about out in life. What I'm trying to say is this. It's not only football them boys learned on the field. It's a desire to be somebody. To make something out of themselves. Football ain't all that we're stressing here tonight. We're stressing a desire to win. If you win on that football field, you're going to win out here in what you do in life.

Football taught me more than any one other thing in life. It taught me to never give up. Never quit. Because so many times in this life I could have given up. But I'd look back at John, and Coach Garrett, and they'd say never give up. Keep punching, keep punching, keep punching. And it just created something within me that's never vanished. It's always confronted me when

I had a problem. Character was the one thing that our coach stressed. And that's stuck with me all these years. I've raised a family, and I've tried to teach them the same thing that Johnny's daddy taught me.

I'll tell you what it did. It put them kids out in the world. Now we graduated in the Depression. It put us out there to where we had a desire that we wanted a way to earn a living. We made our living. And I'll tell you, I can't stand to lose right now.

DAVID EASLEY, MARK BOWEN, ARNOLD CLARK
Thirty-five, forty-eight, and seventy-four, Lineville football coach and former players, white

Mark: Football in a rural area for a long time was the only game in town. There wasn't a lot to do in Lineville. We didn't have a band even when I finished high school. So you either played football or you didn't do anything. Which is good, because it laid the groundwork for people that had a lot of pride in Lineville football. Red and black meant a lot. I was so strong on Lineville that when I went off to school, I'd get aggravated when I went to an intersection and it didn't have a Lineville thirty-six-mile sign. I thought the world was built around Lineville.

Everywhere I went in the state, people knew Lineville football. They knew the red and black. And when that team walked on the field, it meant something. I can remember Johnny Ingram quarterbacking, and he wore the red uniform with the black and white stripe down the side, and that was the best-looking uniform I've ever seen. And Johnny was the quarterback then, and it meant a lot to me. It was a lot of pride. It was a tremendous thing for Lineville.

David: You try to be more than a coach to them. You try to be mama and papa and aunt and uncle and granddaddy and grandmother. We try to let our kids know we care about them. We're interested in what they're doing off the field just like we are on the field. If they've got a problem, we'll try to help them. We'll do everything we possibly can. And then at the same time, you've got to mix in the other things. Academics, discipline, pride, character. You've got to build all those things, and you've got to do it around football. If you put all that together, and you put a kid in a program for four, five, six years, the end product hopefully is going to be a good kid ready to go make something out of himself. It's not an overnight process. It's start them when they're young and work them up through a program, and your finished product when they walk down for graduation and get that diploma is what you want to see.

We don't have cuts. If I've got a kid that weighs forty pounds, and he wants to be a part of it, and he pays the price and all, he's going to get a uniform. If we can't afford to buy him a uniform, I'll go out and buy him one myself.

The values of football haven't changed. You still want to teach those kids how to—what I call suck it up on the goal line, because ten years from now they may have to do it again. They may come home, their house may be burned down, their wife may be run off with the milkman, took the kids, the car may be stole. They've got to learn to handle that. You learn on the football field, when it's time to suck your guts up—I'll just get down to football talk—you learn to suck it up when you have to. That's one thing we try to teach these kids.

*   *   *

Arnold: I'll tell you when the rivalry started. It started back in my daddy's day. When they put the courthouse over at Ashland. Right then. When they put the courthouse at Ashland. And from that day to this—it'll never end.

David: When you move around from job to job, it takes you a while to really understand what's behind what you're coming into. It took me about halfway through the season to realize just how important the Lineville-Ashland game was. You've got your Alabama-Auburns in one class, and to me a class above that you've got Lineville-Ashland. These people down here in Clay County live three hundred and sixty-four days out of the year for the Lineville-Ashland game on the three hundred and sixty-fifth. Just like the people in the whole state live for the Alabama-Auburn game.

The closer it came to the Lineville-Ashland game, the more things started coming together. I started hearing people talk. I started seeing the way the kids were acting about it. And the week before we played Ashland, we played B. B. Comer for the area championship. And B. B. Comer beat us—they had a better football team than we did that night. But for the last two weeks of the season I found that I was thinking about Ashland. I found myself being just like the kids. I had Ashland on my mind. And then it finally hit me just how important this thing was. It was really amazing.

The week that we played Ashland, we worked all week in pads, we hit four days, and it was the only week of the season that I never raised my voice to the kids. Once the whistle blew, it was just like clockwork. You could feel it in the air. You could feel it in the dressing room. You could feel it in school every day. It was the easiest week to prepare a football team that I've ever had in eleven years simply because those kids had one thing on their mind. They was bound and determined that they was going to beat Ashland. That's the only thing they thought about all week. There's not another rivalry in the state like it. Not even close.

Mark: I think a big thing was the fact that it was played on Thanksgiving day for so long. Before you had to get football season earlier for state play-offs. That was the big thing. People came home Thanksgiving to be with their families. But that afternoon they went to the Ashland-Lineville football game. You started building a bonfire Monday or Tuesday—each town would build a bonfire. You'd have the bonfire Wednesday night before Thanksgiving. And you decorated the town, and everybody tried to burn the other school's bonfire, so they wouldn't have one to burn. You tried to cut down the ribbons that was in the town—they used to hang ribbons criss-crossing before they started painting on store windows. And Thursday morning before the game you had a parade. The Ashland cheerleaders would get on the fire truck, and all the cars, and they would parade through Lineville, and then the Lineville cheerleaders would do the same thing, and then that afternoon you had the football game. You would have all the people that you could pack inside that gate. A county that has twelve thousand population would have six or seven thousand at the football game.

David: Your adrenaline runs as high as it'll ever run that night. I played college ball, and played in the College World Series in front of seven or eight thousand people, and it's nothing like it. Unless you experience it you just can't understand. It's hard to describe, it really is. You walk in the stadium, and you talk to the kids, and you get tears in your eyes.

*   *   *

Mark: Football players in Lineville have been looked up to. They were leaders in the classroom, they were leaders on the football field, and they were leaders as far as their behavior. Our coaches told us, don't embarrass yourself, don't embarrass your team, and don't embarrass your family. For that reason, you didn't want to do anything that would take away from it. Our players were not troublemakers. We didn't have any renegades. By the same token, we'd have done anything for each other. It's more than a fraternity. I believe right now that if any of my teammates, or any Lineville football player, called me in trouble, I'd go to their help. I really believe that. Right now, a Lineville football player, I still respect, no matter how old or how young. To me it's a special breed of person. I go to the athletic banquet, and I see these kids graduate, and I want to cry just like a father. It just breaks my heart to see them go.

Arnold: Regardless of whether he's your son, or your grandson, or who he is, if he's got on that red and black, you've got a feeling for him that you have for no other kid.

Mark: I came back from here after I went off to college and went to work in the valley. Came back to Lineville, and I went out there and I saw a football team, and we were in black and *white.* And I said, "This is not my team." I like to had a heart attack. We got started right then getting us back into the right colors. Our colors are *red,* with a black trim. And it's not black with red, it's red with black. That's the colors.

David: When I was growing up, we used to go see Alabama play. When I saw that crimson jersey, it just sent chills up my back. And when I take those kids on the field at seven twenty-five, to see those jerseys walk down that hill, it just makes your spine tingle. When you see that red and black— I just got a chill right then, just thinking about it. Those colors mean a lot. Really they mean it all.

*   *   *

Arnold: Playing was a big highlight. But I'm going to tell you the biggest. Sit up on the sidelines and see your son play. That's the greatest thrill a man ever had.

DAVID GOOD
Eighteen, college freshman, Millerville, white

At Lineville and Ashland they think the football players are gods, or something like that. It was a different kind of atmosphere at Millerville. I was one of the players. And you never knew too much that anybody cared about it.

Football's a lot of fun. You get everybody playing as a team, and you get to work out all your aggressions, and it becomes terribly violent. I guess it's a contradiction, because I'm not a violent person, but it's just a lot of fun. Stereotypes are really no good anyway.

Nobody ever really screamed for us; we didn't win. Year before last we got ranked in the state poll, and people were coming, and we've got all these old bleachers—we never had enough money hardly to buy our jerseys even—and then it was just people packing in the old decrepit bleachers, and that was pretty neat. We were all just like: "Look at this. People actually came to the games."

HORACE SIMS

We used to go to football games over here; we'd go peep in. We didn't have a football team at that time. We'd go over here to the high school to see the white team play. We'd stand on the outside of the fence, and peep in, and we'd get up in the trees. Some of the little white kids—they didn't mean any harm in a way, but they would take rocks and throw at us up there in the tree. They never did hit anybody.

Now I go to that same field, and my son played there and he was the most valuable player in football, and he was the most valuable player in basketball for this same school, Clay County High School. Most valuable player. I looked at him when he graduated, and I looked at him when he played football, and I would visualize myself a lot of nights, where we used to stand and peep through the fence. And I was there when I could sit in the bleachers, and it felt just like I'd been there all my life.

WE DROVE AROUND ALL THE TIME

On most days, Clay County seems made with cars in mind; on those days when the sky stretches clear above you, the wheel needs barely half a hand, and you ease along well-paved and almost empty roads, where the only street lights sit right downtown, and four-way stops are scarce as snow in April. You don't drive in Clay County, you ride. You ride to the funeral home to view a friend. You ride to the store to see what's going on. You ride around.

In a place with few shops over gas-station size, with fewer restaurants and not a single movie house, riding the roads is sometimes all there is to do. Kids speak of distances in numbers—"two," "five," "thirteen"—not bothering to add that they mean miles, and unless you live right downtown almost no number is low enough to be worth the walk. If you don't have a car, or can't hook up with friends that do, you sit at home and watch TV, or spend enough time on the phone to infuriate the others on your party line.

For some, just to ride is not enough, and so they pass spare hours with tools and vehicles, tuning mufflers to the roar that means more than the freedom transportation offers, coaxing engines to swiftnesses that gain status at Sunday drag races on flat stretches of clear road, that reach in the direction of the Indy-class cars which, twice a year, draw such great crowds to nearby Talladega, to drink beer, to laugh or fight amid the thousands that jam the infield of the track and, as the cars circle round and round, to taste speed far greater than anything at home will ever touch.

LYNN SMITH

My dad's always had a fast car at home. I've always liked just fast cars. Able to outrun most of the rest of the people. My dad drag raced a few times. He always had a fast car and drag raced on the street and stuff like that, and I sort of done that too. He's still got one as a matter of fact. It's pretty good.

I got my first car when I was sixteen. A little old six-cylinder—it wasn't fast. And I fooled with it, and then I built me a car. Went to the junk yard, bought an old body. No tires or nothing on it. Built me an engine, transmission. The car was pretty fast, and I played with it, stuff like that. It wasn't a real fast car, but put some loud mufflers on it and you can make it sound fast.

There wasn't many people that had a fast car. They just had factory cars, say in a quarter of a mile run eighty miles an hour or something like that, ninety miles an hour in a quarter. I tried to get mine to run a hundred or so in a quarter. It wasn't real fast, it wasn't a high-priced motor, just pieces and parts put together. Fixed up. I got another one after that one. I done a little work on it, and it was pretty fast. I drag raced a lot over there in Ashland. I'm not bragging or anything, but I beat every car that I ever raced.

We would start there at Wellborn's cabinet shop, and we'd mark us off a quarter of a mile, and we'd run right there most of the time. On weekend nights. Then we had a place down on the Sylacauga highway, out in Millerville. Sundays, there'd be a crowd of us there. Probably ten or fifteen cars, drag racing up and down the road. We could see for probably a mile, mile and a half down the road. We were pretty careful. I've had people to come down from Anniston and Talladega and everywhere around to race. People's always raced. Somebody's got a pretty fast car, and you think that you've got one too, sometimes you'll come and look that fellow up, just to try him, see how his runs.

It was just having something better than somebody else, or being better at fixing it than somebody else. All my life I've growed up around mechanics. My father, he was a mechanic. My grandfather was a mechanic. All my life that's all I ever wanted to be, was a mechanic. I've always liked hot rods, so I'd take and build my own stuff, and try different things. With just a factory engine, you can change the carburetor or the cam shaft or something like that, and you get twenty or thirty more horsepower, or whatever, out of it. I just like to try all that.

You could get away with it over there at Ashland. You've got two police cars to keep up the whole town. We used to go off and get a little tight, come back uptown and cut doughnuts all around the square. Get the policemen to chase us and outrun them. I've done it two or three times a night. Spin the tires and all that stuff. They never caught me. They knew who I was; everybody knows everybody over there. But they couldn't catch me, and they got to where they wouldn't even try to chase me. They'd just come to my house the next morning and tell my father. They would tell him, thinking that he would get onto me. And here he is, he likes hot rodding and all this stuff too. He would want me to tell him how fast the car was run, and how bad I beat them and all this stuff. And he would sometimes go outrun them. They wouldn't know it was him, but he would go outrun them.

*   *   *

It's a slow-moving town. As long as I've grown up there it's been that way. Didn't even have a picture show in town; they closed it down. At ten o'clock they roll up the streets and cut off the water, you know.

We drove around all the time. Now, I don't care much about getting on the road and driving to the store and back, except when I'm racing or something like that. But then, from the time I got out of school, or when I graduated and went to work, I'd stay on the road till time to go to bed. Just riding. That was about all there was to do, especially on weeknights. There's nothing going on. We'd go over to so-and-so's house, see if he wants to run or something. Maybe he's done something else to his car, thinks it's a little faster, and we'll race him. Or just ride around. Drink beer. Talk. Loafer.

WE DIDN'T KNOW
WHAT SOCIAL DRINKING WAS

BILL BRADY
Forty-three, substance abuse officer,
Clay County Mental Health Center, Bluff Springs, white

Drinking's all these people ever knowed. Several years ago there was a liquor still in every hollow, back when moonshine was big. It was just there. There was never no education about what alcohol could do to you. So it was just a part of society, especially in the backwoods.

I started drinking when I was about thirteen years old. With the older guys that I run with. Started out with beer and went to whisky. Beer was hard to come by back then. The nearest place you could get any legal booze was Birmingham or Montgomery. Eighty, ninety miles. It was mostly white whisky.

There was nothing to do then. One theater, and it was just open on the weekends. Then they shut them down. Friday nights after you carry your girlfriends home, the guys get together. Probably the biggest majority of them did it. It starts with that. Saturday nights especially. And it develops into Sunday afternoons, gets into one night during the week, picks up from there.

We'd drink enough to get drunk. We didn't know what social drinking was, because you had to hide to do it. The law frowned on it real bad. It was very hard to even haul booze up and down the road here. They were down on booze worse than drugs now. So when you got it, you carried it and hid it somewhere. And when you drank it you drank. It wasn't like now these guys ride up and down the road drinking beer, or go to the club and drink a few beers. That was unheard of.

People kept it hid. It was one of these family things, you know, they'll handle it themselves. It had to get really big time bad before you went outside the family. My parents separated when I was about six months old, due to his drinking. But I know of a lot of cases where the women were just really entrapped because there was no way they could support a family. Because there wasn't nothing to do. So many of them were so uneducated that there was just no way they could survive. So the only thing they had to do was just stay there and take it. Nowhere to turn to either.

About the time I finished school I was drinking through all the weekends, and once or twice during the week. I straightened up then, got to going with a good Christian girl, joined the church, lived right for about nine months, and then got back in with some of the old guys. Then I quit through the intervention of my family. I was thirty-seven.

It cost me a lot of money. Fines, car wrecks, insurance. I've been in about nine or ten, total. I've never been in but one that I wasn't drinking, and the guys hit me head-on and they were all drunk. They were estimated running a hundred and fifteen miles an hour. I lost a few friends. I was fortunate. I totaled seven cars, and never had no more than seven or eight stitches put in. Of course you'd probably say I was one of those that come up on the wild side. I run with the rough people. Now I'm trying to live my life straight.

*   *   *

It's a hell of a lot worse than you think here. I can leave here and in five minutes have you anything you want. If you take per population, per capita, this Ashland school per capita, Birmingham schools, it's pretty close.

But of course now it's a lot more wide open than what it used to be. Hell, now on Saturdays you can see them riding up and down the road drinking their Budweisers. It's like drinking Coca-Colas now. But back then, man, I'm telling you what, they'd nail your butt to the cross.

Drinking today is an accepted part of society. It's something that's just mushroomed out. And today, you get this kid that's got a bad drinking problem, you approach the parents and they say, "Well thank God it ain't drugs." So it's all right to drink, but it ain't all right to smoke pot or use coke or whatever.

Peer pressure on kids today is astronomical. Probably a hundred times greater now than it was twenty-five years ago. More of them smoke pot than don't. More of them drinks than there is that don't. There's nobody nowhere whose life's not affected directly or indirectly due to alcohol or drugs. Anywhere.

I graduated in '63. You could of probably went through that school, just random checks, say once a month, through the lockers in that school, and in that whole year I bet you wouldn't come up with ten times that you'd find booze or drugs in some lockers. Hell, you'd find twenty-five or thirty now every time you'd check.

I still have people come to me now that say their kid's got a drinking problem, or a drug problem, they come to me to place him in a rehab program of some kind. And they want it kept confidential. And what the parents come to realize, within a week after they go into the rehab program, they realize that everybody knew he had a problem. He's always the last one to know. So we're trying to do a lot of family education.

They get caught up in that vicious cycle, and by the time we get them, they've done been to the bottom. So this is one thing that I feel like our educational process is really helping. It'll show up on down the line. These people now are going to have some insight, and then you won't have to get as low as these people are getting now before they start doing something about the problem.

Like an alcoholic, why does his bottom have to be when they've lost the home and the car, and he's killed somebody in an auto accident, and they're faced with all this? The thing is getting some education now, so that they can create this bottom for this guy, his bottom can still be while he's got a good job, still making good money, still own the home and the automobile. If the family intervenes to bring the bottom up, you can keep the crisis away. This is things that we're seeing, it's beginning to come into focus a lot quicker than we thought it would. We're beginning to see it come now.

God Has Been with Me
All of My Life

Preceding page: Antioch Baptist Church

Beneath the glare of Ashland's football lights, before the game, the restless crowd grows still to hear a broadcast preacher's voice, offering not a vague appeal to some obscure Greater Being, but a prayer direct to Jesus, delivered with the comfortable assurance that among five thousand lowered heads, despite church splits and feuds, despite disputes over the permanence of salvation and the propriety of ornate churches, over alcohol and music and television preachers, few would quarrel with his words.

If Clay County lies far from any font of any earthly power, another world's map gives it, residents feel sure, a loftier position. A worldly traveler in the county has only a scattered few road markers for a guide, but at almost every crossing a sign directs you toward a church—to Mount Pisgah, to Mount Moriah and Mount Zion, to Bethany, Bethlehem, Pleasant Grove, Pleasant Hill, Pleasant Home, Manning's Chapel, Shirey's Mill, Lystra, Sardis, Liberty, Spring Hill, New Hope. The county's map counts close on a hundred, and there are plenty more—those in the two cities, packed too tight for mention, and the scattering of newer, smaller congregations, that have split off from older churches, or grown out of someone's prayertime inspiration. At times, the edges of the walls and hills around you seem to blur, as people talk of dreams, and visions, and hearing words from God, and sometimes, with someone who has led a long and faithful life, those boundaries seem almost to disappear, dissolving into the more permanent landscape the believer has been waiting on so long.

Before Clay County's lines were ever drawn, country churches were defining dozens of small communities, providing their members with both spiritual and social solace, offering sustenance for the hard, unsteady living that small farmers made, and the unjust fate blacks and sharecroppers so often bore. Many of these churches still remain, the same families sitting always in the same pews, and the growth of the new-brick, modern buildings that testify to their congregations' generous prosperity has yet to overwhelm the scores of old, white wooden structures, carefully painted and maintained even where the members have shrunk to just a handful.

The sway of stern church doctrine has softened from the days when parents would not take back a married daughter, no matter what her husband did to her, and when a man who fought the call to preach says he knew God meant business when a chip flung from a sawmill put out one of his eyes. And barring the religious tempest stirred up by a wet-dry referendum, most people, true to the Protestant creed of individual revelation, do not seem much disturbed by the patchwork the practice spawns. Even when a deep believer can barely get his words out fast enough, his feelings are so strong, he often hesitates, and qualifies, protesting that he does not mean to criticize others or their faith.

Revival and regression roll through the county in waves of good and bad Sundays, barren and fruitful years, rising and falling fortunes from one church to another, and although preachers lament the hunting done on Sundays, although many complain that residents now depend more on money than on God, Clay County remains the sort of place where people in trouble turn first to their church members, where politicians would not dream of skipping services, and where, when you move in, almost everyone you meet asks you where you go to church, and then issues an invitation to try out theirs.

Shopping trips, social gatherings, and phone conversations can lead to long, serious and at times impassioned discussions, on questions of whether a person, once saved, can fall again, of when the world will end (which surprising numbers, pointing most often with pain toward rebellion among children, and with disgust-tinged anger at the prominence gay men have recently attained, expect will happen soon), or on more esoteric points, such as who did Cain and Abel marry, that reflect the nights and years spent in private, careful study of what one preacher offhand calls "this book I use." When in the small office of a filling station, amid the Cokes and Baby Ruths and sticks of chewing gum, an attendant and a salesman, preachers both, leave off their talk of battery displays and turn to salvation and apocalypse, they pleasantly, although earnestly, dispute and agree, pausing only when customers come in, as though the place, and the conversation, were the most natural in the world.

ELVADIE WALLACE
Eighty-six, retired nurse, Ashland, white

I've thought about God all of my life. I knew what was right and wrong from the time that I can remember I was a human being. In here. Just on the inside of me. If that said don't do it, all the king's horses couldn't make me do it.

My dad was from Georgia. He met my mother in Amarillo. She lived in Oklahoma, out in Texas and Oklahoma. They got married. And years ago, people, when they changed climates, they'd have malaria. You've heard it talked about, I'm sure. You'd have chills and fever. So it wasn't long after they were married, the doctors told him if he didn't go back home, he was going to die. He got so bad, he sold off everything but a covered wagon and a team, and he put the family and the bedclothes all in the covered wagon, and started back to home. And we traveled eighteen months in the covered wagon.

I just remember two or three little things. The first time I was frightened to death. We was crossing a high bridge. You could look down and see the top of the trees. And it was just raining like everything. And I was just frightened to death. I just knew that the wind was going to blow us off on those treetops. And then another thing, when it was pretty weather Papa would sleep on the ground. And his head would be by one of the wheels. And so one time I told him, I want to sleep out on the ground too. So he let me. I had my head on the other side of the wheel. Your body was under the wagon and your head out. And just look up. And honey, that was the beautifulest blue sky I ever saw. And great big old stars right in it that looked like diamonds. And I just lay there, and to me that was the most beautiful picture I ever saw. That dark blue with the golden stars right in it. They were just all over the place up there.

Then another thing—and these three things is all I remembered about it. We were going along on a big old mountain, rolling around over here. It was on this side, on my left-hand side. And it was a big valley. Just as green and beautiful, you know. And then over there was another big mountain. And the top of it was covered in snow. And it was so pretty. Here it was green down here, you see, part of the way up the mountain, and the rest of it was covered with white snow.

God was in it. I guess I was just born with a love of the creation. It was a beautiful picture to me, what God had created. So anyway, it went on that way, and all my life I have been that way. I feel like God has been with me all my life, honey. It was on the inside of me. I listened to that. I obeyed whatever that was.

*   *   *

My husband, Marshall, was plowing one day, and he fell between the plow handles. Something happened with his heart. He couldn't work the farm any more. So we moved to Talladega. When we was up there, Marshall got him a job. He was with the foundry. And this union business come in. It was a closed shop. Everybody belongs. And the Primitive Baptists won't let you join any other organization, period. He wouldn't join. So they sent him home.

There we were up there with six children. No work. No money. House rent to pay. Utilities to pay. Groceries to buy. Well, he was in his forties and he couldn't find work. And one day I started talking to my God. And I said, "Well, God, I know you wouldn't put somebody in this world and let them perish to death, if they would make an effort. But where can I make an effort sitting up here on cement? If I was on the farm, we could grow us something to eat." And that's what we needed most. And we'd naturally have a house to live in. "What can I do?" And there was just a voice from somewhere, said, "You can answer lights." Work in the hospital and take care of patients. That's what we called it. Answer lights.

So I said, "Okey dokey, I'll give it a try." I didn't know who to see or nothing. But Dr. Cole's office was right up on the other street. And Miss Ophelia Monroe was his nurse. I said, "I'll go up there and I'll ask Miss Ophelia." I was fixing on a dress, so I put it down, got me a fresh bath and put on my one little old dress I had to get out of the house to go somewhere in. I told the children, "Y'all stay in that back yard now. Mama's got to run to town, and I'll be back in a little bit. Don't you get out of this yard." And I went up to see Miss Ophelia. Told her I needed some work. And I wanted her to tell me who and what and how to get at it. And where was the hospital? So she told me, and I went on up there. That was on a Tuesday. Thursday, I got a call, come to the hospital. I worked there thirteen years. I moved here in '59, and I retired in '77.

I was scared. But I wasn't as much as if I had just gone on my own. I felt like I knew where that idea come from. That helped me to go. Because if He would tell me to go, I felt like He would follow up. And to me, that was the start of God's really taking care of me. I'd never worked, other than in a field. It wasn't long after I went to work that my husband died. And that was how come He didn't let Marshall join that union. Because He knew he wasn't going to live long. And He knew He had to prepare me to take care of the situation. I know that was God in that. God has taken care of me all of my life.

LEWEL SELLERS

The big event in the summertime was the revival meeting. They had three churches here. My granddaddy established the Methodist Protestant church in 1875. But eventually practically everybody joined the Baptist church. In the summertime, the Baptists held their revival the second Sunday in August. Every summer. And everybody went. All the young folks, they looked forward to that revival in the summer. I'd say Christmas and this revival in the summer was the two big events, socially, when they'd get together.

They always had a preacher. And he preached fire and brimstone. Those preachers knew a lot about psychology. They'd get them all excited, and then open the doors of the church, and those adolescents'd pile in there. They'd get them in the summertime and then they'd have the baptizing the last day of the revival. Take them to a creek somewhere or other and baptize them. Those were big events. And a lot of them was sincere. Those young people. Adolescents was what it was, most of them. Occasionally some old man would change his ways and become a member of a church or something like that, but the bulk of them that ever joined were adolescents, I'd say.

I'll tell you a story—it didn't happen at that church, but it happened at another one. This preacher, oh, he was preaching away. And this old boy brought a girl to church. He carried her on in the church, and went back out. Of course, another thing, there was always some liquor there. At the revival, or whatever it was, they had mountain dew there. And the preacher was preaching, and this old boy come in and was walking up the aisle, walking and looking around. And the old preacher says, "Are you looking for salvation, son?" He said, "No sir, I brung Sal Jones here and I'm a-going to take her back."

I never did join. I went to those revivals, yes. Me and another boy, as teenagers, we were together. Where you saw one you saw the other. Well the other boy joined the church at one of these revivals. I didn't join. I kind of fell out with the preachers. I learned some things that they had done that I didn't think a preacher should've done. And then this preacher, after my buddy joined the church, he headed me off one night. He talked to me one hour in the church over there. And the more he talked the further away I got. He told me, it's the great fellowships, and such fellowships as Brother So and So, and I knowed what kind Brother So and So was. And I didn't want any fellowship with him.

I remember one boy that had the gift of gab. And he pretended to be very religious. Well I happened to be sitting by him one night, and they called on him to pray. And you never heard such a prayer as he put up. And after it was over, he said, "Damn, that was hard to do." Now you know that didn't get higher than the ceiling. Lot of people say prayers don't get any higher than the ceiling. That never even got out of the bench.

They'd have girlfriends that was big workers in the church. People'd see them in different places, and all such as that. Then another, they wouldn't pay their debts. Beat people out of what they owed. I remember one fellow in particular, this man kept him in wood one winter. Well, he never paid for all of it. He owed him about fifteen or twenty dollars. Well, he saw him over here in Millerville once, and he asked him how about paying that. He says, "I ain't got a bit of money. I ain't got a bit." And he watched him, and in less than an hour, he'd already paid somebody something. Well that's the kind of rotten preachers we had.

There wasn't many God-called preachers. One that I know, he was working in a graphite mine up here. And he decided he'd go to preaching. Well he went over here across the mountain one Sunday to a church and preached. They made up sixty dollars in money and paid him over there. Well the boy he rode with, going to work at the graphite mines, come by that afternoon— they worked on the evening shift—and he told him, "I ain't going to work." Said, "I'm quitting—I'm going to preaching." Said, "They give me sixty dollars over there preaching last Sunday." Now he wasn't a God-called preacher.

I know of several good preachers around here at Millerville. I'd say it's about fifty-fifty. I knew a good man. He never misrepresented anything, and he was always ready to help. Didn't make any difference whether it was his denomination or not. There was a lot of them though, if you wasn't a Baptist, they didn't have much to do with you.

*   *   *

I am not an outwardly religious man. But I do know there is a God, and there's a Heaven and there's a hereafter. And I can think of two instances in my life that I know God saved me. It was just a split second between death and life. I remember out in California, we were going to Sequoia National Forest. And I had a brand-new A-Model roadster. It was at night. I started to pass a big old truck. And just as I pulled out, there was a car coming right at me, it just shot off the road there. I bet there wasn't that much space between us. Then another time when I was out there, I come up to a place where there was the prettiest creek, and I thought shoot, there's no traffic coming by. I'll just go out there and go in swimming. Well I went in a-swimming, went up and down the creek and back. I don't know how deep it was—it was a good bit over my head, I know. Anyway, I pulled back out and looked up and there was a big sign that says "DO NOT ENTER. DANGER, DANGER, DANGER. Erected in memory of my son who was drownded here." There was suction under there that'd pull you under. Well, the good Lord watched over me that time, I know.

FULL OF MOUNTAINS AND VALLEYS

Longtime Baptist preacher Grady Harris, speaks with slow deliberation, leaving one phrase at a time to hang upon the air and be considered before replacing it, often several seconds later, with the next. He shapes every point with care, puts each detail in place, and his words pile one on another, building toward an apparently unshakeable religious edifice. He has been quite ill, and some fatigue shows in his tall, thin, rangy form as he rests in the front room of a house that belies the oft-told stories of preachers who grew wealthy from their call. Despite a gravel-bitten harshness in the lower ranges of his voice, and a sign on his door that tells of oxygen in use, he smokes while he discourses, flicking his ashes into what looks like a large spittoon filled almost to the brim with burnt-out butts.

He rarely lifts his voice, talking about Hell, miraculous experiences, and the bloody details of the car wreck that led to his conversion in the quiet, matter-of-fact narrative style so many county men adopt when describing anything from a flat tire to a murder. But within the boundaries of this even tone his voice travels a tremendous range—rounding out to linger over certain syllables, then tightening to run quickly through a string of others, rising to a pitch so high and soft the words begin to quiver, then dropping to a hoarse growl of disapproval.

Although his lengthy pauses at first seem like hesitation, he never drops the thread of what he's saying, or appears to be unsure of any of his words. This doesn't sound good, but it's true, he says to preface his description of the way he drank before converting. And although some of his fellow Baptists may have softened once-unmoving opposition to dancing or to Sunday fishing, he has not. If something was wrong twenty years ago, he says without apology, it's wrong today as well.

GRADY HARRIS
Seventy-three, Baptist preacher, Delta, white

I was about thirty-seven years old when the Lord called me to preach. Every time I lay down, all I could hear was the word *preach*. Preach, preach,

preach. Well, I was studying the Bible. I was in the bedroom there, reading the Bible, and I was checking out some references. And it didn't tell out what I thought it ought to. I guess you'd say I got angry. I throwed that Bible on the bed and said to hell with it. That's the truth, if there be a God.

I got up and walked out in the yard. And I saw—now this is from out of the world—a yellow rainbow. With my family in that circle. I come back in the house and picked up that Bible. And opened it—it just fell open. And I've never found it—I've searched for it. But what I read said, "Man, open your eyes and be satisfied with bread." So.

I wrassled with the problem, still wasn't convinced. Back across that hill over down there, you've got a big bottom, maybe twenty or thirty acres. Down here where this house is on the left, there wasn't no house there, there was just road. And I got my start up that road, to go over that bottom. And this sounds like a fool. But I could see every tree in that forest. I could see all of them. Some little, some big, some all warped, some with big knots and what have you. I stood there, and a voice said to me, "This is the shape of humanity." Well, I accepted the call to preach. Told the church about what I told you. They asked me to preach, and I preached. The third time I preached, they called me. I ain't been without a church from that day till this day.

*   *   *

I don't just read the Bible like you read a book. I don't do that. I study it in subjects. In contexts. See the Bible tells you, in Isaiah, a little here, and a little there. Line upon line, and precept upon precept. Now you can sit down and start reading the Bible, and if you think that Bible happened just like you're reading it, you're bad off. Because it's not. It'll be talking about different subjects, different times, different places. When I'd preach on a subject, why I'd find out everything that was in that Bible that was on that subject. And that's what I'd be preaching on.

I could just take a verse, open it up. Like getting out there and go on a rabbit hunt and jump a bunch of rabbits running every which way. But I'm talking about staying with a subject. What God has got to say about it, not what I think about it. You can't just pick up the Bible, and open a verse, and begin palavering around. What I want to know is what God says.

I understand "in the hand of God" now more than ever. In the Bible,

Psalms, it says in the hand of God there is a cup. And the wine is red. And it's full, and He poureth out of the same. And it's full of mixtures. And He's going to pour out of that cup. God's doing that today. And in that cup—now you hear a lot of people preach just one attribute of God. That's love. But that's not all of it. God has more to God than love. God's a jealous God. God hates sin. God is long-suffering. God will punish. And we are created in the image of God, and we've got the same attributes. Now you can choose to hate somebody, choose to love somebody, and so forth. God's a merciful God—God has shown me mercy. A lot of times when I didn't deserve it. If He hadn't, I wouldn't have been around. And He's still showing mercy. God's still long-suffering. And when that long-suffering comes to an end, God is going to clean the house.

If you read the Bible, if you read Revelation, the sixth seal in Revelation, when it is opened—up until the sixth seal is opened, John saw in Heaven the saints, dressed in white linen. But when the sixth was opened, the mountains began to tremble, the earth began to shake, the stars began to fall. The sun turned to darkness. Kings and all began to flee. Because the love of the Lamb had turned to wrath, see. That's the description the Bible gives, not what I think.

*   *   *

Thirty-something years ago, the churches of Clay County would be filled on Sundays. Sunday night, they'd be full. Well, it dwindled down until there wasn't nobody Sunday night. Hardly anybody goes on Sunday night now. Well they used to have revivals, they had it day and night, Monday through Friday night. Now it's at night only. That's all happened in my ministry.

There's been a drastic change. Thirty-something years ago, the people of this country wouldn't put up with hunting on Sunday. They wouldn't put up with fishing on Sunday. But today, on Sunday, there's more people goes fishing and hunting than goes to church. When I went in the ministry, divorces were very scarce. You hardly ever heard of one. When I went to Mount Zion, there wasn't a divorce there. Well there're probably seven or eight now. I don't know, the outlook or something has changed. It didn't change the Bible. The change come through the people, see. Actually, in my opinion—of course, my opinion don't count—the Bible said that there'll come a falling away. And I believe we're living in the day of the falling away. Falling away from our values.

*   *   *

The greatest thrill in the ministry to me is to see a church revived and see lost people accepting Christ. That's the highest peak in a preacher's ministry, when he sees that going on. Then you get tangled up in counseling with people, and what have you, and that's not pleasant, stuff of that nature. I've enjoyed marrying a lot of people. Preached a lot of funerals. Seen a lot of heartaches. And a lot of joy. It's full of mountains and valleys.

TIME IS RUNNING OUT

TIME IS RUNNING OUT

By Rev. Steve Robertson

Pastor of the Ashland Church of God

Are you aware that "prophetically" speaking we are living in the last of the last days. I'm sure I do not have to tell you that people's hearts are troubled very deeply, that the divorce rate is alarming with one out of every two marriages ending in divorce court, that AIDS has put a fear in a lot of our nation, that the world is one big pressure cooker, just waiting to explode with world war, that the devil has almost as good as eliminated prayer and spiritual material from the classroom, and that now, more than ever, is attacking, and sad to say, with success ripping apart at the seams what used to be one of the strongholds of our nation, the family. And on and on we could go with the list.

And yet most people are still living as though life here on earth will just last forever, and they seem to being growing more unconcerned every day. . . .

Fellow Clay Countians, I really have a burden for all lost people of this county. Clay County, as does our whole nation, *needs* desperately a Heaven-sent, soul-saving, Holy Ghost–Baptising, Devil-chasing, genuine, true-blue, red hot, Jesus-bought, heart-felt, Holy Ghost Revival! And I'm praying for God to give us that.

Steve Robertson's description of his faith leaves the unmistakable impression of a struggle, of someone forced to grapple with an unruly flow of power that courses through him with enormous force, but which he has not quite learned how to direct. A rapid string of words spills across the counter of the Lineville garage where he keeps shop, complemented by his face's eager youth and the kind of thinness that suggests intensity. But even while explaining he doubles back to qualify, to anticipate questions or attacks; and at times he comes dead to a stop, marking defeat with an uneasy, nervous laugh.

He has to be encouraged to tell about the spiritual experiences stressed by the charismatic Church of God, in part because he seems always ready for the skeptical dismissal he has heard so many times before, in part because it's hard to find the words. He will embark upon a subject with a handful of terms too often used to have much meaning, abandon them part-way through because they don't say what he wants them to, then grope for other, better ones, but only rarely does he hit on something that seems to satisfy him.

Still, in the moments when he does relax, forgetting the surroundings and talking with more ease—the questions still come up, but only as minor ridges in the conversation flow, dismissed almost as soon as they appear—as he works up enough emotion to hit his words with force, to thump a little on the counter and to lean forward in excitement, he comes closer to his goal, as the tenor of his voice, more than the words he uses, sends off flashes and suggestions of the power he is trying to describe.

STEVE ROBERTSON
Twenty-eight, preacher, Ashland, white

I was hungering for more than going to church. And we'd been going up on a mountain close to the house, and praying after service on Sunday nights, and we began to experience things I'd not experienced before. There was revival in those years, 1979 and '80. I'm talking about real revival, not like a sign: "Revival, March the eighth through the thirteenth," but real revival. In fact four present-day Church of God pastors came from this experience that we had.

I went up on the mountain, and these things might sound strange to you, but I saw young men rolling down the hill. You say what's that got to do with salvation, what's it got to do with religion? I can't explain that. I heard people speaking in tongues. I felt something that was real. You may not understand it, but it's real. We'd go up on the mountain and pray for two, three hours and longer, Close to the midnight hours.

I went to Zion Church of God one Sunday night, in Randolph County, and that was it. That night, they had a prayer line. It's similar to going to the altar. Just like in the Scripture, they anoint you with oil. And I got in the prayer line and he laid hands on me. One of my buddies run out of the church. It scared him to death. It scared me, but I knew there was something to it. The shouting. I got a little taste of it in a sense on the mountain, but not in church. People shouting and praising God. Speaking in tongues. Slain in the Spirit—falling in the aisles. You look and you stare and you wonder what's going on, but yet you feel something from it. And when he laid hands on me I knew beyond a shadow of a doubt this is for me.

I've seen a lot of people fake. I've seen a lot of fake in it. That's what hurts it. I see more of it in the Church of God and the Pentecostal churches than I did in the Baptist church. But it still doesn't make me have second thoughts. For people to say it's not real when they haven't experienced something like this, that's like people telling me, "Well, that pie is not good, but I've not tasted of it." It's real.

You go to somebody's house, they ask, "What is it about speaking in tongues?" It's like, Why? Why do you believe in God? How do I know tongues are real? I try to prepare, and I don't know if this'll justify it, but anyway—when I went to the altar I stayed at the altar an hour at a time or longer, seeking for this baptism. Not knowing what I was seeking. Again, in the back of my mind: "Am I making a fool of myself, God, or should I stay here? Is this real?" Something kept pulling me there. I kept feeling—this again is what's hard—a sensation. A warmness. Or a quickening. Something inside of me. I've heard great men that could not describe it. It's hard to tell.

I want to reach the people of Clay County with what I believe God has laid on my heart. I'm trying to get on the radio; I feel like I can reach more that way. People are eat up with tradition. They're missing so much.

*   *   *

I feel something similar, I believe with all my heart, to what Jesus experienced in the garden, when it says when he prayed, his sweat became as great drops of blood. I've given my life to this Gospel, I hope I can say, and it's all that matters to me, and as long as there's one lost, I'll always feel this way. The deeper I've got into this, the closer that I get to the Lord— there's so many Scriptures that I feel now, that I didn't feel. You sense war, and you sense the stock market, it's unstable, and you sense these things. And it's like when I read God's Word, He knew His time was soon. He knew it. He might not have known to the day. And I don't know the day. But I go to bed with that feeling that the next great event is not going to be world war. Some people have that fear. They're eat up with it. Some people think the stock market's going to fall. When I read God's Word, and I read the signs of the times, and I lay down at night, I just get that feeling. When I shave in the morning, when I shower, it's like at any moment someone's going to knock at the door. The closer I get to this, the more I read this Bible—I get absorbed in it until I know I sound like a freak.

I want to go visit. I want to tell the world. I want to minister to a world. It affects my whole life. It's like I can't do enough. When I preach, I'm tireder on Sunday night than if I had dug ditches. Me and my wife, this has been one of the roughest years of our marriage. Maybe at times I haven't shared with her like I should have. Some times I want to quit it, and say, "Lord, let somebody else do it. I can't handle it; I can't stand this that I feel at nights when I lay down." It affects me that much. And then at times I get that outburst. I'm eat up with that zeal, as one prophet put it.

Even two years ago, at nights I would be going with the other guys to play basketball—which there's nothing wrong with. My buddy called me last night. I think the world of him. He wants to get in a tournament. I don't have any desire to go. I don't have any desire for it. I feel that urgency that the time is soon. I feel it's that soon that I don't have time to be doing these things.

I HAVE GROWN SO MUCH

Vadie Wallace leans forward from her chair, her body tense and urgent, and with a force that seems wholly to outmatch the growing frailty of her tiny form, she wrenches almost any question back to the theme that gives her will its strength and her long life coherence. "Don't you see?" she keeps demanding as she tells of God's role in the way she learned to drive, in coping with her husband's death, and in the five bushels of potatoes she brought in from this year's garden, despite a doctor's warning that pulling even one might break her back. "Don't you see?"

In some conversations, the swell of faith breaks with unavoidable insistence into constant view. In others it tends to peak just out of range, the depth unsounded through descriptions of childhood spitballs and corncob fights, of political activity and of country music, although even the most shallow groping can bring forth an outpouring of description, a rush of deep beliefs that even sometimes troubled lives have not exhausted. Older residents in particular shift to talk of heavenly affairs without a trace of hesitation. And whether they mark the change of subject with a suddenly grave tone, with a gathering intensity or with just the faintest hint of extra, easy rhythm, the faith that they describe, in contrast to the steady stiffening in joints and arteries, seems to have grown over the years both stronger and more supple.

ELVADIE WALLACE

I used to be afraid to go to sleep at night. And the reason that it was, we had a preacher that said if you're saved, and you do something wrong, and you don't get forgiveness before you go to sleep at night, if you die that night, you'll die and go to Hell. If you don't get forgiveness from God. I was afraid of that. It started I guess about ten or eleven years old. When I got big enough to understand what God was.

When Marshall and I married, I was Missionary Baptist and he was a Primitive Baptist, what people call a hard-shell Primitive Baptist. I moved up there. And Marshall was a member, and he was housekeeper at the church. Well I'd go with him. I got to listening. You know there's always been a prejudice between the Missionaries and the Primitive Baptists. Well my daddy and Marshall's daddy was just as bad as any of them could be. And naturally they passed it on to us. But when I kept hearing that preacher, it quieted that fright that I had in my mind. And I am proud to say that I believe it now. When you are one time saved, or born, you are all the time saved and born. So I joined the Primitive Baptists. And that's what I am today. And I'm proud of it.

The other day, this came into my mind. I have said sometime that when I was born was when God shed his blood. That's whenever I was born. I was very young when I come in to know it. Well, it seems nobody else ever thought about it like that. But is your child your child until it's born? And doesn't it shed blood? Have you ever heard of a baby coming into this world that the mother didn't shed blood for it? Well, honey, it's as simple as that. People think it has to be some big mountain of a thing. But God planned things—it's His pattern. And He turned it any which way. Haven't you ever wanted to cut a dress maybe a little bigger or a little smaller? And you turn that pattern this way and that way to do it. Well don't you know God's got sense enough to know how to do that too? Don't you see? And that is when you're born.

But then He lets you get old enough after while that He lets you know, "Well, I'm your daddy." You come to know your daddy. Or your mother. Well that's the way it is with us. With God's children, honey. I think you've got to believe it. You've got to believe it if you enjoy and appreciate your mother and daddy. You've got to know that this is my mother and daddy, not that one over there and not this one here and not that one. Then you are saved from all of that worry. Where's Mama or where's Daddy, or where can I get this or where's that coming from. Well doesn't it look sensible to you?

Before you was born did you know you was going to be born? Did anybody tell you about it before you was born? They planned it. They planned to have children; they wanted to have children. Well all right then, when you were born their plans came true. You were in their minds to be a child. But you had to be born, the shedding of blood, before you were really their child. God and Jesus planned before the world was planned. God gave Jesus His people. He knew who was going to be, and who and what and all of that kind of stuff. God's not that dumb, or He couldn't have done what He's done. When God shed his blood on the cross, that's when His children were His children. Well, if you had a child, would there be anything that would undo that thing, that it wouldn't be your child any more. You see the point I'm trying to say? Now don't that seem more reasonable than all this other stuff?

RUBY KING

I'm a believer in salvation. And God is the major part of my life—He's the major part of my life daily. Now how I respond to that, I have daily prayer. I pray in the morning, and I pray at night. Sometimes it's up in the day before I pray, because my husband is retired too, and he's around. I don't even like for him to be here. I like to go alone and pray. I read the Bible, and I have been reading the Bible more. God is really in my life, and I depend on Him. I depend on Him for guidance. And as I grow older, I try to get closer to Him. And He's more the center of my life now. He's just really the center of my life.

And another thing about it, I am so thankful. Because as I look back over my life—and I have told my children this. My son, he was here for Father's Day. I was telling him that the way I grew up, we never had a lot of money. But I said, "You know, through it all I've been a happy person." And I was telling him about when I went to college. Now my granddaughter is a senior this year, and she'll be going to college next fall. He said, "I wish you would tell her what you're telling me."

I had nothing. We had a very humble home. It was clean, but it was so humble. And I didn't have all those fancy clothes, and I just didn't have a lot of material things. But I was a happy person. I never thought about it. It didn't bother me in the least. And it's just a miracle, as I look back over, how I felt like that. Today, I really can't understand that. I really don't understand it at all. When I went to college, I did have a scholarship, but I didn't have anything else. I was in a play. And I had the leading role. And I said—oh, I can laugh about it today—I said, "Do you know, I didn't have a thing on there that wasn't borrowed but what I had on underneath." I had to borrow everything. I borrowed what I wore. I borrowed a hat. In one scene I had to have a bag, and I borrowed that. And everything was borrowed from my friends, because I didn't have it. But in all of that, I was, say— comfortable, if you want to say that. I had friends, and I never felt bad. I can't understand that.

Maybe that was the spirituality. I think it's something that you're not conscious of, maybe the spirituality. Even though you be making mistakes—I was doing everything a teenager would do. I'm not saying I was a saint. I was having fun. But when I say spirituality, I'm thinking of it now as a person not going around in sackcloth and ashes, with a long, sad face. That you enjoy life, but still you feel that there is a Supreme Being that will help in your life. Even as a child. And you think that, and you're taught to pray. And when it gets kind of rough you get down and you pray. And you get up and you go on. And maybe that's the reason.

In other words, I'm saying on one hand I had a hard time. On the other hand, I'm saying I went through this as a well-adjusted, happy person. And my son, the last time they were here, he wanted me to talk to his children. Because they just think they've got to have all this, that and the other. He said, "Mama," said, "I wish you would tell them what you're saying."

*   *   *

On my spiritual journey I have grown so much. As a Christian, I just feel stronger than I ever have. You ask why—it's because of my experiences. I have experienced God in my life. I have had things to happen, and I have had so much faith. That I prayed so hard. And I felt God answering my prayers. And that's the reason I know there is a God. Because I can feel Him. And I used to pray, and I'd just pray for blessings. But now, I have learned that I can pray for specific things. With that faith, you don't pray just for blessings, but for some specific blessing that you need. And you pray for that, and you have patience to wait, and have that faith and God answers that prayer. I had an experience, since I've been retired. I had neuropathy in my legs, and I couldn't walk. And I can't say that I wasn't ever depressed, but if I was depressed then it only lasted a few hours. I had this faith, and I just prayed. I never did feel like I wasn't going to walk again. And through it all I just kept praying and communicating with God. And then I just got where I could walk. And it was through God. And I can feel Him now. I can feel His presence. You know, that's what faith is. I think I could leave here today. I could just leave here today and feel very comfortable about it.

J. C. AND TINY CHAPMAN
Seventy-three and seventy-seven, retired funeral-home worker
and wife, Shiloh, white

J.C.: I'm not superstitious. There's an explanation for anything that happens, if you'll dig in it far enough. If you dig in it deep enough you can figure
it out. Actually if you're in your right mind, you'll know what it was when it
happens. That's sort of like I was one night at the funeral home. I had two
bodies in the preparation room, and the tables just setting side by side. And
I'd propped this one up with these rolls of cotton, to hold the arms. I was
working on the other one, and the cotton slipped out yonder, and that arm
come back and hit me in the back. Just for a split second right there, you
don't know what kind of feeling you do have. Well by the time it happens
you might see what's happened. But there's a split second there that you
don't know what's happened.

Now I'm a-studying the old Bible to find out what people before me went
through, and what was required of them, and all that kind of stuff. There's
one Scripture in there says "rightly dividing the word of truth." I've heard
preachers say that one part of it contradicts the other part. But that ain't
so. If you'll dig far enough in it, you'll find out that it's all the same thing.
Right now, I'm studying the old Mosaical Laws. What them people all went
through, who it was talking about and where it was at and the time that
it all happened and all that kind of stuff under what conditions. We take a
Baptist paper. And we don't go along with these preachers that writes in
these papers, we don't go along together. Because they haven't dug deep
enough to get all that.

They's some things that you won't never find out. You won't never find
out until you leave this walk of life here. There's lots of things in there that
it speaks of that you won't find out while you're here. Well, human beings is
human beings. And they ain't never going to be as smart as God Almighty is.
You just don't worry about it because there ain't no need to worry about it.

*   *   *

The Bible gives you a pretty good description of Heaven. But you don't
know—you ain't never been there. It's sort of like an old nigger told us
once in the hospital over there, when we went to pick up a body. My friend

told me, he says, "We'll just get this one right here, while we're here." And we wheeled that stretcher in the room where he was at. He went under the bed. He said he didn't know but what maybe he'd died and we'd come after him. He hadn't ever died before. So you haven't never been there before, so I don't know exactly what the whole thing'll be like. I don't think any human being does. The Bible says you can't even imagine what it'll be like.

Tiny: Some people thinks they know, though. The way they talk. I've heard people say they know, and when they died, they'd meet their people and said they'd know them. And I don't think they will. I don't believe that you're going to know your people when you get there. Because there ain't nothing there but your spirit. It won't be nothing like here. Because, I want to tell you—it's sort of funny—if when you get into Heaven you're going to know all these people, what is it these people that've been married so many times, what are they going to do if they get there and see all their husbands and wives? [Laughs.] I've thought about that a lot of times. What would you do?

J.C.: Well, it don't exactly say that you ain't going to know them. If you're lucky enough to make it there, there ain't going to be no worrying and stuff like that.

Tiny: But now when that body dies and goes back to earth, there's nothing in Heaven to meet.

J.C.: Well, I think when you get down to the basic part of the whole thing, it's going to be a spirit world anyway. Because the basic principle of the whole thing is the spirit. And whether people believe it or whether they don't believe it, there's going to more or less be a spirit world there.

*   *   *

Well I think the most important thing I've found is it don't matter whether you're a Catholic, or whether you're a Protestant, or whether you're a Jew— in other words, the type of religion ain't going to carry you nowhere. There ain't but one basic principle, and that's accepting the Lord Jesus Christ as your personal savior, and that's it.

When I started work at the funeral home, and started going to different churches, and seeing their customs and all of like that, I started to studying it. Every denomination's got good points and bad points. Some of the best friends I've got are Roman Catholics. I'd always been taught to have a difference between a Protestant and a Roman Catholic. People are peoples. Regardless of what they believe. And when you simmer it down to it, things that you'd do, I won't do. Things that I'll do, you won't do. We's just people. Far as people's concerned, you might as well say that we're all equal. You take alcoholics. If you need help when you're in a strange place, don't go to a church and ask the church people to help you. Because nine times out of ten they'll turn you down. But if you find that old drunk out on the street and ask him for help, he'll help you. Well, he knows what he is. And that's the way he lives, is helping one another from day to day. I don't think it's good to be an alcoholic. But still, that's human nature. Now we've asked a Baptist preacher right over there in Ashland to help us put a patient on a stretcher, and he refused us. And he's supposed to be one of the fellows that's the most eager to help. It makes you look a whole lot closer than you'd ordinarily look.

Well, there ain't but one way a person can serve God Almighty, and that's to serve his fellow man. If you need help and I refuse you, I'm going to pay for that, one way or the other. And that's the reason I like the country so well. Country people, they might walk around you and not speak to you, but if there ever comes a time that you need help, they'll be there.

ANY TIME ANYTHING WAS LOST

LEWEL SELLERS

My guess is Mrs. Teel came here somewhere around 1912. She was a native of Coosa County. I've forgot her maiden name now. It was I guess three or four years before she started telling fortunes. The first time I ever remember, they had a to-do out at the schoolhouse, and she was out there. I was a teenager, and I got her to tell my fortune.

She made a name, and then more and more came, and it got to where you had to have an appointment with her. You couldn't just come, you would have to have an appointment to get your fortune told. That house right in Millerville is where she lived, across from those stores. It was more on the weekends than other times, but there wasn't a day went by, I don't suppose, that she didn't have somebody there.

She was a very small person. Very active. Moved in a hurry. I just called it fidgety. She was moving around all the time, the way I remember her. The way she'd tell, she'd have coffee grounds in a cup, turn that cup around and look in them coffee grounds and tell your fortune. The coffee had already been made, and she'd have those grounds in that cup in there, look in the cup and read your fortune.

Any time anything was lost, they'd head for Mrs. Teel. If they'd lost a dog, a cow, a mule, or something like that. And then sometimes they'd think somebody stole something, and she could tell where it was at. I've known her to tell that a truck backed up to a certain place and got it. She could describe whatever it was in detail. There'd be something there close to that place she could describe and everything. I guess about as good a one as I remember her telling, they came here from Birmingham, and some boy was lost on Double Oak Mountain. I think they found the person. She told them where they could find him, and as best I remember they found the person. That was just before she had to quit. Sometimes people drowned. I remember one in particular, a fellow about two miles up the road got drowned, and they searched and searched and couldn't find him, and they got her and she went and they found the body. I don't know whether it was where she said, but it must have been mighty close by.

Most of the time, she was a big talker. And you told your own fortune. But when you're talking about looking for something, she'd get down really serious about that, and look at the cup, so they said. I never went for anything like that. And then go back and look again. Try to do a thorough job— be sure she was right. I'd say that at least fifty percent of the time it was close, or mighty close, to where she described it. That's why so many people got to coming, because they'd go back and find out about her being accurate, telling them right where everything was.

My Aunt Doris had to know everything—she couldn't do anything without coming up and consulting Mrs. Teel. Any little old thing. If she wanted to make a new dress, or something or other like that—why she just believed Mrs. Teel on anything. When they'd come in the summer I bet she went half a dozen times, finding out. Of course Mrs. Teel never charged her very much, sometimes nothing. She was good to take care of the poor people too, and to donate to good causes. She would always contribute to all good causes that they worked up. She was a good neighbor.

Most people seemed to think it was a God-given gift. It was something that God give her. But there were lots of people who thought it was the Devil. You had two groups there, them that thought it was God-given, and then the others thought it was Satan in her. They wouldn't go to her no way it could be fixed.

I'd say she started telling in 1918, right after World War I. Up till she got to where she couldn't. She's buried up yonder at Salem. I forgot the year. It was in the fifties, as best I remember it. She had to quit about two years before she died. She suffered with cancer. People came right on up as long as she was able. But it didn't take it long to get around to where she wasn't able to tell. Then people quit coming.

THE GRIEF IS GOING TO COME

The little country store up on the ridge looks out on sloping fields gone gold with the dead grass of winter. Rust has worked red along the roof's tin, and the Royal Crown Cola sign on the composition siding has faded, although the Red Man Tobacco logos on both sides of the screen front door look recently put up. The gray-headed owner is watching a group of younger men run a wire across the road to reconnect the building's electricity. He ran the store for decades, he says, and it made him a good living. His house is right next door. But he's letting another man have it now. Ever since he lost his wife he hasn't done much of anything, he says, pain breaking sudden in his face, and cracking in his voice. Every night, he says then, he goes to bed and hopes he won't wake up.

E. Z. BENEFIELD
Sixty, owner, Benefield Funeral Home, Lineville, white

The endeavor is to treat the person just like you would if he was living. He was due respect when he lived; he's due respect when he dies. I don't allow nobody to go in that prep room that ain't supposed to be in there. I don't allow nobody to leave one of mine uncovered. He's uncovered when we're working, but he is covered back up. I don't allow them to come out of that room, and leave him just laying there. That's one thing about the dignity of dying that you can do something about.

Once the initial embalming is done, you take and you try to restore that face back. This is where you can really make a remains look good. If they don't have dentures, or teeth, then we have a form that we use to fill that face back out. If you care enough, you'll take your time. You work the faces back out, you work the eyes back out, you get the hands placed where they look good. The whole thing being that you care about that person laying on the table. As far as I'm concerned, if Mr. Smith dies, and I've got him on that table, then that's Mr. Smith. And again, if he was due respect when he lived, he's going to get it here when he's dead.

You ask them, "How did he part his hair? Was he ruddy-complexioned, was he fair, what kind of complexion did he have? Did he keep his hair cut neat, or was it a little long?" Every little aspect that you can ask them about, that helps you improve their looks, make them look like they looked before they got sick or whatever. This is what you want to do. It's easier when you fix somebody that you know. A man that I see every day, I know his complexion, I know the way he parted his hair, I know a lot of features about him. Whereas if you get somebody that you don't know, then you can't move the features back to what he looked like, because you didn't know what he looked like.

Most of the time, before death, they get to looking so bad. They get so hollow; their color is so gaudy-looking—it'll be gray, it'll be pale, it don't even look like a human being. So if you bring that face back to where it looks good, then this helps a family.

Death is bad. Most people accept it well, but a lot of people have a hard time accepting death. Even the grandchildren have a hard time with grandmas. And if Grandma looked real bad before death, if you can bring Grandma in here, you can fill her face out, you can put a little lighting on her cheeks and a little color to her lips, get her hair fixed good: "Well, my goodness, Grandma looks so good." This takes away a lot of the heartache that they have. So if you can bring them out to where they look good, then you've accomplished a lot.

You make the family feel welcome here. This is my ideas, my way. This is their place while they're here. They should feel free to go out the front door forty times if they want to, and come in forty times. You get them, and you get your remains in there, and let them get the grief out in the beginning. Some people have a hard time doing that. I can make them feel like this is their home, and if you want to stay till midnight, you stay till midnight. If you want to cry, you cry. If you want to get a chair and sit over here by the casket, you get a chair, you sit it over there by the casket. If you want to stand at this casket for eight hours, you stand there eight hours. If you'll do this with them, you'll see the grief start gradually leaving. And the first thing you know, they're out here drinking coffee, they're up front, they're talking, and it just makes it a lot easier. They see that remains, and they know that it looks good. And they're pleased with the way it looks. They look comfortable the way they're laying. They know they're not suffering any more.

If they hold it in, and they don't cry—now here's the thing about it. When a person dies, say a wife dies, or a husband dies. They bring them over here, and we handle them just like I told you we handle them. Everybody and his brother, boy here they come. They're hugging, and they're telling them they love them, and all of this. Then we have the funeral this afternoon at two o'clock. Nine times out of ten, you can go to that husband or wife's home later, and maybe a child or two'll be there, but that's all that's going to be there. You're not going to see friends. Down the road the grief really comes. So you get it out of them as best you can.

You let them know you did everything you could do. Down the road, they won't sit down when they get by themselves and say "Well, I wish I'd of done so-and-so. I wished I'd got a better casket. I wished I'd of had so-and-so say some words." The real grief comes when Mama or Daddy is sitting at home alone, a week or a month after you bury that mate. Or the child, after you bury a child, when they sit at home, and the little one ain't there. Try to help them get that grief out. Because honey, the grief is going to come. And it's tough for them.

As you know, maybe about twenty percent of the population goes to church. I want you to think of that. Maybe twenty percent of the population goes to church. No more than twenty-five percent. Invariably, this family hasn't been together, prayed together, in a long, long time. A lot of times I've had to find a minister. But we're in the Bible Belt; we're going to have a Christian funeral. Everybody wants a Christian funeral. There ain't no doubt about it, when they get in trouble they want a preacher.

I try to get my families in here, because of the far-awayness that families have from one another. I know—I've got it in my family. I tell my families in the office, would you like to come and have prayer together as a family? I've only had one family that objected to it. You'd be surprised how mellow that makes a family. How they will listen to me. How they won't run. If you don't do this, and they leave here, they just go every which way. But if you hold them together, you don't have that problem.

Let me tell you something. Anybody can bury a remains. Ain't just anybody that can care enough to see after a family this way. I spend my time with the family. I get out here and I sit with them. I talk to them. And I think this is part of me doing what I'm supposed to do. I average about sixteen to eighteen hours a day, when I'm busy here. But I know I'm doing this family good. I *know* I'm doing them good. I feel in my heart that I've given them part of me. So if I do this, I ain't got anything to worry about. I think probably I'd rather be what I am than anything else I know. See, you really don't know. I can talk till I'm blue in the face. But you really don't know till you've went down the road with me. I like this business. I like being able to do something for somebody.

It puts a lot of stress on me. But I've been dealing with it long enough that I know how to handle it. I've been doing this since 1950. When I get through with a family—and honey I'm telling you, this family's mine, they're going to be mine till they get them buried—then I have ways of getting away from it. I go home, and I want everybody to leave me alone. I want to sit there in my chair, with my TV, with my paper. And I don't want to be bothered. One night is all I need, and I'm fine the next day.

A baby's funeral is tough, when you have a young parent. Maybe this is the first child. Or the second child. This is tough. Or you take a fifteen-year-old. Honey, that is tough. Because their parents are young. This child just begun to live and realize what this world was all about. And then probably a twenty-five year old, that's just married and got a couple of little ones. That's tough. And some people handle grief and some people don't.

I compose myself. I'm the leader. I've got to be able to talk to them. Any consoling, I should be the one to be able to handle it. Sometimes I break down. But I try not to. I try to go out behind the shed if anything's going to happen with me. I got to hold up. I've got to be able to lift them up. It's just a matter of I've been doing it a long time, and I care, and I know when, and when not to. I know how, and where to. But your baby, your fifteen-year-old, your twenty-five-year-old. . . .

I had a funeral one time, it's been several years ago, and I can hear this child just as clear today. The man was fifty-five years old, and he had shot himself. His health was bad, that was what was wrong with him. I'll never forget this little grandchild, four to five years old. We went in the church, we had the funeral. Then I opened the casket afterwards. And that is the hardest type funeral you can have. You bring out more grief, they get to playing these old church songs, "Farther Along" and all this, and the preacher talks, and he gets them all revved up, and it's just killing them. It just starts over everything we went through at the funeral home a little while ago. But this particular family, I had all of the friends went around, and then I brought the family. Then before I could close the casket, about a five-year-old grandchild ran up, and he went to saying, "Paw-paw, don't leave me. Paw-paw, don't leave me." This child—it just remains in my mind. That kid tore me and everybody else on the staff out of the frame. I had to get a parent to come up there and get him, so we could close the casket. The little people get you. Honey, they get you. I'm glad they can. Because if they couldn't get me, I wouldn't care.

Sometimes you get discouraged. You get a family in here—and I have them, honey—that couldn't care less. I have them that'll sit, and talk about their mama, and say it don't matter. Just whatever you want to do—it don't matter. And that kills me. I mean sit and look at me, and that's their mother back there, and they tell me it don't matter. That's hard for me to handle. But I go right on with it. And I treat them just like they cared. And all the time I'm burning up inside, because I know they don't. But I can't ever get to the point that I say, "Oh, what the hell. It's useless. I can't help them." I don't ever get to that point. Sometimes I feel like it. But I don't. Because maybe down the road, maybe something I said, or something I did might make them think, well, maybe it does matter.

We were talking about the singing once. "It don't matter." I said, "Yes it does matter. You're not going to do this again. This is your mother—you ain't going to do it again." So I guess it did matter, because about three hours later he called me back and says, "We've decided that we're going to get somebody to do the singing." See what I did? It did matter.

Why does it matter? Because I've got to feel like that I have done everything that I can to make it easier for them. I have got to do everything I can. If it hadn't of mattered, he wouldn't have called me three hours later and said how about we go ahead and get some singing. The caring and the mattering is what's important. If we don't do this, down the road you're going to die, they're going to come get you, and they're going to roll you in a sheet, and they're going to take you to the cemetery. And everything that this nation was founded on, our beliefs and everything, it ain't going to matter any more. I don't want to be rolled up in a sheet and dumped in the ground. It's the end. When you're born it's your beginning, and when you die it's the end. And I believe in it. It does matter.

You Always
Think of Home

Preceding page: Lizzie and J. C. Colley

L. D. LAMBERTH

I wanted to go in the army and see the world. Or the navy, one. Well, I was going to be a cowboy to start with. Wound up sitting under this apple tree.

Even for someone who has never lived there, Clay County reaches out to tug at images that living in this country often lodges in a person's heart, where the waves of untouched, grassy fields, the neat barns built so many years ago, and the lines of clean white laundry swaying in the wind evoke the sort of quietly persisting calm you might well hope to find in a place you would call home.

Many of those now in the county have tried the world outside—sometimes for a few months, sometimes for a whole career—and from almost all of them you hear the same set of refrains. You lived too close together. The noise weighed on your nerves. You didn't know your neighbors' names. Over and over they tell you that coming to Clay County is like reaching back in time, like living on among the values and surroundings that in so many other places have somehow disappeared. For many in nearby towns who remember county life, and even those whose parents or grandparents left before their birth, the mention of Clay County brings forth a smile and the sudden, opening nostalgic warmth that marks them as people living still a sort of exile, who have had to leave the innocence of country life and country folks behind.

Such constancy does not live always free from trouble—some residents leave less as exiles than as fugitives and are rarely, if ever, seen again. An at times near-blind adherence to old leaders, old ways, and old ideas can, with the kind of lacerating anguish that results when strife breaks out within a family, tear at those who love so much about their home, but who despair at its resistance to the things they think would render it more prosperous and more just. A woman who has been there close on three decades, and whom many laud for what she's done for those around her, says there are times when she still feels like a stranger. One black man, who left Lineville for Chicago almost that long ago, has been back only once, when his wife got sick while on a visit, and he had to make the trip to bring her home.

Most people, though, have made peace with their surroundings, and the pain and problems that confront them seem often lightened by the soft curves of the hills, by the cool air underneath the trees, and by the vanishing light at dusk, when the fields grow dark, woods rustle with the sounds of moving deer, and lights have come on in the houses and the few small stores that stay open after nightfall. Even with the changes it has not been able to avoid, Clay County remains an image, a feeling, a belief that you can fix within your mind and not worry that its substance, as time goes by, will somehow slip away; a friend on whom age has worked some alterations, but who in essence is the same; a place where you can spend an afternoon in unhurried, small-town talk, where you can still sleep deep and undisturbed; a quiet and enduring refuge.

I DON'T THINK I'LL WANT TO COME BACK

DAVID GOOD

I was probably about three when we moved here. So I've spent practically my whole history here. Mama was from Sylacauga, and Daddy was from Kansas. They let Daddy come back from Vietnam and do an extended tour over here. Then he quit and just farmed. We used to live down in the valley over here in a trailer house. Then when he got some money together we built the house. We used to have mostly beef cattle. Now it's chicken houses and brood cows.

I like it around here, but I don't have any real massive ties to any of it. I think I'd like to live in New England, but I don't know that. I've been to Washington—me and my friend went to Washington for graduation. And we drove around up in there, and it was neat. I don't think I'll want to come back. Not after all my friends move out.

I don't know what I'm going to do. I'm thinking about architecture. One of my friends wants to be a neurosurgeon, so he's probably going to end up in Birmingham. Or in New York, if he makes it. And one of them, he hated it around here, but now he kind of likes it. He was going to be a lawyer, but now I think he's going to be a teacher.

With a college degree here, you could either be managerial at a plant, and there's a need for lawyers and doctors and things, just like anywhere else. But there's only a very finite number of them that can be around. You could teach school. That's the biggest body of professionals in the county. There isn't much engineering or architecture that you could do around here. I'm sure if you were good enough people would come to you, but you'd have to go somewhere else to attract attention to yourself. So I don't really know.

I doubt I'd like the big city. I hate wasting my time standing in line and waiting in traffic. That's just the biggest waste of time I could think of. I guess I'd have to be some kind of suburbanite. I guess just an average-size town, something like Sylacauga or Talladega that was pretty close to a big city where you could get access to everything. I guess I'll have to live in a big city for a while if I'm going to be an architect. But I don't have any idea if that's what I want to do or not. I'd love to be a musician, but I'm not good enough at it. I might try, though. I might like to be a college professor.

The farm's nice. Kind of get out in nature and work; it kind of takes your mind off things. But I wouldn't want to do it all the time. Farming has got to where you've got to work all the time on books and everything else. You've got to be a financial genius to make any money farming. And chicken farming's not laying in the meadows and gathering berries. It's like slugging through crap.

*   *   *

In college, the everyday people are different. But I hang around with the same kind of people that I did in high school. People that can think. Philosophical discussions and things like that. People who don't think everybody else ought to be just like them. We used to talk about all sorts of things. I remember one big discussion we got into about the origin of thoughts. I thought that was pretty fascinating.

People here don't like different things, I don't think. I guess they thought Daddy was fine and everything. But it seems like a lot of people like to cling to regional things. Rebel flags on trucks and everything. I don't feel like I'm one of them, but I don't feel like I'm an outsider.

You can do what you want to. It might not be popularly accepted, but they're not going to come burn your house down. People are very much nosy around here, but that isn't going to bother me. I doubt many people ever too much worried about what I thought. Or what I did. I don't know. After I got this earring, that was a big topic of conversation forever. "What's that mean, you're a faggot?" I didn't really understand that at all. It was at the beginning of summer. It amazes me. I'm glad I did it now, because it tells me how much little things like that can just blow people's minds.

I used to have real shaggy hair, and wear concert T-shirts to school. One of my friends in Ashland, he's got hair down to about his waist, he used to. Bleached blonde. He was pretty bizarre. It's kind of like if you've got different views, and you get caught up in a place that doesn't appreciate different views—rebellion's pretty common among kids anyway. I guess long hair and everything else is just that.

There's a lot of good things about Clay County. I like the woods and everything. You can find solitude, if you want it. And there's a lot of nice people around. Most of them, the older people, have very much a Christian neighbor sense; they've got a sense of community. And that's all good. I never really thought about it much. I think it's all a great idea. But I don't want to say I feel a part of it. I guess I'm more transience than permanence. And they're extremely permanent.

DIANA GRIFFIN
Thirty-eight, building-supply dealer, Spring Hill, white

I had always thought—and I guess this is the way you are when you're young—I'd always thought we would live some place other than right there. But my husband's not going to live anywhere but right there.

It's like you said—the ones that stayed, liked it. The ones that came back, they like it too. So who's to change it? Every once in a while you've got somebody like me who'd like to see things change, or this one or that one. And, well, they're just a troublemaker. Or if you don't like it here why don't you move? There's been lots of things that could have changed. But it was resisted. They do resist change, very much. They like it like it is. They think it's God's country.

There are some nice things about it. And I really like it now that I can come to Talladega during the day to work. And I can go back there at night. I think I have the best of two worlds. I have an out, and then I can come back here to this quietness and this peacefulness and this countryside. And I like that.

You know, I just can't help but believe you'd be bored in Heaven, if it was all the same. If nothing ever changed and nothing ever happened. And I'm not talking about big excitement either. I'm just talking about growing. Growth in general.

But it is nice at night. It's quiet, and it's very rural. I enjoy that part. My husband tells me I wouldn't be satisfied anywhere. Maybe I wouldn't. Who knows?

IT SEEMED LIKE IT WAS HOME

MORLAND FLEGEL

There's people for big towns, and there's people for little towns, and I'm not a person for a larger town. Now they're great, don't misunderstand me. But I feel that raising the children this would be a much better place, and I'm convinced that it is.

I was born in Kulm, North Dakota. I grew up on a farm three miles from town. In 1963 I moved to Clay County and started my business, the dry cleaning and laundry business. And I've been very happy and very much stayed put since. My business was just something I thought I would enjoy. And it was. I have very thoroughly enjoyed my work. Making my own decisions. If it's a good decision, fine. If it's a bad decision, I'm the one that made it. And I have confidence in myself.

There's something fascinating about the person to person contact with my customers that I love and enjoy tremendously. It has been one of the highlights, I think, of my life here in this business. You sit there ironing—every time I do a pair of trousers for someone, or whatever, I'm employed by them, contracted by them to do this. It's been a real good experience, and frankly, the relationship has been real, real good.

*   *   *

A lot of times I think we have been handed so many things in life that we couldn't handle an adversity. This possibly was exemplified in the crash in 1929. People losing their wealth and their money, and there were suicides and people jumping off of buildings when the stock market broke and they couldn't face it.

In this county I think you see great strength. I think you see a lot of ingenuity. I think you see a lot of ability, great natural ability. I see that. They can not only handle one small adversity, but they can handle even a greater adversity. I feel that there are a lot of people that I've seen that have the inner strength and the knowledge of life—all these things and the assurance, you might say from their Maker, that they can pretty well handle it as it comes.

With many people you can feel it. Things that they say. Their actions. Knowing them, you know. Seeing them from one day to the next, you might say. Seeing them handle various situations that arise. Their philosophies. I think that our actions reflect our philosophies, and our philosophies will be reflected to the other person. Like seeing a pair of eyes on a roadside of a deer. It's not that those eyes are great big shiny objects. It's because of the light striking, and it reflecting. To me, life is somewhat that way. Seeing people and getting to understand them through their actions and their words. Here, I see people that are concerned about their neighbor, and that truly love one another. Go out of their way to help. There is without a doubt that. Now as far as people thinking that they missed the boat, so to speak, in life, no. Not at all. Because they've lived a good life, in all honesty. Something to be proud of.

BECKY AND JERRY HOLMES
Twenty-seven and thirty-two, teacher and construction worker, Delta, white

Becky: We moved down here a little over a year and a half ago. My husband's a big hunter, loves to hunt and fish. And he had been interested in moving out of Calhoun County into the country. We were looking for a place with nice neighbors, and closer to Atlanta, for him to work. We had looked for about five years, and had never settled on one place. Then I came down here, and looked at this, and fell in love with Clay County. It seemed like it was home. I went home and said, "I've found the place. We're going to move."

Jerry: I've always talked about living so far back in the sticks they'd have to pipe sunshine in to me. I've always wanted to live out in the country. Ever since I've been old enough to know anything about living. I've always been a pretty good hunter, and I'm a pretty big fan of the cowboy movies. I've really enjoyed it out here. I don't go into town unless I just have to. She brings everything to me. I stay right here.

Becky: I'd never lived anywhere where I wouldn't be at a store in five minutes. He didn't want to buy this at first, because he said I wouldn't live down here. But I feel safer down here than I did in Anniston. I'm not as nervous about being on my own at night. I'm happy down here. Wouldn't want to move back.

I was kind of scared about moving because I had heard that people that have lived here all their lives won't welcome newcomers. And I thought this is going to really be hard, and we're going to really have to watch everything we do. But we hadn't been here a week, and the knock come on the door one morning about seven o'clock, and I went to the front door and there stood Cub Haynes with fresh vegetables from his garden. Everybody made you feel so welcome till you soon got over your uneasiness.

When we went to the first community center meeting, I backed out and said I wasn't going in. This is it, take me home, we won't belong to anything down here. And Jerry took me in and took me over to Betty Haynes. And he said, "Mrs. Haynes, will you stand over here with Becky so she won't be afraid. I think she's going to cry and run home." Then I was OK. And they were just so friendly till it wasn't hard to get used to going. They invited us to join, and it just grew from there.

It's more relaxing down here. It's kind of silly to say, but I've told Jerry every afternoon after I turn off of Highway 9, I can feel myself relaxing, because I know I'm fixing to be home. In the summertime you can sit out on the porch in the mornings, and you drink your coffee, and you walk to the lake, and it's just so peaceful and quiet, and I like that. I've never been where it's quiet before. You can even hear hoot owls out here.

I think it really changed me. It changed him too. We've both changed. It's made me more willing to give and to take. I'm more relaxed. I guess I'm kind of a hyper-tense person. I just go on this nervous tension all the time. And I relax more down here and I'm outside more and I'm doing things I've never really done before. I'm willing to put in a garden. I cut grass. I canned this past year. I made jellies and things. And I fish and I help clean them. It's just changed me.

Jerry: It's made me lazier, is what it's done to me. Made me lazy. When I lived in Anniston I'd come in, hit the front door, sit down and eat a bite, and get mad if supper wasn't ready. Go out in the yard and I'd stay out in the yard till eight or nine o'clock, and I'm talking every night. Down here you come in, you eat a bite of supper, you get in this chair right here. It's a good place to live.

Becky: He's serious. He's not stretching it. A lot of nights, he wouldn't even come in the door when he would pull up in the driveway. He'd just head straight out back in the shed and go to doing around. And I wouldn't see him till he come in and showered and went to bed.

A lot of people don't believe it, but living in the city, or even on the outskirts like we did, keeps you in a nervous tension, just with the hustle and the bustle all the time that goes on. Hurry and get to sleep, you've got to get back up and get going the next morning. Here we have less time to do, but it seems more like you have more time to do. It seems like I get more done.

It's made a total difference in us as a family. Before, we had so many things around us to distract us that we never took the time to be a family. We'd grown apart. Because we led separate lives, really. He went his way, and he was gone all the time. I had my own life. We were kind of like strangers passing in the night. See each other every couple of days, and a little bit on the weekend, because he hunted and fished, and I never got to see him because he wouldn't take me with him. And down here, see, I'm the only one he's got to take. We had gotten to the point where we never seen each other, we never done anything together. We were just always so separate. And when we moved down here, it just pulled us all back together.

WHERE THE SUN SHINES THE BRIGHTEST

JOHN WILSON
Forty-two, textile-plant worker, Millerville, black

I got sick of Alabama. Just the whole thing of Alabama. Like when the civil rights started. Because this black lady sits on the front seat in the bus. This white lady asks her to move, and she refused to move because the old lady was give out from working hard all day. And then the bus driver was going to demand that she move. I'd rather be somewhere else than be in this junk. So I said, "Well, up North I know it's different."

I had an uncle up in Massachusetts, and I said, "Well, I'm going to go up there with him a while." Every time he would come home, he'd say, "Tell John to come on up and stay a couple of weeks and see how he likes it. I know he can get a pretty good job up here." Back then, here, you either pulpwooded or you worked at a filling station pumping gas. That's all there was. I knew good and well that doggone tree would be too heavy on my shoulders. And I ain't never liked pumping gas and checking oil. And plus you wasn't going to be getting paid nothing for it. Let me go somewhere where I can get a job in a factory or something like that.

It was a lot different from what I thought it would be. It wasn't a friendlier place. I lived in Massachusetts for two and a half years, and never did know my next-door neighbor's name. Didn't know their first or their last name. Then you don't know who to trust. Down here, you know just about who you can trust and who you can't. If you know them, you just about know how they feel.

While I was up there in Massachusetts, I told a guy, I said, "Well, I think I can deal with the South better than I can the North," I said, "because in the South, if white people don't like you, they'll let you know." I said, "Up here in the North, peoples'll skin and grin in your face, and then you turn your back, they're ready to cut your throat." I said, "I'd rather be in a place where if I'm liked, let me know I'm liked. If I'm not liked, let me know I'm not liked. And I'll make myself as scarce as possible around you." If there's a prejudiced joker, he'll stick out like a sore thumb. You know it. He knows it. So you just don't bother about being around him.

I was living in Springfield, Massachusetts, and I was working in New Haven, Connecticut. Pratt & Whitney Aircraft Division. Building dependable jet engines. Back then that was one of the highest-paid jobs around there. I worked there for about two and a half years, and then they opened up the armory up there in Springfield, building guns that they were using in Vietnam. One-fifty-five-millimeter machine guns. And I did that for about two years. And then after Vietnam started ending, that closed down, and I started working at A. G. Spalding, sporting goods.

When I came back, I didn't come back to stay. I said, "Well hey, I go home, I stay two or three weeks—I'm going to stay as long as I want to. And then when I get tired I'll come back." And this thing led to that thing, and next thing I knowed I was married, hooked up, tied back in Alabama again.

BOBBY FABLES
Forty-seven, retired soldier, Mellow Valley, white

Along about 1965 I was stationed at Fort Benning, Georgia. They asked us to volunteer to go to helicopter maintenance school. And at that time I'd never even heard of Vietnam. So one day there was three or four of us talking, and there was two of us said, "Well, let's sign up." So we signed the little old paper, and turned it back to headquarters, and about a week later a man came to see us. He said, "We're looking for some good men," said, "You'll go to helicopter maintenance school, and then you will go to Vietnam." I had to get down the world map to see where the country was. So we left Fort Benning and went to school six months, and upon graduation we had orders for Vietnam. We was assigned to the military advisory command in Vietnam.

For the first month or two, it was just like being on a vacation in Florida. But then as time went on, and things picked up, it just got worse and worse. About the time I had been there six months is when the fighting actually started. The snipers and stuff started picking on us, at our compound. Every time an aircraft would take off, they'd shoot at it. Every time we went anywhere, downtown or any place like that, we would be shot at. So then in February of '66, they brought in about three or four thousand marines around the area where we were. It was only a handful of Americans there to start with. Before I was wounded, we was operating twenty-four hours a day. You'd just sleep a little when you could. Aircraft went out day and night, picking up wounded, dead.

They finally attacked our compound. They overrun our area and wiped out just about our whole company. In our group, they killed twenty-nine, and wounded seventeen of us. I was one of the lucky ones. They transferred me from there to the Philippines, and then they transferred me on to Washington, D.C., to Walter Reed Medical Center. I stayed there a year. It took a year for everything to heal, get patched back up, where I could go to work.

After I was in the hospital for three months, I came back to Clay County. I never run into any hard feelings against the war there. Now we went to New Jersey—me and my buddy got out of the hospital one weekend, and we went to Elizabeth, New Jersey—and that was the first time I had ever run into any demonstrators that was really bitter against the war. There was a few there. In Clay County I've never heard anybody say anything real bad against the war. Except they couldn't understand why we were there to start with.

They had an idea of where the country was located and stuff. But they didn't have any idea of what was going on. I found out that most of them were interested in what was going on. They wanted to know how I felt about it. There was always a bunch of questions being asked when I was home. Did I think that we could win the war? Did we think that Congress and stuff was supporting it? Or, should we have ever been there to start with, and why was we there? Just questions.

You've heard talk about the drugs they used over there. Well, a guy's sitting out there, he's looking at it this way—"They don't give a damn about me back home. I'm stuck here in the middle of this jungle. I'm going to die anyway, so why not go ahead and take a little of this?" I found that to be the case a lot of times. But those from Clay County, they didn't have that feeling as much. You talk to some of the guys that was from New York and California—California was the worst place. But just about everybody from Clay County felt like that people really cared about what was going on, and cared about them.

*   *   *

I was hit with shrapnel, mostly. I lost part of my right foot, and a piece went in my hip, and in my head, and my right eye. Pretty well all over. The blast was on the outside of a concrete wall. That's where I got most of the concrete stuff from.

I really didn't think about home until I guess it was the next day. When you first come to, and you're realizing where you're at, trying to figure it out, then your next thought turns to home. The old doctor, he said when I woke up, the first thing I asked him was when was I going home. I didn't even remember asking that. The closer I got to home, when I'd wake up, the more I would think about it.

After I got to Walter Reed, then my family was there. And that made it worse—you're really homesick then, after you see your family. Then most of the time I spent in the hospital, that was always on your mind— "I want to go home. I want to get out of this place and go home." After about three months, my doctor said, "If you can stand up, and learn to walk with crutches by Friday afternoon, you can go home." This was on about Wednesday. And I said "Well, I'll be on that plane. Get me a ticket." And I was.

You miss everything. You miss your family. You miss just the way of life. I liked to fish then, and I like to deer hunt and stuff. You're laying in the hospital, you get tired of just laying there looking at the same walls. And no matter wherever in the world you go, or what you're doing, you always think of home.

I stayed in service twenty-one years. I retired in '81, came back here. You meet a lot of people in the army that says, "I'm never going back home." I used to always tell them, "Well, if you was ever in Clay County, and drank that Clay County water, then you'd always go back." I don't guess over the years the thought of staying gone ever occurred to me.

MIRA CARMICHAEL

You can't quite put it into words. The feel that I had for Father. The feel that Father had for family, and friends. And the feeling that I had that people here were my friends. I've made very few friends that are as close as some of those have been. I don't know what it is. I still see the beauty in our hills. I still see the colors. In the springtime, and in the fall—the changing trees, and all the things like that.

When I was growing up, there was a couple of old unmarried brothers that were so nice to young girls who were growing up. They weren't dating anybody especially. But they taught us all how to—how to let our friends be nice to us, I guess is what I'm trying to say. Somebody asked one of our friends to write something about our brother Omer one time. And she said Omer didn't date any of the girls. He was part of the group. We played together. We didn't ask anything of each other particularly. We'd just be together and just be. Well now, that seems to me to say a lot about the pull that I just never get away from.

I finished high school at Goodwater, had two years in college at Montevallo, and later went to Nashville to business college, and worked in business. I worked just ordinary office work for a good many years. I went to New Orleans with a government agency in 1934. Later I switched and took a job with a millinery company, selling hats, and went up into Pennsylvania, spent a year in Reading, and then a couple of years in Chattanooga. Finally I wound up working for Uncle Sam in Washington, D.C. Started as a clerk-typist, worked with the War Department and the Veteran's Administration, and then transferred to Maxwell Air Force Base. I spent the last nineteen years of my career at Maxwell, and worked up to a base procurement officer. So I'd lived round and about, and done a number of different things. I've lived here since 1971.

I missed home, I guess, as much as anything else. This might tell you. I remember I was active in my church in Montgomery, and one Sunday night, after church, somebody said, "Where were you last Sunday?" I said, "I went back home last Sunday—to Clay County." And I said, "That's where the sun shines the brightest, the stars twinkle the greatest, and the moon is the prettiest." And he said, "Oh you needed to go home."

J.C. AND LIZZIE

The rampant green growth of summer has come up long and wild around the wood frame house where J. C. and Lizzie Colley, both with eighty years of life behind them, have spent most of their earthly sojourn. Pine trees have grown up in all directions, and the sunny circle of the house and garden is like a lighted island in a restless sea.

They would like, says Lizzie, to get someone to cut the grass, and clear the fields, and maybe even plant again, as they did year after year when farming was the only work they knew to do. But the farm is too small, she says, and too far out from town to interest anyone today.

J.C., who loves the country life, says with confidence that the once-lively community of Mountain, founded by his pioneer great-uncle Joe, will live beyond his lifespan. His children have made other homes, some far away, he says, but there are grandchildren, and at least one of them will be glad of the house his father helped him build back in the depths of the worst depression the country ever knew.

His wife says she is not so sure.

J.C. has cast his lot with an uncertain group of allies, with the elusive longing for the sweep of open fields and the solitude of untouched woods, with the need for family and for home, against the multiple attractions of a distant, prosperous world. For decades it has been a mostly losing fight.

But still those like him watch and hope that in the coming generations at least a few will love the county well enough to make the sacrifice that living there requires, to fill the hills and hollows with something other than the shades of recollection, to move into their houses and protect them for a few more years from the relentless world outside.

Once the home J.C. and Lizzie made is left alone, it will stand defenseless to the swell of vegetation that has already reclaimed the field and, in a short few decades, has overwhelmed so many spots nearby, treading the steady path back to the age when the woods stretched unbroken all around.

But for a moment yet, the grass is held at bay.

J. C. AND LIZZIE COLLEY
Eighty and eighty-one, retired farmers, Mountain, white

J.C.: I was born up the road a mile in 1906, in July. I left home one time—
I went to work for fourteen cents an hour. In a cotton mill. It was 1925. I
had an old T-Model car, and an old friend went with me. He lived up the
road a little piece, and he had a family, and he wanted to get on and get him
some money. And we went down at night, come out at West Point, Georgia,
up in the morning a while, and give forty cents for some ham and eggs for
breakfast. Went on down to the mill and got a job, and went to work that
day. It wasn't hard to get a job.

I stayed gone a while, but I got homesick, and they got another grade
in school, and they wanted me to come home to get enough pupils to get
another class. I come back. And she caught me.

My dad told me he'd help me build this house. He lived up yonder. He
says, "I'll help you build a house if you'll build it close enough that we can
holler." In hollering distance. They was getting old, you know. We moved
here in '33. People were leaving here at that time. We didn't give them a
thought, I don't guess. Just let them go.

You nearly had to work all the time. You made a crop, then, in the summer. But when it got laid by, you had about a month, and we'd go to singing
schools and revivals, have about a month that we just had a pretty leisured
time. Then we went right back in to save our crop. That would last till you
got through on up near Christmas, then we had to go to cutting wood.

Lizzie: Well, the women had to can and dry fruit, and stuff, they really
didn't get off [laughs]. Of course, there was nearly always something to do.

J.C.: She wouldn't have no boy babies, had girl babies. Well I had to have
some help, and they'd help me plow. She said if she had any boys, they were
going to help in this house. She did, she had two boys then, and she put
them to milking. They'd go to the barn and come back with milk all over
them; they'd squirt milk on one another, and the old cat'd sit up, and they'd
squirt milk in his mouth—they played more than they worked.

Lizzie: Lot of difference from now and when we started. I'm glad young
people don't have to work so hard.

J.C.: But we've been sort of lucky, though. My brother-in-law bought an
old Chevrolet pickup in 1937. Well, things didn't work out so good for him. I
drove a school bus two years, and I swapped him my old school bus for this

pickup and taking up his payments. And so we had a good truck in 1938. We was doing as about good as anybody in the country, because we had a good pickup truck.

We've been pretty lucky all our lives, I guess. Never did have very much. But we did have a way to go about as early as anybody else here in this country.

Lizzie: In the community.

J. C.: In what?

Lizzie: In the community.

J. C.: Yeah, down in this community.

Lizzie: We've got a lot of pasture. Our son comes and works a little bit of it, trying to keep it from growing up. It's terrible—I just hate it. We tried to get somebody to cut it, but it wasn't a big enough place for anybody to come in and cut. I wish somebody'd tend it; it'd look so much better around here. But nobody wants to get off down here.

J. C.: I don't think it's way out nowhere—I like it down here.

Lizzie: I can understand young people don't want to get off down this way. Most of our young people go somewheres to work for money. And I don't blame them, they couldn't make a living on a farm. Just couldn't do it now.

J. C.: I went to Alexander City and got a job in 1960. We quit growing cotton then. I got that job and we quit. We needed a little more money. Times began to change, and you had to sort of change with the times. Just to live, and to have things like other people had.

Lizzie: We didn't stay but eight months. I loved it. There were lots of people. Where I lived, I had neighbors close by. And there were people, and I could hear the children playing. I just loved it. He wouldn't stay. We ought to be down there now. We'd be close to somebody.

J. C.: I just liked home. We come back, we had a garden. And corn, we had some here every year. I just wanted to come home. I don't know what it was.

Lizzie: It wasn't that bad.

J. C.: I kept my cows here all the time.

Lizzie: You could have sold them. We had everything we needed. I didn't have any neighbors close to me when we was off in here. I couldn't walk, couldn't drive—I couldn't go anywhere unless he carried me. In Alexander City, I had neighbors all around me, and a pretty house. I just liked it. Well, if I can better myself, I want to do it. But he wouldn't stay.

J.C.: I don't know that I was bettering myself.

Lizzie: Well you was, if you could just of took it like that.

*   *   *

J.C.: The community's going to stay on somehow, I guess. We'll move out some of these days, and we've got some grandchildren, some of them'll want to live here.

Lizzie: I doubt any of them want to live here.

J.C.: They'll come here. They'd have to build a house, and a lot of them can't build a house.

Lizzie: They've all got jobs now. They're not going to come.

J.C.: But they stay at home. They'll live around here, they'll want to live around here.

Lizzie: I don't know about that. I can't tell.

*   *   *

Lizzie: We dated two or three years. We lived in the same community, and I guess just knew each other a-growing up.

J.C.: At recess, we all got out and played ball—she was a tomboy. Then got to playing basketball. Just growed here together. Yes, sir, if there was anything to do, we both went. Sometimes her mama'd go with her.

Lizzie: My mama never did go with us.

J.C.: Yes, she has been.

Lizzie: On a date?

J.C.: Well I'd carry you home, we'd be at church or something, and she had to go home, and you'd be with her, and of course we all went.

Lizzie: He's dreaming things.

J.C.: No, I'm not, either.

Lizzie: It's getting hard to remember that far back. We've been married sixty years.

J.C.: Last February. Sixty years. That is a long time to live with the same old woman, ain't it? I guess we get along better now than we did a few years after we were married. I believe she'd agree.

Lizzie: Well, we don't have to work so hard and do things like that now. We had to work all the time. Didn't have much time to rest, then. That's all we've got now.

EDITORIAL METHOD

This book contains material from 100 taped interviews, involving 134 people. Almost all the sessions were conducted in Clay County between May 1987 and June 1988. Age and identifying information for each speaker in the book are given on first appearance and omitted in subsequent appearances. Both ages and descriptions reflect circumstances at the time of the interviews.

All consultants had the opportunity to read over their transcribed remarks before giving permission for publication. Most were remarkably generous with their words and feelings, and I at no point felt the need to turn to pseudonyms to salvage essential material. Of 134 people interviewed, fewer than a dozen declined to let their statements be used. Those interviews for which permission was not given are not included in the following list.

I decided whom to interview on the basis of recommendation, prior acquaintance, and, often, chance. Earlier interviews generally involved life histories; later ones tended to focus on more specific topics. I did attempt to reflect the distribution of age and race set forth in the 1980 census, and to include people from all areas of the county. If I had a central purpose, it was to illustrate the diversity of feeling and experience in a region and a place often portrayed in the flat uniformity of stereotype.

In editing, I cut material from all of the interviews and rearranged parts of many. The only additions or changes I made involved words or short phrases when they were needed for clarity. Some people chose to correct their grammar, or asked me to do it for them, but the sections that appear here on the whole do not reflect extensive rewriting. For what it's worth, the county's speech departs at several points from standard English, local patterns are used even by college graduates, and words that on paper look perfectly grammatical would ring quite odd in a county conversation. The unedited tapes, with some restrictions, will be available at the University Archives, Auburn University, Auburn, Alabama.

Constraints of space and of design did not allow me to include everyone I interviewed, although the words of those who were omitted were often as eloquent and meaningful as anything I used. This book would never have been possible without the efforts of many county residents, and I am extremely grateful to all the people who took time, both on and off tape, to help me with it.

INTERVIEWS

Adair, Mary. Retired farmer, Millerville, 16 December 1987.

Bailey, Theron. Fish-pond operator, Mellow Valley, 4 November 1987.

Belk, James. Methodist minister, Ashland, 7 March 1988.

Benefield, E. Z. Funeral-home owner, Lineville, 12 April 1988.

Bowen, Mark; Arnold Clark; F. D. Clark; David Easley; Johnny Ingram; and *David Proctor.* Lineville football coach and players, 18 May 1988.

Brady, Bill, and *Karin Christopherson.* Employees, Clay County Mental Health Center, Bluff Springs and Lineville, 23 February 1988.

Browning, Kiffin. Local historian, Ashland, 3 May 1988.

Buchanan, Larry. Store owner, Delta, February 1988.

Burdette, Jamie. Student, Cragford, 12 September 1987.

Burney, Ricky. Security guard, Lineville, 1 April 1988.

Carmichael, Mira. Retired air-force procurement officer, Brownville, 4 December 1987.

Carter, Mark, and *William Carter.* Student and retired chicken-plant worker, Lineville, 28 October 1987.

Carter, Mike; L. B. Gibson, Jr.; Olen Farrow; John Stanford; and *Allwin White.* Cragford raconteurs, 23 June 1987.

Cavender, Carol. Ashland store operator, Cleburne County, March 1988.

Chapman, J. C., and *Tiny Chapman.* Retired funeral home worker and wife, Shiloh, 3 June 1987.

Clarke, Stanley. Student, Delta, 16 April 1988.

Clarke, Sonny, and *Dianne Clarke.* Bank officer and mail carrier, Delta, 25 February 1988.

Colley, J. C., and *Lizzie Colley.* Retired farmers, Mountain, 2 June 1987.

Cowan, Jim. Mining enthusiast, Idaho, 22 June 1987.

Crawford, Ida Lee. Ceramic-shop owner, Bluff Springs, 16 January 1988.

Creed, Lois. Retired farmer, Campbells' Crossroads, 2 July 1987.

Creed, Wayne. Retired engineer, Campbells' Crossroads, 2 July 1987.

Denney, Rubye. Senior citizens' companion, Shiloh, 12 September 1987.

East, Hubert; Katherine East; Kay East; and *Christy East.* Pulpwooders, Shady Grove, 20 February 1988.

Evans, Odessa. Housewife, Delta, 8 February 1988.

Fables, Bobby. Retired soldier, Mellow Valley, 19 April 1988.

Farr, Walter Jr. Retired school administrator, Barfield, 3 November 1987.

Farrow, Delon. Student, Cragford, 9 July 1987.

Farrow, Mildred. Store clerk, Cragford, 24 July 1987.

Fetner, Woodrow. Retired school-bus driver, Cragford, 24 August 1987.

Flegel, Morland. Owner of dry-cleaning business, Ashland, 26 May 1987 and 22 September 1987.

Ford, Rickey, and *Michael Wilkins.* Foresters, Talladega County, 5 February 1988.

Good, David. Student, Millerville, 4 October 1987.

Green, Hubert. Truck farmer, Ashland, December 1987.

Griffin, Diana. Owner of building-supply business, Spring Hill, 14 January 1988.

Hamil, Howard. Fiddler, Mellow Valley, 27 May 1987.

Hardy, Lisa. Wood-products worker, Ashland, 11 November 1987.

Harris, Annie Pearl; Allie Mae Ragland; and *Sarah Simmons.* Quilters, Millerville, 11 November 1987.

Harris, Grady. Baptist preacher, Delta, 16 February 1988.

Heard, John, and *Estelle Heard.* Retired pulpwooders, Delta, 17 October 1987.

Higgins, Harold. President of sewing plant, Lineville, 13 January 1988.

Higgins, Otis Jr. State trooper, Lineville, 13 October 1987.

Holmes, Jerry, and *Becky Holmes.* Construction worker and teacher, Delta, 24 March 1988.

Horn, Alvin. Retired electrician and former Ku Klux Klan grand dragon, Idaho, 4 November 1987.

Horn, Cecil. Medical doctor, Ashland, 24 February 1988.

Ingram, Kenneth Jr. Lawyer, Ashland, 26 May 1987.

Johnson, Curtis. Methodist minister, Ashland, 7 March 1988.

Johnson, Tom, and *Eunice Johnson.* Retired railroad worker and retired housekeeper, 26 August 1987.

Jordan, Judith. Painter, Mellow Valley, 8 June 1987.

Kennedy, Annie Maude. Retired farmer, Mountain, 26 May 1987.

Kerr, Angelia. Dairy farmer, Ashland, 14 July 1987.

King, Ruby. Retired teacher, Ashland, 23 October 1987.

Lambert, Bruna. Retired, Lineville, 10 June 1987.

Lamberth, L. D., and *Allie Maude Lamberth.* Retired postmaster and wife, Cragford, 13 July 1987.

Lett, Charlie, and *V. L. Lett.* Retired construction worker and wife, Highland, 14 July 1987.

McKinney, Emma Jean. Director, Clay County Learning Center, Ashland, 5 June 1987.

Moore, Lois. Retired farmer, Barfield, 26 September 1987.

Morris, Walter R. Retired, Cragford, 1 September 1987.

Nolen, Dick. Retired navy officer, Ashland, 26 April 1988.

Padgett, Willis. Car salesman, Mount Zion, 20 January 1988.

Patterson, Aubrey. Retired state trooper, Bluff Springs, 10 July 1987.

Pettus, Mike. Special-education teacher, Delta, 10 April 1988.

Reynolds, Susan. Nurse, Delta, 8 March 1988.

Roberts, Annie Pearl. Sewing-plant worker, Highland, 12 December 1987.

Robertson, Buster, and *Maryjo Robertson.* Garage owners, Cragford, 13 July 1987.

Robertson, Larry. Mechanic, Cragford, 22 August 1987.

Robertson, Steve. Preacher, Ashland Church of God, Cleburne County, 8 March 1988.

Rochester, John. Circuit-court judge, Lineville, 23 February 1988.

Rochester, Linda. Director, Clay County Department of Human Services, Lineville, 4 December 1987.

Scott, Amanda. Retired teacher, Lineville, 7 October 1987.

Sellers, Lewel. Retired farmer, Millerville, 9 October 1987 and 29 March 1988.

Sims, Coolidge. Pharmacy owner, Ashland, 5 April 1988.

Sims, Hop. Retired store owner, Delta, February 1988.

Sims, Horace. Social worker, Ashland, 14 October 1987.

Smith, Annie. President, Clay County Fair Association, Delta, 24 February 1988.

Smith, Lynn. Mechanic, Bluff Springs, 24 November 1987.

Sprayberry, Mark. Sewing-plant worker, Cragford, 25 August 1987.

Toland, Charles. Retired city employee, Ashland, 25 March 1988.

Traylor, Lillie. Chicken-plant worker, Lineville, 15 January 1988.

Upchurch, David, and *Darlene Upchurch.* Farmers, Barfield, 9 February 1988.

Walker, L. D., and *Lula Walker.* Retired store owners, Cragford, 23 June 1987.

Walker, Mark. Blueberry farmer, Bowden Grove, 10 April 1988.

Wallace, Elvadie. Retired nurse, Ashland, 14 October 1987.

Watts, Johnny Ray. Fiddler, Shinbone, 10 July 1987.

White, Jan, and *Wendell White.* Sewing-plant workers, Pine Grove, 14 January 1988.

Williams, Cornelia. Juvenile parole officer, Ashland, 10 June 1987.

Williamson, Jimmy. Clay County Rescue Squad member, High Pine, 12 April 1988.

Wilson, John. Textile worker, Millerville, 26 November 1987.

Winsor, Zenus. Baptist preacher, Corinth, 5 June 1987.

Wood, Monroe, and *Flossie Mae Wood.* Retired army-depot worker and nursing-home worker, Delta, 28 May 1987.

STATISTICAL INFORMATION

Although the concept of this book did not include detailed statistical discussion, a brief survey of economic and population figures both supports residents' statements and helps place the county within more general historical and economic trends. Table 1 portrays shifts in county farming, most specifically the change from independent cultivation of subsistence crops to cotton tenancy, followed by the massive drop in agricultural production. The second table shows patterns of population rise and fall, marking economic and social alterations both in the county and in the nation as a whole. The instability of many county jobs shows in the third table's unemployment figures. Monthly numbers, which often rise far above the yearly averages, reflect the wide swings of employment in a place where work depends on seasonal labor and often marginal industrial operations. The employment profile shown in Table 4 makes clear the almost total shift from farming to factory production. Finally, income statistics for 1979, the most recent year available, reveal the county's unusually high number of elderly residents, and emphasize its widespread poverty, particularly where black families are concerned.

TABLE 1

Agriculture

Year	Total farms	Average acres per farm	Percentage of land in farms	Total farmed by owner or part owner
1880	1,979	123.0	63.0	1,447
1890	2,258	108.0	63.0	1,590
1900	2,887	89.6	67.0	1,671
1910	3,459	73.8	65.0	1,812
1920	3,576	68.0	61.8	1,889
1930	3,032	70.6	54.5	1,464
1940	2,624	87.6	59.5	1,329
1950	2,188	95.2	54.0	1,613
1959	1,027	126.7	33.7	862
1969	603	184.5	28.8	590
1987	439	192.0	21.8	421

Source: U.S. Census.

*The 1880 and 1890 censuses did not separate farm operators by race.

Agriculture (*continued*)

Total farmed by tenant	Farms owned wholly or partly by blacks	Farms operated by black tenants	Acres corn	Acres cotton
522	—*	—*·	24,503	13,921
668	—*	—*	26,391	20,950
1,063	64	173	30,456	26,430
1,645	76	275	30,932	33,690
1,685	89	294	43,868	26,915
1,567	77	282	28,528	20,382
1,294	54	210	38,306	16,752
573	73	119	22,983	8,276
164	44	29	8,931	2,230
13	4	2	1,221	53
14	—	—	153	—

TABLE 2

Population

Year	Total	White	Black	Other	Percentage black
1870	9,560	8,823	737	0	7.7
1880	12,938	11,870	1,068	0	8.3
1890	15,765	14,061	1,704	0	10.8
1900	17,768	15,215	1,884	0	11.0
1910	21,006	18,358	2,648	0	12.6
1920	22,645	19,466	3,179	0	14.0
1930	17,768	15,041	2,727	0	15.3
1940	16,907	14,289	2,618	0	15.5
1950	13,929	11,719	2,209	1	15.9
1960	12,400	10,372	2,016	12	16.3
1970	12,636	10,578	2,041	17	16.2
1980	13,703	11,408	2,267	28	16.5

Sources: Louis Vandiver Loveman, *Alabama Book of Facts and Historical Statistics* (1975; typescript, Jacksonville State University Library); 1980 U.S. Census.

TABLE 3

Percentage of Work Force Unemployed, 1980–89

Year	United States	Alabama	Clay County Average	Clay County Highest month
1980	7.1	8.8	8.2	11.5
1981	7.6	10.7	10.1	21.2
1982	9.7	14.4	15.1	17.7
1983	9.6	13.7	15.6	19.0
1984	7.5	11.1	12.2	13.6
1985	7.2	8.9	11.0	14.8
1986	7.0	9.8	15.2	26.2
1987	6.2	7.8	8.9	18.3
1988	5.5	7.2	7.7	9.5
1989	5.3	7.0	7.2	14.2

Source: Alabama Department of Industrial Relations.

TABLE 4

In-County Employment Patterns, 1987 *

Number of wage and salary workers[†]	3,820
Manufacturing workers	2,110
Durable goods	630
Lumber and wood products[‡]	570
Other durable goods	60
Nondurable Goods	1,480
Apparel	820
Other nondurable goods[§]	660
Nonmanufacturing workers	1,710
Construction	100
Transportation and utilities	150
Trade	370
Services	230
Government	780
Number of farms	439
By standard industrial classification	
Beef cattle	329
Dairy	14
Poultry and eggs	41
Farms with sales greater than $2,500	280
Farms as principal occupation of owner	139

Sources: Alabama Department of Industrial Relations;
1987 U.S. Census of Agriculture.

*The 1980 U.S. Census counted 70.4 percent of county
workers as employed within the county.

[†]Totals are rounded to nearest ten.

[‡]Category includes logging, sawmills, cabinetmaking.

[§]Category includes chicken and egg processing,
rubber tires.

TABLE 5

Income Status for 1979

	United States	Alabama	Clay County total	Clay County white	Clay County black
Number of families			3,792	3,351	441
Number of unrelated individuals*			990	855	—
Per capita income (in dollars)	7,298	5,824	4,855	5,309	—
Total persons (in percentages)					
Below poverty level	12.4	18.9	21.0	17.7	—
Below 125% of poverty level	17.0	25.2	28.7	25.3	—
Age 65 and over	10.9	11.1	15.1	16.5	
Families (in percentages)					
Below poverty level	9.6	14.8	16.8	15.0	30.8
Below 125% of poverty level	13.4	20.6	25.1	23.3	38.8
Householders age 65 and over	14.9	15.8	22.7	23.2	—
With Social Security income	22.1	33.7	31.9	32.7	26.3
With public-assistance income	8.0	10.3	10.8	9.1	23.6
Unrelated individuals (in percentages)					
Below poverty level	25.1	38.7	51.4	49.0	—
Below 125% of poverty level	33.3	47.2	59.8	57.5	—
Age 65 and over	28.2	50.2	59.1	61.4	—
With Social Security income	29.5	52.7	55.9	59.1	—
With public-assistance income	6.7	16.0	23.5	21.9	—

Source: 1980 U.S. Census.

*Many unrelated individuals are living alone.

WORKS CONSULTED

Agee, James, and Walker Evans. *Let Us Now Praise Famous Men*. Boston: Houghton Mifflin, 1941.

Blythe, Ronald. *Akenfield: Portrait of an English Village*. New York: Pantheon, 1969.

Browning, Kiffin. "Clay County History: A Club Talk." Address delivered in Clay County, 4 October 1972.

Browning, Ned. "Agriculture in Clay County." Information Services, Mississippi State University, 1989. Manuscript.

Coles, Robert. *Migrants, Sharecroppers, Mountaineers*. Vol. 2 of *Children of Crisis*. Boston: Little, Brown, 1971.

Flynt, Wayne. *Poor but Proud: Alabama's Poor Whites*. Tuscaloosa: University of Alabama Press, 1989.

Garrett, Mitchell B. *Horse and Buggy Days on Hatchett Creek*. Tuscaloosa: University of Alabama Press, 1957.

Glassie, Henry. *Passing the Time in Ballymenone: Culture and History of an Ulster Community*. Philadelphia: University of Pennsylvania Press, 1982.

Hamilton, Virginia Van der Veer. *Alabama: A History*. New York: Norton, 1984.

————. *Hugo Black: The Alabama Years*. Baton Rouge: Louisiana State University Press, 1972.

Hicks, Roderick. "Clay Opens Its Heart to Learning Center." *Anniston Star*, 15 September 1986.

Jordan, Judith. *Our County, Past and Present*. Ashland, Ala.: Ashland Printing Company, 1978.

Painter, Nell Irvin. *The Narrative of Hosea Hudson*. Cambridge, Mass.: Harvard University Press, 1979.

Patterson, Joyce Ann. "History of Clay County, Alabama." Master's thesis, Jacksonville State University, 1970.

Raines, Howell. *My Soul Is Rested: The Story of the Civil Rights Movement in the Deep South*. New York: Putnam, 1977.

Rogers, William W. *The One-Gallused Rebellion: Agrarianism in Alabama, 1865–1896*. Baton Rouge: Louisiana State University Press, 1970.

Rosengarten, Theodore. *All God's Dangers: The Life of Nate Shaw*. New York: Doubleday, Vintage Books, 1974.

Rozelle, Eddie B. *Recollections: My Folks and Fields*. Talladega, Ala.: Privately published, 1960.

Saylors, G. C., with Andy Hall. *Shinbone*. Columbia, S.C.: Privately printed, 1979.

Shofner, Jerrell H., and William Warren Rogers. "Joseph C. Manning: Militant Agrarian, Enduring Populist." *Alabama Historical Quarterly* 39 (1967): 7–37.

Strickland, Vista. "Shinbone Valley." Privately printed, n.d.

Terkel, Studs. *Hard Times: An Oral History of the Great Depression.* New York: Pantheon, 1970.

———. *Talking to Myself: A Memoir of My Times.* New York: Pantheon, 1977.

———. *Working.* New York: Pantheon, 1972.

Williams, William Carlos. *In the American Grain.* New York: New Directions, 1956.

PHOTOGRAPHS

1. Steve, Dale, and Josh Brown; 2. Ada and Lee Smith, with Bob; 3. Nona Phillips; 4. Tammy Rude and Adam McCain; 5. William James Buchanan; 6. Leonard Price Nunn; 7. barn owned by Adell and Carvel Haynes; 8. Amelia D. Twilley and Kenneth Ingram, Jr.; 9. Amelia D. Twilley; 10. old store near Horn's Valley; 11. James M. Jones; 12. Robin and Rhonda Ogle; 13. J. Aubrey Patterson; 14. James B. Sellars; 15. Bret Ellison; 16. Lois Moore; 17. Hosea Chappell; 18. Bill and Tracy Morrison; 19. Virginia and Jim Cheatwood; 20. Nelner Jean Welch; 21. Erika and Stephanie Smith; 22. Danny Davis and Dora Parsons; 23. O. J. McCoy; 24. Beulah Moses; 25. Adam Watts, Gerald Sewell, and Jody Watts; 26. Christy Watts; 27. Clay County Courthouse; 28. Annie Maude Kennedy; 29. Icy and Earl Griffin; 30. Connie Harkins and Tony Strickland; 31. Nancy Hardy; 32. Emmett Horn; 33. Polly Pace; 34. Travis Leonard; 35. Tad Hardy; 36. Lisa, Aaron, and John Wellborn; 37. Helen Powers; 38. Dessar Davidson; 39. Larry Willis and Ed Lowery; 40. Virgia Martin; 41. Darlene and Jimmy Harris; 42. John Simmons; 43. Littie Lett; 44. Eva and Henry Luker; 45. rural Clay County

INDEX

Ace Products. *See* Amerace
Activities, out-of-county, 141, 164, 165–66, 169
Adair, Mary, 111–14, 262
Aging, 9–10, 32, 74, 75, 76, 79, 91, 189; and spiritual growth, 224–30. *See also* Death; Elderly
Alexander City, Ala., xviii, 43, 165, 257
Amason, M. D., 25
Amerace, 42, 80, 126, 132, 134
Anderson, Michael, 26, 30
Anniston, Ala., xiii, 11, 37, 50, 68, 86, 116, 118, 127, 165, 171, 181, 195, 202, 248; New South growth of, xviii
Anniston Army Depot, 8, 9, 11–13
Ashland, xii, xiii, 33, 37, 61, 64, 66, 75, 85, 109, 112, 119, 120, 125, 126, 139, 141, 142, 149–53 passim, 158, 164, 169, 170, 172, 177, 195, 197, 198, 202, 209, 210, 220, 221, 230, 244; founded, xviii
Ashland Church of God, 220
Atlanta, Ga., 42, 83, 247; New South growth of xviii; commuting to, 86–87
Auburn University, 36, 37, 194, 197

Bailey, Theron, 262
Banks, 54, 98; and blacks, 126, 127, 130, 132, 134, 135
Barfield, 59, 65, 93
Bears, 33–34
Beauty pageants, 133
Belk, James, 262
Bellview, 194
Benefield, E. Z., 233–37, 262
Bethany Primitive Baptist Church, 5
Better Citizens' Club, 121
Birmingham, Ala., 17, 38, 50, 86, 101, 114, 118, 152, 157, 171, 172, 204, 205, 231, 243; New South growth of, xviii
Black Belt, x
Black, Hugo, x, xvii, 139, 149–56, 157–58; memorial and library project, 149, 150–51, 153; and blacks, 153

Blacks, ix–x, xx, 8–13, 18, 46–49, 68–70, 80–84, 109–16, 118–35, 152, 153, 168–70, 181, 182–84, 200, 209, 226–27, 228–29, 241–42, 250–51; statistics, 268, 269, 272. *See also* Businesses; Education; Integration; Poverty; Race Relations; Segregation; Work
Blueberries, xiii, 165
Bluff Springs, 89, 144, 145, 204
Boll weevil, 63
Bowen, Mark, 196–99, 262
Brady, Bill, 204–6, 262
Browning, Kiffin, 262, 274
Browning, Ned, 274
Brownville, 162
Brownville-Hatchett Creek Presbyterian Church, vii, ix
Brown vs. the Board of Education of Topeka, 149, 154
Buchanan, Larry, 262
Burdette, Jamie, 30, 262
Burney, Ricky, 128–29, 132–35, 168–70, 262
Businesses: closings, 18, 23, 39–40, 42, 164; family-owned, 36–39, 77–79, 86; starting, 37, 40, 68, 77, 246; centralization of, 60, 68–69, 85, 88; decline of, 60, 69, 85, 167; black owned, 120, 132–34. *See also* Amerace; Country stores; Higgins Company; Industrial employment; Industry; Russell Manufacturing; Tyson Foods
Bynum. *See* Anniston Army Depot

Calhoun County, xviii, 134, 168, 247
California, 115, 214–15, 252
Canning, 5, 6, 183, 190, 248, 256
Carmichael, Mira, ix–x, 162, 253–54, 262
Cars and driving, ix, 16, 17, 33, 85–90, 92, 146, 157, 164, 201–3, 204, 224, 256–57; Japanese, 14, 85; repair, 23, 36–39, 87–90, 202; racing, 36, 201–3; trucks, 44, 68–69, 87; T-model, 85, 86, 256;